PRAISE FOR *A THOUSAND* ℎ

"Grip your chair. This mind-boggling account of a family's naive-yet-determined move to one of America's challenging urban neighborhoods will lay its hand on you. Maria Garriott's descriptions pull you in, her characters insist you stay. The narrative pays its rent up to the last page, which arrives all too quickly. I envy those about to read this story for the first time."

—Steven Estes,
co-author (with Joni Eareckson Tada) of *When God Weeps*

"I have virtually 'grown up' with the Garriott family and I count Maria and her husband, Craig, as dearest of friends. Their work at Faith Christian Fellowship church has gained the heartfelt respect of all who know them. In her book, Maria shows us what it truly means to practice Christianity with its sleeves rolled up, and to love when push comes to shove. This is not so much a story about urban ministry; it's about reflecting Christ where the rubber meets the road of real life. You hold in your hands a book which is not only insightful, but powerfully encouraging!"

—Joni Eareckson Tada,
founder of Joni and Friends, author of 30 books

"I pray I will be as faithful to my ministry calling as Maria Garriott has been to hers. With the language of a poet, Maria writes of raising kids, shaping a marriage, and serving a church and neighborhood caught 'in the crossfire of America's racial war.' Maria's words capture the brokenness and healing, the grief and joy that lie at the heart of every true story of personal or community transformation."

—Lynne Hybels,
Willow Creek Community Church, author of *Nice Girls Don't Change the World*

"This book is an emotional roller coaster. I laughed, I cried, and I was continually amazed at God's merciful protection of Maria and her family. *A Thousand Resurrections* is a primer for urban ministry that is poetic instead of didactic. It is testimony to the greatness of God—revealed, not in triumphant saints, but in fragile sinners."

—Ned Bustard,
editor of *It Was Good: Making Art to the Glory of God*

"*A Thousand Resurrections* is not a how-to book about urban ministry for every eager idealist. It is the truth about urban ministry, which at its core is God's work of restoring and redeeming people to Himself time and again. The city does not need another well-intentioned savior, but more servants following God's heart and his call. Maria tells the story of following God's call to Baltimore, and the joyous surprise that God was at work long before she or Craig ever got there."

—Rev. Carl F. Ellis,
author of *Free at Last? The Gospel in the African American Experience*

"Effective urban ministry depends upon healthy and growing families. This book is a must for those who are serving in the city and have run into various issues on how families can go through problems and yet be healthy and committed to their calling. Maria provides a great deal of insight that is both specific to her journey and general for many of us who have labored in the urban context. I highly recommend this book to urban practitioners."

—Manuel Ortiz,
Professor Emeritus of Mission and Urban Ministry at
Westminster Theological Seminary, author of *One New People*

"Having watched this story unfold over the years, I believe this book presents the raw intensity of the pains and joys of urban ministry. My friend Maria writes as an urban pastor's wife, mother, neighbor, musician and worker. *A Thousand Resurrections* will give you a true glimpse of how simple people, committed to experiencing, proclaiming, and living the gospel of Jesus, can make a difference for eternity in the city."

Rev. Stan Long,
co-pastor, Faith Christian Fellowship—

"Maria made me care about her neighborhood and the lives she portrayed. Her stories moved me and propelled me from chapter to chapter. *A Thousand Resurrections* encouraged me to keep looking for ways that my life could more effectively bring the Light of Christ to my own world."

—Joyce Sackett,
author of *Goodbye, Jeanine*

A THOUSAND RESURRECTIONS

An Urban Spiritual Journey

BY MARIA GARRIOTT

A Thousand Resurrections: An Urban Spiritual Journey

© Copyright 2006 — Maria Garriott

Published by CitySongs
a division of Riott Publishing LLC, Washington, D.C.

Interior design and cover by Jeffrey M. Hall, ION Graphic Design Works

Printed in the United States of America

Library of Congress Control Number:

ISBN 0-9762004-1-4

Photo credits:
Bill Bolling, p. 11, 245; Jesse Dortzbach, p. 263; Steve Hwang, p. 81; all other photos by Craig and Maria Garriott

www.AThousandResurrections.com

1 2 3 4 5 6 7 8 9 10 / 10 09 08 07 06

CONTENTS

AUTHOR'S NOTE

I have changed names and supporting details to protect the privacy of some individuals. Some conversations have been reconstructed to the best of my ability. Wherever possible, I have verified my recollections with others.

I am grateful for the friends who read this book and offered suggestions. Cora Teter read my earliest few chapters, and gently told me that I needed to tell the story in just one voice. Then she and Ann Maouyo, sharp-eyed editors, read the whole book twice and saved me from a thousand errors. John Yates, our theologian-rocket scientist friend, and Kim and Gerry Sütter were unflaggingly encouraging. Steve Estes, Margaret Osburn, and Joyce Sackett put aside their own projects to give valuable editorial suggestions. Other readers included Manny Ortiz, Bob Lynn, Christine and Bob Harter, Dottie and Jim Taylor, Bruce and Marlene Gustafsen, Krista Herwig, Stacey Allen, and Linette Hill. My brother-in-law Chuck Garriott provided publishing advice and assistance.

Faith Christian Fellowship would not exist without the constant support of our parents, Cleo and Pete Garriott, and Don and Yvonne Dawkins.

I am profoundly grateful to my children, who believed there might be redemptive lessons in their stories and allowed me to share them.

My husband Craig helped me squeeze out some writing time, endured endless book consultations, listened patiently to a thousand nights of writer-angst, and read more drafts of this manuscript than anyone should reasonably have to read. I would not have completed it without him. He is still, after all these years, my favorite.

If you spend yourselves in behalf of the hungry
and satisfy the needs of the oppressed,
then your light will rise in the darkness,
and your night will become like the noonday.

Isaiah 58:10

Charleston, 1979

FOREWORD

WHAT would make a young, gifted college student well postured to achieve her place in the American dream of personal peace and affluence decide to pursue another kind of American dream—one that would force her to take food stamps and move into a violent urban community plagued by entrenched drug trafficking? What would sustain her for over two decades while she raised her five children in a context of failed educational systems, lead poisoning, and chronic theft? What would eventually compel her to move and yet still embrace the heart matters of the city?

This is one woman's story of a return flight to a city that many have fled. It is echoed in thousands of men and women of faith who have returned to distressed urban communities across America in response to a higher calling. It is about the challenges, heartbreaks, lessons, and joys of a woman participating in the transformation of the city while being transformed herself. This is my wife's story.

I first met Maria in the summer of 1979, in Charleston, South Carolina, where she worked as a historical guide for the National Park Service at Fort Sumter, whose bombardment in 1861 began the Civil War. She was a singer-songwriter whose song "Women's Lament" expressed the losses of that great war. Maria lived next to the Sullivan's Island lighthouse in an old, un-air condi-tioned Coast Guard station. She told me that she could still sleep through those sultry summer nights, even though she was occasionally awakened by thumb-sized cockroaches crawling over her. I was smitten by this poet warrior.

Within four months of meeting we were engaged. Six months later we were married. Within four months of our marriage, Maria was expecting our first child and within a year, we had relocated into a blighted urban communi-ty of Baltimore where we raised our family. Our desire was to follow God, who was already at work in the city, and become part of growing a reconciled com-munity that pursued doing justice while celebrating His grace. I was the pas-tor but Maria was much more than a pastor's wife.

Twenty two years and five children later, we took a much needed sabbati-cal. Besides seeking the rest and renewal that we desperately needed, we had intended to write a book of practical theology for those interested in growing reconciling communities. We started the sabbatical by taking a weekend trip to Gettysburg, Pennsylvania. There, Maria told me that in the process of writ-ing she had conflicting voices. One was the theology with the stories of the mission and vision of the church and the other was her own personal journey as a woman, wife, mother, and community developer. It was clear that we had two books. It was also clear that the most needed theology of our day is that which flows from the wisdom of those "veterans of creative suffering" who have fleshed out their faith around the core issues of the gospel in the city. Maria's book must be first.

In his Gettysburg address, President Abraham Lincoln spoke about "a new nation, conceived in Liberty, and dedicated to the proposition that all men are created equal." He also added "Now we are engaged in a great civil war, testing whether that nation, or any nation so conceived and so dedicated, can long endure." In many ways this war defined our nation and its issues of liberty, unity, race, and class. These issues continue to be the testing ground, not only of our cities and nation, but of the world. The challenge is not only knowing how to engage redemptively but also how to "long endure." The good news is that God cares, God has spoken, God has come, and God will revive. I am deeply honored to be married to, loved by, and partnering with Maria and am a personal witness to the resurrections she speaks of. Read, weep, rejoice, engage and endure.

—Craig Garriott
January, 2006

Charleston, 1979

WHAT I DIDN'T KNOW

*He has shown you, O man, what is good. And what does
the Lord our God require of you? To love justice, to do
mercy, and to walk humbly with your God.*

MICAH 6:8

WHEN I was twenty-two, my husband Craig and I took our two-week-old daughter and moved to the inner city. We traded our apartment in the country for a hundred-year-old house previously owned by a slumlord, and known more for its drug deals than décor. The once-spacious Victorian had been carved into five miserly apartments to maximize profits from low-income tenants. The roof leaked and old trucks lay rusting in the rear yard. The front and back wooden porches looked like shredded wheat that had banged around in the box too long.

We put glass back in the window frames, scrubbed the chipped, green tile floors, picked up bags of broken bottles from the yard, and mowed the foot-high grass. We dreamed of starting a church where black and white, rich and poor would come together to fulfill the mandate of the Old Testament prophet Micah. We envisioned a spiritual community committed to racial reconciliation and social justice, a church bridging the gap between the educated and the street-wise, between those who lived on the edge and those who rose to the top like cream.

I didn't know we would scrape by just above the poverty line for years. That I would live with people who heard voices or had spent most of their lives in juvenile hall or prison. That I would share a house with women who sold their bodies, snorted cocaine, or whose boyfriends choked and punched them. That we would be robbed over and over. That we would give a second chance to young men who would rummage through our drawers to steal Craig's wallet or my grocery money. That the boy next door would deal drugs and that gun battles would sometimes erupt. That a man would be murdered in front of my house for his radio.

I didn't know my children would be lead poisoned. That they would be mocked for being white, then scorned for acting black. That their friend, who ate at our table like a godson, would go not to college with them but to prison. That a little boy with no daddy at home who had baked cookies in my kitchen and hunted snakes with my son would one day lie on the street in a pool of blood.

I didn't know that several times a week my husband would wake in the night agonizing over whether we were failing to reach the neighborhood, whether an African American pastor would be more effective, whether God was still calling us here. I didn't know depression would stalk me.

I didn't know that when I was scraped raw, Jesus would heal me. That when I was broken, God would use my brokenness. That he would use us in spite of ourselves. That Jesus would shine so clearly where race, class, and suffering intersect.

I didn't know I would witness a thousand resurrections. That church members who struggled to pay rent would adopt nieces and nephews to save them from drug-addicted parents. That a woman who saw a teenaged mother roll her baby's stroller into an empty house, and abandon it, would raise that baby as her own. That men who snorted cocaine would get clean and love Jesus. That women sexually abused by their fathers would be healed and would rescue other children. That Muslims from Iraq, atheists from China, and Hindus of Indian descent would find Jesus and encourage my faith. I didn't know that they would become my heroes and friends. I didn't know they would be braided into my heart.

CHAPTER 1

Charleston, 1979

AN IMPECUNIOUS SEMINARIAN

CRAIG pulled at his tie in the sticky, late summer heat as the Maryland farmland of his childhood faded in the rearview mirror. Even in dress clothes, he looked younger than twenty-six, the boyishness clinging to his slender face. His left arm rested jauntily on the open window, and his hair flitted in the wind like a blond flame. Beads of sweat made my thighs stick to the Honda's cracked, black vinyl seats. I pulled at my skirt and shifted in my seat. He turned his blue eyes to me and grinned, a flash of white.

Behind us lay rural Baltimore County, where acres of Silver Queen corn backed up to his parents' modest brick rancher. After our wedding two months before, we had moved into a two-room apartment above their detached garage, where we were lulled to sleep by the rustling of ripening corn. In front of us lay suburban neighborhoods of manicured lawns and the white-steepled church where Craig had begun his pastoral internship just one week after our May wedding. In our album photos, we look like two giddy high schoolers who had skipped out of the senior prom to march down the aisle.

Beyond the suburbs, some thirty minutes ahead, lay the city line. It was an urban world as unfamiliar to us as Ethiopia or Estonia. As our old Honda hurtled towards it, I reflected on how much had changed in twelve months.

Craig had burst into my life the previous summer, after my junior year of college. I was twenty, and had returned to Charleston, South Carolina to work a second summer for the National Park Service. I wasn't interested in starting a serious relationship. And marrying a minister? Not a life choice considered by good Catholic girls.

Dating a seminary student had never entered my mind the evening I sat on a stage in a restaurant in Charleston, where I had landed a weekly gig singing and playing guitar. Unlike proprietors of the coffeehouses and college bars where I had previously played, the owner allowed musicians full artistic license: I could sing about Jesus. Singing about Jesus had recently become important to me. And that night, a long-legged seminarian sat at a table, listening intently.

During my sophomore year in college, I had attended a non-denominational campus Bible study that expanded my view of God from flat to three-dimensional. I had always believed that Jesus was who he claimed to be—the Son of God. But I had conveniently compartmentalized God, and had no plans for him to break out of that box and interfere in my life.

That year, the Bible study leader talked about knowing God personally, and showed me a little stick-figure drawing: a circle and some symbols. A few lines on paper. It blew my world apart.

"Let's say this circle is your heart," she said. "There are many things we can place in the center." She pointed to different symbols outside the circle. "Our dreams, money, status, or relationships."

I could see where this was going. My little gods were slipping from my hand, falling, shattering. She continued. "Jesus wants to be in the center—on the throne of our lives." She drew a cross in the center of the circle. "So the question is, Maria, is Jesus on the throne of your life?"

I knew who desperately wanted to be on the throne of my life: me. At that moment I understood that I had created an a la carte god, a manageable handmaid god, but one only distantly related to the God of the Bible. I had justified myself. I was basically a good person, I had argued whenever my conscience pricked me. I now recognized the fallacy of believing that God graded on a curve. I knew from the Bible study leader that my relationship with my boyfriend did not honor God because he was not a Christian. But I was convinced—with all the accumulated wisdom of a nineteen-year-old—that I would never find love again. And wouldn't getting serious about God change other things in my life, too? I felt trapped, unable to break from my old life, too scared to close my eyes and leap off a cliff into a future I couldn't imagine. I pushed Jesus away for months, yet still felt him pursuing me. Finally, I gave up. "O.K.," I prayed one night in my dorm room, "I'll follow you."

I changed, as if my magnetic North Pole shifted. Jesus became the relationship through which I evaluated other relationships, other decisions. I broke up with my boyfriend. I began to study the Bible every day, to see God as the center of my world rather than a once-weekly check-up or obligation. I didn't know what Jesus wanted me to do with my life, but whatever it was, I wanted to do it. My friends found my zeal—and me—as weird as snowsuits in Alabama.

A few months later, I landed a summer job as a park ranger at Forts Sumter and Moultrie outside Charleston. With several other seasonal employees, I moved into the former Coast Guard lighthouse-keeper's cottage. The Park Service had tastefully furnished it with hand-me-down gray metal office desks and tables, worn green vinyl sofas, and metal beds. It was like living in a government warehouse, but with scenery. The NPS had never gotten around to affixing a sign designating it as seasonal employee housing. Unsuspecting tourists regularly interrupted our lunches, dinners—and in at least one memorable instance, my roommate's post-shower dressing—striding unannounced through the door and asking for tours of the now-closed lighthouse. Flying roaches the size of my thumb —palmetto bugs—crawled in my sheets and flew out of kitchen cabinets. It was so hot that cotton clothes felt like a punishment, and polyester was a death sentence. Even the breezes were like blasts from on overheated engine. But to me, it all seemed like a fabulous adventure, especially with the ocean a short walk from our back porch. On days when I worked at Fort Sumter rather than Fort Moultrie, I rode in the park boat out to the fort. "Can you believe it?" a coworker whispered to me one day. "We ride a boat to work. We actually get paid to do this." I liked it so much that I stayed on part-time during the fall, and returned for more the following summer.

Craig had made his way to Charleston after his college buddy Ron offered him a well-paying summer construction job. The fact that Craig had recently been corresponding with a Charleston belle he had met when she had visited her brother in seminary some months earlier—well, that seemed providential! But when that relationship fizzled shortly after his arrival, Craig considered throwing in the towel on the wife search he had begun back in high school. He prayed. "You've been faithful to me through twenty-five years of singleness," he sighed. "So I guess I can trust you for twenty-five more." His world had now shrunk to his all-male construction job (demographically similar to seminary), church on Sunday, and quiet domestic evenings with Ron, his wife Ann, and their baby. When they returned from a restaurant dinner date and urged him to come hear me sing, he shrugged. "What have I got to lose?"

Since some of my songs were original, Craig felt he had a window into my soul. It was, he would later profess, love at first sight—or at least heavy infatuation. When I put down my guitar, he lost no time introducing himself.

"I really enjoyed your singing." His blue eyes bored into mine with an intensity that eventually made me drop my gaze. His face was tan, his shoulders broad, his waist narrow. "How long have you been playing guitar?"

"Since I was thirteen or fourteen."

He told me that he, too, played guitar, and the bass as well. Then he had invited me to sit with him and Ron and Ann, whom I had briefly met the previous week.

"Thanks, but I can't. A friend is waiting for me." I nodded to a corner table where a young man sat patiently. "It was nice to meet you."

I joined my friend, but still felt Craig watching me. A few minutes later, I headed to the salad bar for my on-the-house meal. As I heaped on lettuce and tomatoes, he materialized at my side, plate in hand. It took him two minutes, tops, to state his case.

He had put himself through college, earned a degree in building construction, and worked several years, but then decided he wanted to invest his life helping people grow spiritually. He had just finished his first year at Covenant Seminary, a Presbyterian graduate school in St. Louis. "I don't know where God will lead me," he explained. "Maybe a pastorate here in the States, but maybe overseas or urban ministry." He flashed a dazzling, almost goofy smile. Something about him—a mix of boyishness and spiritual maturity, humility and boldness—impressed me.

Returning to the small plywood platform for my second set, I still sensed Craig's gaze. But I did not look at him. Somehow, eye contact would have felt...too forward, too intimate, an invitation. Craig later told me he had despaired at this point. "Maybe I said something wrong. Maybe she doesn't like me. Maybe that guy is her boyfriend...or a fiancé!"

A few minutes later, Craig and his friends pushed back their chairs and slowly walked to the door. But Craig lingered, stalling, fiddling with the toothpicks at the register, ducking his head then glancing my way one last time. I looked back. And smiled.

The following week Craig asked me out, and within a month, declared his love for me with ardent intensity. A few weeks later, when he returned to St. Louis for the second year of his three-year Master of Divinity program, he love-bombed me with letters and long phone calls. In October, using money from his meager student loan, he flew me out to St. Louis. His seminary buddies slapped him on the back, amazed that he had gone to Charleston to check out one woman and with blitzkrieg speed had won over another. In November, just four months after our first date, he sold his 1968 Mustang fastback to buy an engagement ring. He flew to Charleston, where we jumped in my car and drove to Florida. Craig, meeting my parents for the first time, asked to marry me.

"But what about the religious difference?" my mother asked. I explained, as gently as possible, what I had not wanted to tell her in a letter. While I appreciated many aspects of the Catholic Church and my liturgically rich upbringing, I had decided to leave on theological grounds.

My mother looked like she'd been punched. How could it not hurt? I was the child she had baptized Maria Virginia, the latest in generations of French and Irish Catholic girls named after the Virgin Mary. All those years of Catholic elementary school, ironing my little plaid uniforms and Peter Pan collars. The angelic First Holy Communion dress and veil she had sewn, the fish on Fridays. I was throwing over the One True Church, papal infallibility and all the popes since Peter. I was leaving the rosary for the Reformation.

"It's just that you're the only one who ever cared about the Church," she choked. I had been playing guitar in folk masses since age thirteen. It was an open secret that my two older brothers had spent their teen years playing hooky from Mass.

My father, more sanguine, sighed. "A few hundred years ago, you would have been burned at the stake. I'm glad that's no longer true!" His concern was Craig's present status as an "impecunious seminarian"—with no income at all. "But after seminary, in another year and a half, you'll be a pastor in a Presbyterian church?"

"Yes, probably," Craig replied.

My father envisioned stately churches in comfortable enclaves with well-heeled parishioners. "Well, you'll never be rich, but you'll make a decent living."

I often thought back to my father's words and wondered if, during our years of struggle, he remembered them.

I had no idea what it meant to be a pastor's wife. During our engagement, I read up on the subject with the zeal of the converted. I found plenty of evidence of ministerial marriage meltdown. A prominent ministry magazine devoted an entire issue to the pastoral family. One article chilled me: "Minister's Wives: The Walking Wounded." I read of absent, overworked husbands, neglected wives, grumbling parishioners, skimpy paychecks, and unspoken expectations. Parishioners traipsed unannounced through the manse at all hours, female church members demanded counseling time and angled for more, board members erupted over the color of the new carpet. Is this what I've committed to? Shell-shocked, I showed it to Craig.

"It won't be like that for us," he promised, embracing me. "Besides, manses are largely a thing of the past in our denomination. Most couples own their own houses."

Another book for pastor's wives opened with a neglected wife staring at a bare light bulb in a camp cabin while her youth-pastor husband worked sixteen-hour days. "No way," I thought, pushing back uncertainty. "Anyway, Craig's not going into youth ministry."

But two weeks after our wedding, I lay staring up at a bare light bulb in a cabin in Colorado. Our double bed was separated from ten giggling teen girls by a floor-to-ceiling curtain. Each morning, Craig slipped out of bed before seven and returned to my side, exhausted, near midnight.

As part of his internship, we had driven a station wagon full of high school teens across the country to this church camp. Craig had agreed to serve as head counselor for a week, and I to serve as a girls' counselor. He had volunteered here for several years, and his addition of a wife did not meet with universal feminine teen approval. A few girls eyed me suspiciously. "So you're his wife? I thought he would wait for me!" pouted one girl in tight shorts and a cropped t-shirt. Others nodded in agreement.

I tried so hard. I hiked up a fourteen thousand-foot mountain in borrowed boots that left my feet blistered and bloody. I led girls in devotions every morning at seven, and prayed with them to get along better with their little brothers or parents. I ate with them, joined them in the lodge for kitchen duty, swam with them during free time.

One night, Craig told me that the pastor who was speaking at the camp had privately expressed concerns about my bathing attire. Apparently, my one-piece, chocolate-brown suit with the deep slit and 34A cleavage was a little provocative.

"He said that?" I gasped. I felt like a scarlet woman.

"Yes," Craig said. His face lit up. "But I really like it!"

I stuffed the bathing suit at the bottom of my drawer.

Because we had agreed to spend our week focusing on the kids, Craig and I spent little time together. The girls noticed, and peppered me with questions.

"Why don't you eat with your husband?"

"Why don't we ever see you together? Don't you like each other?"

I tried to explain that we were camp counselors, not honeymooners, and we wanted to focus on them. They looked skeptical. They did not weep with gratitude at our sacrifice.

One afternoon, I trudged up the steep hill to our cabin to find Craig's underwear thumb tacked across the front porch railing, resplendent with giant red lipstick hearts. His flapping Fruit-of-the-Looms greatly amused the gaggle of girls. Mortified, I yanked them down. As a new bride, I was a tad oversensitive. I snapped to the girls that I was hurt that they had violated our privacy.

"We just thought it would be funny," they said innocently.

"Where did you find them?" I interrogated. "Did you go through our drawers?"

"No," they defended themselves. "He left them on the bathroom floor."

Now I was irked at Craig.

By the end of the week, I felt marital doom stalking us. My loneliness and feelings of trailing a distant second to the ministry burst to the surface. When I heard that a prominent Christian couple had filed for divorce, it was like squirting lighter fluid on smoldering embers. As Craig stumbled into the cabin at midnight, I was a tight, frayed cable, ready to snap. I struggled to articulate my feelings, but was nearly incoherent. "I don't want to get a divorce!" I sobbed.

He was stunned, struck by lighting on a clear summer day. Poor guy, married only two weeks and his wife was using the "D" word. We talked for a long time, and renewed the covenant of communication we had formed during our engagement: to share openly with each other, to never let the sun go down on our anger. That resolve would serve us well as we returned to Maryland for Craig's pastoral internship.

CHAPTER 2

AN URBAN GENESIS

A S Craig's Honda neared the Baltimore city line, the four-lane road narrowed to two and large retail chains gave way to shabby storefronts with barred windows and advertisements for cheap liquor. Hair braiding shops and dollar stores dotted every other block.

A week before, Craig had returned home from the church office radiating excitement.

"I've been asked to fill in at a struggling mission church in the city," he announced.

"What mission church?"

"Just a few people attending an afternoon worship service right now, but the presbytery hopes it will grow."

The presbytery consisted of leaders—pastors and elders—from the denomination's Maryland, Delaware, and Virginia churches. They had realized the scantiness of their impact in urban Baltimore. Most churches in our denomination, the Reformed Presbyterian Church, Evangelical Synod (which later merged with the Presbyterian Church in America, or P.C.A.) sat safely in the suburbs. Some city congregations, unable to adjust to the changing demographics, had moved to the suburbs. Many of the urban churches in other denominations had strayed from what we considered Biblical absolutes, such as the deity of Christ. The presbytery recognized that new churches do a better job attracting unbelievers. Thus, they had decided to plant a church in the city.

"It's called the Charles Village Fellowship," Craig said.

"Sounds interesting," I said. "When will you start?"

"Sunday afternoon, four o'clock."

He paced our tiny living room furnished with a hand-me-down sofa, mismatched chairs, and the chipped desk where I would type papers that fall when I transferred to a local college for my senior year.

"We'll visit this Sunday. Check it out. This is a great opportunity to see if urban ministry is for us."

Urban ministry sounded exciting, cutting-edge—and a bit daunting. I had dated a guy who spent a summer volunteering in a Catholic inner city church, and his letters had been a window to a world far different from my middle-class, all-white, suburban upbringing. During our engagement, Craig and I had met men and women who worked in inner city St. Louis.

"Tell me about this mission work," I said. "Why does it need someone to fill in?"

"The last leader quit after two months," Craig admitted. "There's no pastor right now, so a guy who once attended seminary has stepped into the gap, but he isn't working out either."

"Isn't working out?"

Craig hesitated. "He's become mentally unbalanced."

We had prayed about where God might lead us following Craig's internship and final year of seminary. One of his professors had challenged the students to consider overseas missions or the city instead of competing with each other in the suburbs. We wanted to follow Jesus anywhere he could use us. We were willing to go where others might be unwilling to go. We wanted to make a difference, to be challenged spiritually, to take a leap of faith and watch God catch us.

What better target than urban Baltimore for two fresh-faced, untested newlyweds?

The name Charles Village Fellowship reflected the denomination's original plan to target the middle-class yuppies and students in the neighborhood around the Johns Hopkins University. But somehow this church plant had migrated to poorer Waverly, several blocks east, where the 1980 annual median family income was below $15,000. Waverly's tenuous hold on integration—what cynical observers of America's racial demographics described as "that period between when the first black family moves in and the last white family moves out"—was already slipping. Middle-class whites and African Americans had been leaving Waverly and other city neighborhoods for over a decade, fleeing crime, drugs, and crumbling public schools. Waverly's once-diverse mix of thrifty students, young professionals, senior citizens, aging hippies, gay activists, the unemployed, and the working poor was giving way to a more homogeneous low-income, minority population. Pawnshops, check-cashing outlets, and rent-to-own stores had sprung up when Woolworths, Hardware Fair, and the A & P grocery fled. The Kentucky Fried Chicken had installed bulletproof barriers and turnstiles where patrons exchanged crumpled dollar bills for hot, spicy food. A neighborhood bank—which had once posted a hand-lettered, misspelled note saying, "No Mone Orders Today," closed its branch.

We parked on a tired, littered street in front of a sooty red-brick Baptist church that had agreed to rent space for an afternoon worship service. A man in his early thirties stood outside, smoking intently. A pair of old, seventies-style striped bellbottoms were fastened under his ballooning belly and topped with a loud, mismatched shirt. He drew hard on the cigarette, and as we approached, ground the butt into the sidewalk and thrust out a nicotine-stained hand.

"How ya doin'?" he said in an aggressively friendly way. "I'm Larry." He stepped close, keeping eye contact for a few seconds too long. His brown eyes were troubled but intelligent. His straight, dark brown hair needed a wash and trim, and he smelled stale.

We introduced ourselves and followed him inside the church, which smelled of old books and dust. At the front of the sanctuary, a half dozen or so white adults sat on folding chairs arranged in a semicircle. They included the former seminary student, whose mental illness was lapping at his heels, and his thin wife, stretched tight with the care of two small children and a collapsing husband. To Larry's left sat an equally disheveled and hygienically-challenged dark-haired fellow. On his right, a skinny thirty-year-old whose thin, blond hair nearly touched his threadbare collar. "I'm Steve," he said with a shy smile.

Craig led an informal service. A Peabody Conservatory student with waist-long, dark hair rose to play a few hymns on the piano, and Craig taught from the Book of Psalms. Afterward, everyone gathered for a potluck dinner in the church basement, digging into casseroles the women had brought, which were heavy on noodles and rice, short on meat. Plopping down at one of the chipped, folding tables, Larry pulled a Budweiser six-pack from a paper bag, popped one open, and lit a cigarette. I was a bit surprised by this.

The Baptists were even more surprised. Finding Larry's empties later that week, they ejected the group.

On the way home, Craig and I talked about this odd gathering. What Larry and the other street-smart men lacked in social finesse, hygiene, and mental stability, they made up for in honest struggle. We found it refreshing to be among people who were trying to follow Jesus as they struggled with poverty, mental illness, unemployment, and other issues. We dreamed of a place for people like Larry to be embraced by the Gospel, to know God's unconditional love.

Over the next few months, duties for this mission work would expand like a patch of kudzu, gradually taking more and more of Craig's time. We started a midweek Bible study and a social time that included informal discussions on how to apply the Gospel to life. Crisis situations erupted often; once a man from our fellowship was coughing up blood, so Craig took him to a local emergency room. They waited over five hours. Desperate for treatment, Craig finally raced the man to a suburban hospital where he was diagnosed, treated, and released within forty-five minutes.

While officially Craig was still interning at the suburban church, its leaders agreed that our city ministry should become his main focus. As we commuted from country to city for Sunday afternoon worship, midweek Bible study, social events, and intermittent crisis intervention, our pre-urban lives faded into the background. We began to wonder if God was calling us for the long haul to a place with more concrete than cornfields.

CHAPTER 3

Maria in labor/Craig's cousin Tim

A PREGNANT REVELATION

ABOUT this time, I began the fall semester of my senior year at a nearby university. One morning, shutting off the alarm and putting my feet to the floor, I felt queasy. Strange. Not quite right. When this persisted for several days, I pulled out my calendar and started counting backwards. Then forwards. It was a revelation. Suddenly it became clear that, in addition to incubating a fledgling ecclesiastical group, we were incubating something else.

We had been married three months. If I had gotten pregnant any faster, it would have been a scandal. We were one month into our urban ministry.

Craig and I stared at each other, dazed, excited, disappointed, terrified. We both came from families with five children and had hoped to have several of our own. But not now. Not when we could barely support ourselves. Craig's internship paid six hundred dollars a month, and offered no health insurance. His school loan hovered over us. I was a full-time student with a tiny part-time job. We would also need to pay for his upcoming, final year of seminary. I had planned to take classes in Biblical studies or counseling when Craig returned to seminary. Goodbye, M.A., hello, M.O.M. "Children are a blessing from the Lord," we reminded each other, quoting Psalm 127.

We knew our parents would be surprised but ultimately supportive. We decided to share our news with Craig's mother, Cleo. Looking out her kitchen window, Cleo saw us approach from our garage apartment, cradling something small in our hands and laughing. She thought she knew what this meant. As we tried to enter, she threw her weight against the kitchen door.

"Get that thing out of here! I don't want to see it!" she commanded.

This only made us laugh harder. "No, no, you'll really like this," we choked.

"I don't think so! Get that thing out of my house!"

"Mom, seriously, what do you think we have?" Craig asked.

"It's a mouse! You've caught a mouse in that apartment, and I don't want to see it!"

After repeated assurances that we were rodent-free, she cracked the door and peeked out. I held up a little plastic wand with a color strip inside.

"Oooh, and what is this?" Cleo asked.

"A home pregnancy test," Craig told her. "A positive home pregnancy test."

"Well, well, well!" Cleo beamed, throwing open the door.

I began to read books about pregnancy and childbirth and made a list of everything a new baby needs—crib, changing table, car seat, the hundred accoutrements of infant life. I prayed over the list every day. Somehow, over the next nine months, God sent me every item we needed.

Because Craig's pastoral stipend did not include health insurance, I received prenatal care at a Catholic hospital clinic near the city-county line that charged on a sliding scale. I waited in long queues for brief appointments, lined up with other pregnant girls like lunch hour shoppers at a crowded deli, a captive to the banal soap operas that blared from a television in the waiting room. At twenty-one, I was one of the oldest: most were high school girls from Baltimore's economically depressed east side. The nurses called me "Miss Garriott," and I gave up correcting them.

I learned that our income qualified us for WIC (Women, Infants and Children) vouchers, the government's food stamp program for pregnant and nursing mothers. I had grown tired of standing in the grocery aisles, trying to decide which staples I would have to put back. Vouchers for milk, cheese, juice and cereal would ease that burden—they don't call it "relief" for nothing. The program's nutritionist asked me to write down the foods I had eaten over the previous twenty-four hours. My list made her ecstatic: lean meat, cottage cheese, an apple, spinach, whole wheat bread.

"A lot of the girls eat a bag of chips and a soda for lunch," she mourned.

The humiliation of poverty felt raw and shameful and new. Embarrassed to redeem the vouchers at our suburban grocery store, I slipped them to the cashiers as quietly as possible. But people noticed, and I could feel their eyes on me. Once, a cashier yelled across the store to a supervisor, "Margaret, how do I punch in these food stamp coupons?" I cringed.

I had grown up in McLean, Virginia, outside Washington, D.C. My father's salary and mother's prudent home management had not only sent five children to college but purchased a summer investment home as well. They knew we were on a tight budget, but would have been shocked to learn that for our first married year, we qualified for food stamps. Craig's father, Pete, owned his own plumbing business and built houses on the side, and Cleo had been a hairdresser. They had never needed government assistance. We justified the pain of accepting WIC vouchers by recognizing that God was helping us identify with the poor. But we knew there was a difference between being broke and being poor. At any time Craig could use his bachelor's degree in architecture from Virginia Tech to pull us out of poverty. We—unlike the truly poor—had options. This was the first of many lessons in our urban education.

CHAPTER 4

Steve Stahl, 1982

CON GAMES

WE were lily-white suburbanites woefully unprepared for urban ministry. We didn't know a chicken box from a Happy Meal. We didn't know a step dance from a fox trot. We didn't know an unlicensed taxi driver (a hack) from a freelance writer (a hack). We couldn't sing a single verse of James Weldon Johnson's "Lift Every Voice," often called the black national anthem. We didn't know what God was already doing in the city and whether or not he would use us there.

But this was about to change. We would learn that a chicken box is an urban staple: several pieces of fried chicken and a heap of French fries, sometimes slathered with cheese or hot sauce. We would thrill to watch step dancing, the tightly choreographed, athletic movements drawn from African roots (sort of like Irish dancing on steroids). We would choke up at all five verses to "Lift Every Voice." We would learn that God had his people in the city, and that he would use us—the ignorant and unprepared—to build his kingdom.

While the priests of my Catholic childhood had periodically preached about God's care for the poor, little had prepared me for a struggling urban neighborhood. Nor had Craig's two years of seminary fully addressed the issues we now faced.

How do you serve an economically unstable, racially mixed area? How do you attract African Americans to a denomination that largely sat on the sidelines during the civil rights movement? How do you show Jesus' love to people scraping for the basics of food and shelter? How do you survive on income from a tiny congregation rife with unemployed and under-employed members? Few people in our branch of the Presbyterian church had experience in urban church planting—let alone in multiethnic, low-income city neighborhoods. We desperately needed mentoring.

Within a few months, I began to express my frustrations in my journal.

Matthew 7 says, "Not everyone who says to me, 'Lord, Lord,' will enter the kingdom of heaven, but only he who does the will of my father in heaven.'" But what is God's charge to me? I have been struggling with the inner city work. It is so demanding and draining with so few tangible rewards. I've been frustrated and upset with some of the people. But this is not how God wants me to deal with all this. He wants me to pray and trust Him and do His will...

God was teaching us to hang onto the promises of Jesus just as a rock climber rappelling down a cliff grasps his rope.

Thanks to Larry's six-pack, our first crisis was to find another meeting place. In many municipalities, start-up churches lease space in public schools or recreation centers, but Baltimore City facilities were closed to religious groups. Until we found more suitable arrangements, we decided to rotate among members' homes.

One young couple had space, but like us, lived too far away. The Peabody Conservatory student's second-floor apartment boasted a grand piano, but had almost no chairs. Steve's rented room was in a house so decrepit I wondered if it could bear the weight of twelve additional people. Larry's nicotine-stained basement apartment qualified for an EPA air-quality warning. The cramped apartment of the former seminary student and his wife exuded a tense sadness; once, when he tried to give us a dozen eggs from the local farmer's market, his wife burst into tears. She had little else to feed their children.

Craig and I cut our ecclesiastical teeth on Larry, Steve and several other members whose lives seemed to teeter on the edge. We spent endless hours hashing out the issues they presented. They seemed to have no relationships with healthy people, and little family. Steve rarely saw his father, though he lived in the area; another fellow's dad paid for his apartment, but they seemed perpetually at odds. Larry was rumored to have spent time in prison for attacking his father with an axe and setting his house on fire.

Larry and another attendee, who lived off government disability checks, frustrated us with their manipulation and irresponsibility. Their code seemed to be "get over or get by." But they taught us invaluable lessons about mental illness and street culture. They forced us to constantly think about the spiritual and emotional lives of the mentally ill. For example, was it in Larry's best interests to not work at all? To live an idle, aimless life, not contributing to society, excluded from the normal workday world? If God had created all people to work, to create, and take dominion, wouldn't volunteer work build him up? Wouldn't he be healthier with productive tasks, a regular schedule, and more contact with healthy people?

Larry had little sense of work or sleep schedules: he often called at two or three in the morning to chat about the Bible, discuss a problem, or ask for cash. He slept, ate, played guitar, wrote poetry, and hung out with other unemployed or mentally ill men. He generally came outfitted with Twinkies and a 7-11 Big Gulp. I secretly suspected his mental state would improve dramatically on three squares a day with a little wheat germ thrown in for good measure. Within days, Larry would squander his disability check on Chinese restaurants, new clothes, and paying back loans from the previous month. The rest of the month, he would hit us up for money, using charm and con games to talk Craig into a loan or a new pair of sneakers or jeans—until we learned that his check was more than our income.

One night Larry phoned, demanding that Craig come down to the city and give him some money. When Craig refused, Larry erupted. "If you were really a Christian, you'd come down here. You call yourself a minister, and you won't help me? F—- you!"

Craig hung up. When Larry called back, I answered and refused to let him talk to Craig. "F—- you, too!" Larry roared. He later apologized.

But Larry could also be charming and witty. He offered opinions on local and national politics, and even thought up a more modest slogan to replace the hyperbolic "Baltimore is Best." "How 'bout this," Larry said, "'Baltimore—It'll Do.'" He had a fondness for puns and lame jokes, which he related in his thick, local, "Bawlmerese" accent. During the Reagan years, I heard this one over and over:

"Hey," Larry poked me with a fleshy, brown-stained finger. "What kind of gun do you find in the White House?" "I don't know Larry, what kind?" I humored him. "A Ray-gun! Get it? Ray-gun."

I often thought how different he could have been had schizophrenia not overtaken him. Periodically, he stopped taking his medicine and a revolutionary persona named David Michael Blue emerged. He phoned in the middle of the night: "God has called me to raise an army to liberate oppressed people and punish wicked institutions," he ranted. "I'm going to go down to Mexico, gather some people there, then head up to Canada, too."

Craig tried to reason with him, urged him to take his medicine, offered to drive him to the hospital, but to no avail.

When the former seminarian told Larry that God had raised up prophets in Old Testament times to preach violence against Israel's enemies, this unseated Larry completely. As David Michael Blue, he painted "666"—the symbol for the beast in the Book of Revelation—on several bars near his Waverly apartment and threw a brick through the window of a pornographic bookstore. This landed David Michael Blue in jail.

At Larry's arraignment, the courtroom buzzed with irate Waverly businessmen. The judge's gaze moved from Larry's dirty jeans and stringy hair to the baby-faced blond man in the suit standing next to Larry's public defender. "And who are you?" the judge asked Craig.

With some awkwardness, Craig explained that he was Larry's pastor. We hadn't expected that Craig's pastoral duties would include going to court on behalf of delusional, rock-throwing congregants.

"Does your church encourage these kinds of actions?"

"No, sir."

"What am I dealing with here? Is he the kind of person to pick up a machine gun and start blowing people away?"

"Not to my knowledge, sir."

Unable to post bond, Larry spent several weeks in jail. When his trial came up, Larry found himself standing before a female judge. He refused to submit to justice dispensed by a woman. "Down with women, down with the E.R.A., and down with you, judge!" he roared.

Whack! The gavel fell. "Thirty days, contempt of court."

Larry's arrest stirred up impassioned debate among our tiny band of believers. At our next meeting, in Steve's rundown apartment, the former seminarian defended a position known as radical theonomy—"God's law"—calling for government imposition of Old Testament statutes. Craig argued that Christ had taught that the authority of the Church is a spiritual one. He pointed out that Jesus rebuked Peter for taking up the sword. The group decided that Craig's theology was correct. The whole event had a surreal tint, like an old sepia photograph where the colors are no longer true.

Working with these new believers flooded us with headaches and hope. We found it exciting to engage this raw, unchurched culture. For instance, we watched Steve, a quiet loner in his early thirties, blossom. Steve had dropped out of school in the eighth grade and sporadically painted houses for his brother's company. Before coming to Christ, he had difficulty keeping a job because of his lack of education and low self-esteem. But after his conversion, Steve spent several hours every day reading the Bible. As his confidence grew and his emotional health improved, he worked steadily. Church members embraced him and invited him over for dinner. The fears and insecurities that had marked his earlier life faded. In its place, a gentle spirit emerged.

Larry and other street men seemed to exhibit a genuine faith, even if their way of expressing it occasionally dumbfounded us. During a part of the worship service set aside for silent confession, they blurted their sins out loud with earnest repentance. Lust was a prominent theme. "God, You know I've been wanting a woman pretty bad. And I've been goin' places I've got no business goin'. I'm asking you to forgive me. And send me a girlfriend. Amen."

They met God in worship with gutsy confidence, without any masks, in a transparency that made me squirm and marvel at the same time. Larry, Steve, and some of their friends would never be rich or even middle class, never be eulogized in the *Baltimore Sun*, never be considered important or valuable in the world's eyes. But they were valuable to God. And he was with them.

CHAPTER 5

Trip to Voice of Calvary, 1982

"ISN'T JESUS BIGGER THAN RACE AND PLACE?"

THAT winter of 1980, the presbytery officially asked Craig to pastor the mission work, which was still known as the Charles Village Fellowship. He would work full-time to develop and lead the church. He would receive a modest salary (subsidized by presbytery the first year). He would finish his Master of Divinity degree part-time by commuting to Westminster Seminary in Philadelphia two days a week for the next few years.

Our sense of God's call was based on several factors. The Scriptures clearly instruct believers to extend the Gospel to all people groups and care for the downtrodden of society. The presbytery had confirmed Craig's leadership, and we felt a conviction in our hearts to stay. Circumstances seemed to point to remaining in this ministry. And God was blessing the church, slowly but steadily bringing in new believers.

The members—now numbering a dozen—met to decide on a name. While most church plants, or start-ups, are named by the organizing pastor, Craig wanted to build consensus. Members floated possibilities. Someone offered Faith Christian Fellowship. Craig suggested Rock Fellowship, because "Jesus is our foundation, our fortress." After more discussion, quiet Steve spoke up. He measured his words like a frugal housewife counting coins: "Faith Christian

Fellowship. That name just explains it all. We have faith. We're Christian. And we believe it's important to have fellowship and encourage one another."

Unimaginative, I thought, but several heads nodded in agreement. When it was time to vote, everyone scribbled his or her choice on a piece of paper, and put it in a bowl. When the tally was taken, Steve's choice prevailed. We became Faith Christian Fellowship.

In 1980, Baltimore was hurting.

The blue-collar jobs that had put food on the family table for generations were evaporating like drops of water on a hot griddle; thirty thousand manufacturing jobs had disappeared during the previous ten years alone. Every day, thousands of city residents—one in ten—faced the empty days, slammed doors, and empty pockets of unemployment. Joblessness stalked youths and minorities; fifty percent couldn't find work. More public-school kids took permanently to the streets than stayed to stride across an auditorium stage, shake a principal's hand, and palm a diploma—while in surrounding counties, high-school graduates outnumbered dropouts at least four to one. Economy-related crimes—burglary, larceny, and robbery—spiked, jumping almost fifty percent during the first half of 1981. The "white flight" triggered in the 1960s sped on without a backward glance. Residents were fleeing the city at the rate of 10,000 a year.

What an opportunity for the Gospel.

Everywhere we looked in the Bible, we saw God's concern for the city—and for the poor, who are often disproportionally warehoused in cities. About sprawling Ninevah, God challenged Jonah: "Should I not be concerned about that great city?" Approaching Jerusalem, Jesus wept over that ancient metropolis. Of King Josiah, God complimented, "He defended the cause of the poor and needy, and so all went well. Is that not what it means to know me?" And hadn't Jesus declared that his mission was "to preach good news to the poor"? That when we serve "the least of these" we are serving him?

But how do we bring Jesus into this crucible of relentless needs? How do we introduce Jesus to people who are different from us culturally, educationally, and economically? Baltimore was primarily a black and white city, but its Asian, Latino, and international population was increasing. How do we build a church that unites these diverse groups? Many urban churches in Baltimore struggled to stay afloat even with one ethnic group. None of the churches in our presbytery had sought such a messy mix.

We devoured books about urban outreach, cross-cultural strategies, multi-ethnic ministry, and ministry to the poor. We learned that in addition to our lack of urban experience and meager resources, an even bigger hurdle loomed: according to many church growth experts, the sort of church we were attempting to build simply would not work.

At that time, most how-to-grow-your-church books advocated the homogenous unit principle. It went like this: "Focus on one people-group. Grow a black church, a white church, or a Korean church. Mixed churches won't fly." People are uncomfortable crossing ethnic and class barriers, sociologists argued. Multiethnic churches are too problematic.

"But where is that in the Bible?" Craig countered. "Sure, we have to contextualize the Gospel to different cultures. But shouldn't love for Jesus supersede affinity groups? Isn't Jesus bigger than race or place?"

Having scoured Scripture from Genesis to Revelation, Craig read only of a God who unites diverse people to worship him. After all, Jesus didn't build tidy segregated groups of followers, or choose people who felt comfortable together. He tapped militant Simon the Zealot (a Jewish patriot) and Matthew, the tax collector (who had cooperated with the occupying Romans). Outside of Christ, they would have had little tolerance for one another.

In its first decade, the early church wrestled with race—and set a precedent. When Greek-speaking widows complained of being neglected in the daily food distribution, the apostles resolved the dispute by appointing leaders from both the dominant (Hebrew-speaking) and subdominant (Greek-speaking) cultures. The church didn't split into Greek and Hebraic congregations.

Paul's proclamation to the Galatians must have left them goggle-eyed. "There is neither Jew nor Greek, slave nor free, male nor female, for you are all one in Christ Jesus." The Ephesians must have been similarly stunned, too, when Paul declared that Jesus had destroyed the dividing wall between peoples and made them one. Following Jesus Christ transcends cultural differences.

"But where is this happening?" we asked. In the 1950s, Billy Graham had refused to allow segregated seating at his crusades, lamenting that eleven a.m. on Sunday was "America's most segregated hour." Martin Luther King, a decade later, also decried America's segregated houses of worship. But who was listening to Graham? What had happened to King's eloquently articulated dream of racial reconciliation? Why wasn't the church embracing it?

We knew only a few exceptions to this de facto segregation of the American church. Most of these had sprung up in the 1970s; a few had already split along racial lines. When Randy Nabors, who called himself "a white boy from the projects of New Jersey," and his African-American wife Joan started New City Fellowship in Chattanooga, few expected their multiethnic church to thrive. But it did. John Perkins, the son of a sharecropper, founded Voice of Calvary Ministries in Mississippi, where blacks and whites worshipped and worked together. His books, *Let Justice Roll Down* and *A Quiet Revolution*, outlined his three Rs of Christian community development: Reconciliation (between man and God, and between races), Relocation (into the community of need), and Redistribution (sharing one's resources and empowering the poor).

Craig and I didn't believe that there was anything wrong with wanting to be with people who look like you, who share the same racial and cultural background. But we believed God was calling us to a richer, deeper experience. We had no way of knowing how rich, how deep, and how difficult at times building a diverse church would be.

We thought John Perkins best articulated the practical, Biblical principles to reach a struggling urban community. But most people thought we were wrong or misguided.

"I predict disaster," intoned a fellow seminarian, when learning of our vision.

"Only the blacks can reach the blacks," warned one family member.

But Craig refused to give up. "People from every tribe, nation and tongue will worship God together in Heaven," he said. He paced back and forth, warming to his topic. "Why not here? If the neighborhood is multiethnic, then the church on the corner should reflect that. Most New Testament epistles address the issues of uniting race and class. And the apostles didn't split into ethnocentric congregations."

For the next fifteen years, Craig said this again and again. On Sunday mornings, he preached it with confidence from the pulpit. In afternoon workshops, he taught it through the books of the Bible. He blurted it out at our kitchen table, head in his hands as if to assuage the pain from banging it against the walls of race and class. He said it in great agitation, pacing back and forth in our living room, as various crises threatened the church. He sighed it at night in our bed before rolling over into exhausted sleep.

"It's a whole lot easier to focus on one people group," he said. "It's just not in the Bible."

CHAPTER 6

Bill Bolling, Bob and Jean Jenkins, Craig

"THIS IS A WEIRD GROUP"

"I'LL tell you one thing," Craig said one day in the spring of 1981 as I labored over a paper for one of my classes and shifted my uncomfortably large belly. "If this church is going to get off the ground, we need strong African American leadership. I know just the man."

"Who?" I asked.

"Bill Bolling, my old buddy from Virginia Tech. He's mature, focused—and he has a heart for the city. I'm inviting him to the worship service this Sunday."

Bill agreed to visit. That same day—Palm Sunday—two other future leaders, Bob and Jean Jenkins, attended as well. We gathered in a low-ceilinged basement apartment belonging to a friend of Larry's. Incense burned, not for liturgical purposes but to mask the musky air and the lingering aroma of a previous pot-smoking session. A floor-length curtain of glass beads separated the hall doorway from the living room. Larry and Steve sank into the sagging couch. The rest of us perched on folding chairs.

For our opening song, Steve tapped his bongo drums and I played guitar. Great with child in my denim maternity jumper, I shared my Bible with one of the young men whose mental illness had precluded any recent contact with barbers, showers, or washing machines. He kept nervously rubbing his hands up and down the thighs of his dirty jeans. Seeing me sharing my Bible with him, Jean Jenkins assumed I was his wife or girlfriend. Later she told me, "I just couldn't figure out how this smelly guy ended up with this sweet, young thing."

Bill and the Jenkinses were underwhelmed by the possibilities in this odd mix. A pastor who looked eighteen, his pregnant wife, a handful of mentally ill white guys, and a couple of college students or recent graduates?

"This is a weird group," Bill thought to himself. "I'd better plan my exit strategy. I'm telling Craig, 'See you later.'" But somehow, the three decided to visit again the following Sunday. And the next.

After the second week, Bill began to see possibilities. "These are people who know the Lord," he decided. "Maybe I'll stick around a while."

God had given us uniquely qualified men and women for this oddball work. Son of a devout mother and an alcoholic father, Bill spent much of his childhood hungry and cold in Baltimore's Cherry Hill housing projects. Even though his mother worked several jobs to support her six children, the family struggled to survive. Bill remembers watching snow fall on their few possessions, tossed onto the street in one of several evictions. His parents hung a blanket over the kitchen door and the whole family slept in front of the open stove, their only source of heat. On payday, his mother sent Bill to the corner bar to beg his father for money before he drank it all away.

Bill excelled academically and earned admission to the city's best magnet high school. He still remembers the first day he saw the school's large parking lot. "Man, they sure have a lot of teachers!" he thought. It was the student lot.

After graduation, Bill headed for Virginia Polytechnic Institute, where he met Craig in a Bible study. Four years later, a degree in engineering hung on his wall. He bought a renovated townhouse in Baltimore, and his mother and several younger siblings moved in with him.

Bob Jenkins looked the part of the distinguished, middle-aged successful lawyer he had become. But Bob had spent twenty years of his life living on the streets or in downtown missions, in and out of jails and institutions for petty crimes associated with his alcoholism. Bob had married three times, been divorced three times, and had fathered three daughters, from whom he was estranged. Although he clocked forty separate admissions to the state hospital, it seemed that nothing could break the cycle of drinking, drying out, and drinking again. But in 1972, he converted to Christ and dried out for good. Then he met and married Jean, a librarian and Bible teacher. At forty, he enrolled in law school at night and took his first full-time day job in years. After graduation, he started his own law practice. Although they lived in the city, Bob and Jean attended a suburban church, where they learned of our fledgling congregation.

Bob and Bill became Faith's first elders. Jean mentored younger women, taught a midweek Bible study, assisted with crisis food distribution, and led several committees. Bob and Jean Jenkins would serve for twelve years before retiring to Maryland's Eastern Shore. Bill Bolling is still with us today, beloved, faithful, and steady.

God was providing the core leadership we so desperately needed. But Craig and I still lived forty minutes away in the green country, in our tiny nest above his parents' garage. We longed to plant ourselves in the Waverly community. Jesus had become the Incarnation—God with us—and had relocated to Earth. We wanted to follow his model and move into the neighborhood.

Craig's salary was modest, and although I would finish my bachelor's degree in English in a few months, I planned to be a stay-at-home mom and assist in ministry. What could we possibly afford to buy in our $20,000 price range, even in a low-income neighborhood?

CHAPTER 7

Greenmount Avenue house, 1981

GREENMOUNT AVENUE AND
A DIFFERENT AMERICAN DREAM

WHILE I concentrated on college papers and prenatal visits, Craig and his father, Pete, a plumber and home builder, went house hunting in Waverly.

For houses within our financial reach, the phrase "needs work" failed to convey the magnitude of the task at hand. Craig and Pete toured a discouraging succession of tumble-down wooden homes and burned-out row houses. They examined an abandoned auto parts store with an apartment on the second floor. It squatted next to a series of rundown storefronts on a busy street, and instead of a yard boasted a weed-laced parking lot. "We could have services there, and live upstairs!" Craig said. Mercifully, God closed that door.

I kept waiting to hear of a house worthy of a second look, but after every expedition, Craig and Pete shook their heads sadly. Until one afternoon, a savvy realtor called Craig. "I know this property is out of your price range, but it's been on the market for a while and they might take less," she explained. "It's owned by a real estate company liquidating its assets. It's a five-unit apartment house, so it has income-producing potential, which…" she said diplomatically, "might help in your situation. It does need a lot of work, though."

"It's in Waverly?" Craig asked.

"Yes," she said. "On Greenmount Avenue."

In every city, certain street names raise eyebrows. To many Baltimoreans at this time, Greenmount Avenue was a place to be avoided. Dangerous. Foreign. Other. It epitomized the worst: pawn shops and check-cashing outlets, gutters choked with litter. Men loitering on street corners, boom boxes pulsating, teenage boys jaywalking, drugs passing through quick handshakes, snatch-and-grab robberies. Some of this reputation was undeserved. Long blocks of neatly kept single-family residences and row houses testified to the pluck of urban dwellers who refused to give up.

Greenmount Avenue runs north-south, dissecting the city like a scar. At its southern end, it gasps to a stop amid housing projects, City Jail, and the Maryland State Penitentiary. At its northern end, it delineates an abrupt socio-economic schism typical of many cities but especially pronounced in Baltimore. To its west, primarily white, professional residents of Guilford tend stately homes or million-dollar mansions. On its east side, the mostly black, working-class residents of Pen Lucy—nursing assistants and aides, security guards and retired Bethlehem Steel workers, the unemployed and the under-employed, grandmothers and mothers, uncles, aunts and children—crowd into row houses, apartments, or older, sometimes poorly-maintained wooden houses. Greenmount Avenue passes through Waverly's hard-pressed commercial district of pawn and pizza shops, liquor stores, rent-to-own furniture outlets and beauty salons. Just four blocks west, Johns Hopkins University presides over more prosperous Charles Street. But that is a different world.

The realtor met Craig, Pete, and me at a rundown apartment house a few blocks north of Waverly's commercial district. Vandals had broken several windows, and paint chipped and peeled off the wood frames. Abandoned cars and piles of trash littered the vacant lot in the back.

The realtor opened the heavy, Victorian front door and we stepped into the dim hallway. A terrible odor hit us—dust, urine, mouse droppings, and something worse. We later learned that an elderly tenant had died in one of the first-floor apartments; the putrid smell lingered.

A carved wooden banister lined the central staircase, a reminder of the house's former grandeur. But someone had taken a hatchet to it to make room for a code-required firewall. It was obvious that the realty company had collected rents but had done no maintenance for years. All five kitchens and bathrooms dated to the 1940s. Broken furniture and empty bottles of Mad Dog and Colt 45 littered the vacant units. Every wall needed repairing or replacing. Neighbors complained that drug dealers conducted business from the house, and that the grass grew up to a foot high.

As we opened one apartment, an emaciated cat burst out; it had been trapped inside for weeks. The building's only tenant—not counting the mangy cat, of course—occupied the small, third-floor apartment. She had finally refused to pay rent, indignant at the lack of heat and hot water.

Craig and Pete poked around, murmuring about the radiators and plumbing. They seemed optimistic. I was excited and terrified all at once. Could God really give us this house? Would we want it if he did?

Pete pronounced the house structurally sound.

"We can fix it up ourselves," Craig exulted. "Just think of how we could use the other apartments for ministry!"

Ah, yes. I had married a visionary. In comparison, mere optimists looked like gloomy Eeyore. Craig saw things that were not and imagined what could be. This was more than the gift of faith, it was idealism squared. And I was right there with him, because we shared a dream—a different sort of American dream. In this house, we would relocate into our target neighborhood. We could also live with other believers eager to do urban ministry. With Craig and Pete's construction expertise, we could renovate it over time. I had no idea we were picking up a spoon to dig a mine shaft.

The owner had received few bids, and interest rates had spiked to fourteen and a half percent. No one was interested in a broken-down apartment house in the inner city. No one except us. We offered $25,000, and the owner took it. I sold my Toyota Corolla for a down payment, and Cleo and Pete co-signed a loan.

A month later, as the ink still dried on the settlement papers at the lawyer's office, we stopped by our new house to thank God, eat lunch, and celebrate. As the four of us parked behind the house in Cleo and Pete's beat-up old Pontiac station wagon and unwrapped Subway sandwiches, fire engines came screaming up Greenmount Avenue. We scarcely noticed this everyday occurrence, but when the blaring stopped in front of our house, we froze. Then loud pounding boomed from the front of the house.

"I think I'd better check this out," said Craig.

As he sprinted towards the front yard, I waddled behind, seven months pregnant. Rounding the corner, we saw a burly fireman in full gear kicking our front door.

"Wait!" Craig yelled, fumbling in his pocket. "I've got a key!"

"Got an emergency call from this building," the fireman said. "Suicide attempt on the third floor."

Craig threw open the door and the fireman, followed by a paramedic, bounded upstairs to the apartment. The house's sole tenant lay semiconscious on the bed, her long, strawberry-blonde hair spread across the pillow. Minutes earlier, despairing, alone, she had swallowed handfuls of pills. Before blacking out, she had gotten cold feet and called a friend.

She was still breathing. The fireman bent over her and she struggled to sit up. The paramedic strapped a blood pressure cuff on her pale arm, pumped it, and watched the dial. They lifted her onto a stretcher, tucked a blanket around her, and carried her to the waiting ambulance. A month later, she moved out.

This settlement-day suicide attempt marked the beginning of an era of sharing an apartment house with humanity's spectrum: deeply committed volunteers, missionaries, alcoholics, drug addicts, and people suffering from schizophrenia, paranoia, and manic depression. For the next ten years, Craig would spend nearly every free hour tackling century-old plumbing, aging appliances, and rotting porches. Rather than swinging a golf club on his day off, he would swing a hammer.

But before any interior repairs, we needed a roof. Our next door neighbor, a roofer, offered to do the job for one thousand dollars. But he might as well have said fifty thousand: we were penniless. "Lord!" we gasped. "Help!"

One morning a few weeks later, Craig paced outside our rural apartment, praying and fretting. "What was I thinking? Where am I going to get a thousand bucks?"

That afternoon, a long white envelope peeked from the usual stack of bills and advertisements in our driveway mailbox. The return address was from a fledgling mission church the presbytery had been trying to start in a nearby town. Craig had preached there at two services several months earlier. He ripped it open.

> *Dear Craig,*
>
> *We are dissolving our mission church, and voted to send the balance of our missions budget to you. We heard you are starting a new church in the city. May God bless you and your work.*

A check fell from the envelope. Craig picked it up. On it was a simple number one, followed by three zeroes.

CHAPTER 8

Summer Urban Project team, 1981

TWO BIRTHS

AT three o'clock one June morning, pain awakened me. It felt like a massive charley horse hardening my abdomen. I watched the hands of the clock sweep slowly around the lighted dial. Seven minutes apart: twenty-five seconds long. Six minutes apart: thirty seconds long.

Craig slept at my side, exhausted from long days in the blistering sun preparing our Greenmount Avenue house for our move. I didn't have the heart to wake him yet. Finally, at seven a.m., I rolled my swollen body out of bed, leaned over, and whispered, "Good morning, love. I'm in labor."

Craig's eyes flipped open. "Should we go to the hospital?"

"Not yet. But I'll call the doctor."

Fully awake, a realization dawned on him. That afternoon Stan Long and Dan Korzep, who led ministries at two local colleges, would begin training their students for a six-week Summer Urban Project. And we wouldn't be there.

Craig had looked forward to this for weeks. Stan, Dan, and Arlette Lindsay had recruited a dozen students from their InterVarsity groups to spend most of their summer learning about the city and serving its kids. InterVarsity, a non-denominational Christian organization, encouraged short-term, cross-cultural

37

service opportunities. The students planned to distribute flyers door-to-door inviting neighborhood kids to weekly Bible clubs which would feature puppet shows, songs, and short lessons about God and Jesus. Since we lacked a church building, the clubs would be held wherever kids could gather—on sidewalks, on front porches, or in living rooms. Parents usually appreciated this safe, healthy investment in their children, and would be invited to bring their kids to our church services.

Craig had managed to make several of our apartments livable enough to house the Urban Project students and leaders. Steve Stahl, our ministry's first convert, had pitched in with what seemed to be endless painting. (Larry, Big Gulp in hand, would drop by periodically to check on our progress, tell a joke, and shake hands all around.) Because we had not yet moved into our partial-ly-renovated apartment, the students and leaders would meet in our empty living room for prayer and training.

My college graduation ceremony two weeks before had been anticlimactic. For months I had struggled to focus, doodling baby names on the margins of notes. My interest in poetry and literature had been eclipsed by the drive to finally hold my baby and to nurture the infant church we were birthing in Baltimore.

Craig carried my little suitcase of baby clothes and labor supplies to the car—tennis balls in a sock for back rubs, lip balm, a lollipop to suck on when my mouth dried out from gasping and rhythmic breathing—pitiful ballast against a tidal wave, but I didn't know this yet.

We waved goodbye to Craig's family and drove to the hospital, located in a grimy, congested area near the city line. In a tiny labor room, nurses glided in and out, asking questions and hooking me up to a fetal monitor. Finally, a resident entered the room, introduced himself, and squinted at the printout from the monitor. He examined me, looking off into space while gauging the dilation of my cervix. The latex gloves snapped as he pulled them off.

"Labor will take another ten or twelve hours," he told us. "Do you want to hang around here, or go home and come back later?"

I repacked my little suitcase and wedged myself back in our car. Craig slid behind the wheel.

"What do you think? Should we head into the city, see how the Urban Project is going?" he asked, glancing at me sideways. He tried to sound casual, but I heard the excitement in his voice.

"Sure, might as well." I wanted to help birth this church, too. It was our call, our mission, our adventure. We drove to Greenmount Avenue.

Stan and his wife Terri, Dan, Arlette Lindsay, and fifteen eager college students had squeezed into what would soon be our living room. Craig had created our living quarters by knocking out a wall between apartments on the second floor, giving us four rooms. Laborious scrubbing and a fresh coat of paint had slightly improved the drab interior. To inexpensively cover the damaged plaster walls, Craig had mixed white paint with gallons of spackling to create a textured finish. Several students sat swallowed up in a massive, 1960s era couch. The tiger couch, we called it, after the orange and yellow stripes splashed across its fabric. Too big to fit out the door—and with no money to replace it—we had thrown a blanket over it to silence its loud roar.

Stan greeted us with surprise. "I thought you were in labor!" He eyed my belly cautiously.

"I am," I admitted, embarrassed. "But it's early labor. It's going to be a while."

The students watched me with fear and awe: is she going to have the baby here? This moment burned into their memories; years later, when they saw me at conferences, they would exclaim, "And you were in *labor* that day!"

We watched a movie about an inner city ministry founded in Watts by a young white man after the 1964 riots decimated that area of Los Angeles. His ministry had expanded to several cities, and focused on reaching children for Christ through Bible clubs. Urban missionaries in his organization were urged to commit to a particular community for life, or at least until they could raise up indigenous leaders to take their place. At the end, he looked into the camera and said, "Come die with us." Was he speaking literally or figuratively?

Squeezed into the back of the hot room, my discomfort increased with every contraction. Beads of sweat rolled down my face and under my arms. Periodically, Craig touched me, asked if I was all right. I checked my watch, timing the contractions.

"We need to go now," I told him. With a nod to Stan and Arlette, we slipped out the back. As we descended the steps, I clutched Craig's arm, stopping to breathe deeply every time a contraction hit. We bounced down potholed urban streets in our twelve-year-old Honda, its shock absorbers long gone.

At the hospital, Craig donned scrubs and wrapped footies over his size-thirteen shoes. As the clock ticked into the night, he watched the monitor outline the jagged peaks and valleys of contractions, warning me of each new offensive in this battle.

My room connected to another via a shared bathroom, and I heard the hysterical screaming of its occupant. "How far along is she?" I whispered to the middle-aged nurse whose hands smelled of cigarettes. I feared I would reach that stage and dissolve.

"She doesn't have to carry on like that," the nurse replied with disgust. I later learned that the other patient was young, alone, and had not gone through childbirth classes. She had not spent Wednesday nights for two months propped on pillows on an auditorium floor watching movies about the stages of labor, learning to breathe to outwit a terrifying pain.

I panted and breathed until my mouth was arid. I was drenched with sweat. Craig repeated his mantra over and over. "You're doing a great job. Keep it up! Almost there!"

The nurse looked at me and shook her head. "Are you sure you don't want an epidural?" she asked.

"No," I gasped. "No epidural." Lamaze instructors, who were fond of euphemisms like "discomfort," had convinced me that childbirth was a natural process and epidurals were not best for the baby.

The nurse harrumphed. "I don't know why anyone would do that," she said, rolling her eyes.

Finally, the Asian doctor who attended me spoke. "Ten centimeters. Baby coming."

The atmosphere changed. Energy and tension filled the room. Another nurse appeared, bustling around with basins, a bassinette, and shiny, cold instruments. They swabbed my twitching thighs with sticky orange iodine.

"With the next contraction, I want you to push. Push right here," he said intently, massaging me.

The nurse grabbed one knee and pushed it hard against my chest.

"O.K., Dad, hold the other leg, like this," she ordered Craig. "These contractions won't hurt because you'll be pushing," she told me.

It was another childbirth lie, and a big one. It's like concentrating on an algebra problem while someone pries your fingernails off.

They all yelled at me. "Push! Push!"

I ripped apart.

They all shouted. They saw the baby's head. I tried to look in the giant convex mirror behind the doctor's head, but there was so much blood...

In the middle of one massive push, I heard a long, high-pitched squealing echo off the tiled walls far away. It grew closer, louder. Suddenly, I realized that this noise was....me. The nurse with the cigarette-smell hands spoke.

"You really don't need to make that sound," she said abruptly.

I pushed again, and again, and again. I felt a popping and more fluid gushing out. A Greek chorus called out at once. "There's the head! One more push!"

After twenty-three hours of labor, Rebecca was born on Father's Day. She weighed eight pounds, and she had a perfectly round head, tiny rosebud lips, and wise, quizzical blue eyes. She had her father's long limbs and narrow feet.

I was in love. As they took her out of the room to examine her, waves of protectiveness washed over me. I fretted until they brought her back. When I tried to sleep, I closed my eyes and saw blood. I remembered the curse in Genesis: "In pain you shall bring forth children…" God wasn't kidding. But when I held Rebecca, the pain of labor felt utterly inconsequential compared to this tiny, perfect being. It was a modest expenditure for such a treasure.

The next day, my Lamaze coach called me at the hospital, her perky voice floating through the receiver. "How was your childbirth experience?" she asked.

I wanted to say it was excruciating, that she had not prepared me for this, that nothing could, and who was she kidding about this breathing business? "It was okay," I lied.

On the third day, the nurses put me in a wheelchair and placed my tightly wrapped daughter in my arms. We stopped at the front desk where Craig wrote a check for fifty dollars—the hospital's fee, charged on a sliding scale based on our income.

Two weeks later, we moved to Greenmount Avenue. We could little imagine how this decision would affect our daughter.

CHAPTER 9

Becky and Melissa, 1984

"YOU LIVE WHERE?"

A blank stare. A furrowed brow. A double take.

"Where? You live where?"

Friends and strangers alike questioned the wisdom of our move to Greenmount Avenue. Our new home sat on a notorious street in a racially divided city gasping for its economic breath. In hypersegregated Baltimore, we were the wrong race to move to Greenmount Avenue.

A woman Craig had known since high school collared him one afternoon at his parents' house. "Shame on you, Craig Garriott! Shame on you for moving your family into the city!"

I had expected this from nonbelievers, but not from Christians. Believers who thought nothing of waving goodbye to missionary families boarding planes to far-flung countries balked at Baltimore. To some, Bangladesh, Belize, or Botswana seemed more acceptable.

Urban living did offer its own kind of entertainment. Gil Nadolny, who had participated in the Urban Project and just taken his first teaching job in a depressed school in east Baltimore, found that his first-floor apartment offered unexpected adventures.

Late one night, alone in the cavernous house, Gil heard a fierce banging on his back door. "John! Let me in!"

Gil moved to the back door but didn't open it. "There's no John here. He's moved out."

"Quit foolin' with me, man. I left my gun here. I need my gun." More banging.

"John's not here. I'm the new tenant. Go away." He lifted the curtain on the back door to prove that his slender white face, short brown hair, and wire-rimmed glasses did not belong to John.

"Then where's my gun?"

"I don't know," Gil replied, exasperated. "I don't have it. Leave or I'll call the police."

Another night, as Gil relaxed in his bedroom, he heard voices. They appeared to be coming from his living room. Spooked, he walked into the adjoining room—no one there. Then, voices again, floating up from under his feet. Two homeless men, seeking warmth on a chilly night, had discovered the outside door to our basement boiler room—unlocked and right under Gil's living room. They happily chatted and passed a bottle, unaware that the formerly vacant house now had tenants.

The next morning, Craig put up a padlock.

Our décor was the fruit of the entire extended family's recycling efforts. Doors salvaged from a hospital appeared on our closets, and kitchen cabinets arrived from an apartment complex under renovation. An elderly great-aunt donated dining room furniture. Dozens of red-and-white checked curtains hung in nearly every apartment, compliments of a dumpster behind a Ponderosa Steak House. As if that wasn't enough, I sewed several together to make a matching tablecloth. It's a wonder visitors to our dinner table didn't yell "yee-haw!" and order steak.

When we finally moved in, carefully placing Becky's bassinet next to my side of the bed, our first night was an auditory awakening. Craig had grown up in the country, hearing only crickets at night. I was raised up in a quiet suburb, then for several years had lived along the beach, where the sea had lulled me to sleep. Most nights, Greenmount Avenue offered a cacophony of rumbling buses, booming car stereos, and wailing sirens.

For the next several months, the congregation met in our living room. This provided a modicum of stability; rotating among members' homes had been disruptive and probably felt cultish to newcomers.

"Come to our church," we coaxed people we met through our jobs, schools, or neighborhoods.

"Where is it?" they would ask.

"Well....we don't have a building yet. We're meeting in different homes." Or worse—one week it came down to this: "We don't know where we're meeting this Sunday. We're praying that God would provide. But if you give me your number, I'll call you and let you know."

Our living room was available, and drug-and-odor-free. We pushed the tiger couch into the corner, and arranged twenty or thirty folding chairs in rows. Craig played acoustic bass and I played guitar, our backs nearly against the wall to provide room for more seating. Our bedroom doubled as a nursery for rambunctious toddlers. Eventually, we spilled out into the hallway and kitchen. When the weather warmed up, we held services in our backyard.

Our need felt especially acute because so many children from the neighborhood worshipped with us. Some belonged to members, but many attended without a parent, drawn by our Bible clubs and Sunday school. We welcomed them, but where we would put them?

By fall, we were desperate. "Lord, please send us someplace to meet!"

Those first three years, we moved eight times—urban pilgrims, a start-up congregation with no building. Craig pursued a meeting place with the tenacity of a marathon runner. He called a local businessman, who owned a defunct disco a few blocks to the south. "No," the man dismissed him. "We want to open a bar or something like that." A bar? Now there was a novel idea. Within four blocks of our house, tipplers could already stop in at twelve liquor establishments. A local coffeehouse seemed promising at first, but its owners were more interested in hosting left-wing activists than Jesus freaks. Another meeting room down the street turned out to be owned by the proprietor of a local pornographic store. That didn't seem like the right fit, either.

Hoping for a warmer reception from area churches, Craig phoned the pastor of a Presbyterian church in Waverly. "I know who you are!" the reverend blasted. "You're part of that schismatic group!" He was referring to our denomination, which had formed as a more conservative alternative to his larger, mainline group. "I don't want any part of you!" And he hung up.

Finally, a local hospital agreed to rent us a physicians' meeting room on Sunday mornings. Five months in the same place! This stability helped us catch our breath, and we grew slowly but steadily.

Late that summer, my parents drove up from Florida to see the baby. During their tour of the house, they silently took in our "alternative" lifestyle— patched, unpainted plaster walls, rotting steps that threatened to dash them to the concrete below, and a conspicuous absence of air conditioning and even towel racks. I knew it was a stretch for them. In my letters, I had been careful not to pass on any bad news about the neighborhood—the "grandparent version" left out tidbits like "Someone got shot across the street today." But Mom and Dad had grown up in New York City and were not naive.

While I knew that our living situation was not up to the family standard, I was nonetheless immensely proud of what God was doing. Wasn't this *exciting*?

They remained remarkably composed. "An apartment house," my father sighed. "Well, your Grandma Dawkins kept the whole family afloat during the Depression running a boarding house. Must run in the family." Years later, my mother confided that she had cried all the way back to Florida. "Your Dad was none too happy either," she added. "He saw combat in World War II and didn't want his daughter under fire in the inner city."

Living only forty minutes from Craig's childhood haunts in the country, we frequently visited friends and family there. But culture shock battered me as we moved between two worlds. I came to feel not completely at home in either. Attending bridal and baby showers in the suburbs felt like a jaunt to foreign territory: I staggered through stores to find a gift, numbed by wealth, then watched as piles of Williams-Sonoma kitchenware and Laura Ashley linens piled up in tastefully appointed living rooms. I couldn't help but think of Larry, Steve, and others who subsisted on a few hundred dollars a month in depressing, dingy, or even dangerous apartments.

Laura Ashley linens were as far from our lifestyle as Lear jets. My main homemaking issue was ridding our quarters of mice. Mere traps were helpless against generations of rodents who had, until recently, enjoyed the run of the place. The Pied Piper of Hamlin might have been useful, but we settled on sticky paper, spooning a dollop of peanut butter in the center and stationing the traps where Becky wouldn't crawl into them. One square of it went under our bed. One night, in the wee hours I heard a faint rustling and squeaking. I switched on the light, got down on all fours, and lifted the bed skirt. There huddled a family of six, marooned on a paper island but with plenty to eat. We started a contest with Gil, Arlette, and the others in the house, posting each apartment's results on our living room wall: wry little sketches of mice, crossed out.

When Becky first learned to talk, she couldn't quite manage the word "apartment" and dubbed our residence "our a-poor-pit." Out of the mouths of babes...

But our modest surroundings stemmed not just from necessity, but from principle. John Perkins' three principles of Christian community development—reconciliation, relocation, redistribution—resonated deeply within us. Wouldn't a self-denying, we-live-here-too ministry best allow us to reach our neighbors for Christ? Wouldn't wealth be a stumbling block, separating us from those we wanted to reach? Shouldn't Craig take as low a salary as possible, freeing up church funds for other things?

The reality proved complicated. When our friend Carl Ellis, an African American pastor and author, visited, we sat around a bag of Oreos late into the night, talking about race, reconciliation, and the church. The next morning, Craig's parents called to tell us they had found a used washing machine for sale for eighty-five dollars. Did we want to buy it? Carl watched as Craig and I debated.

"Most of the families around here probably don't have washing machines," Craig said. "They have to use the Laundromat."

"But Craig, I'm using cloth diapers," I said. "Pampers are just too expensive. I can't haul diapers to the Laundromat all the time."

Carl shook his head. "Come on, now. Get the washing machine. Don't you think that if black folks in this neighborhood had the chance, they'd get a washing machine?" To be incarnational, he pointed out, did not necessarily mean to be as impoverished as our poorest neighbors.

So we bought it. And it was a good thing, too. Craig was dreaming up ministry plans for the house that would keep that machine—the communal washing machine—humming for years.

CHAPTER 10

C.U.D. dinner, 1982

C.U.D.: FOOD FOR THOUGHT

A year or so after we moved in, Craig formalized his vision for the house: a Center for Urban Discipleship (C.U.D.), where people interested in urban ministry could learn and volunteer in a supportive environment. We hosted weekly potluck dinners, studied the Bible together, served in the church, and discussed books about urban ministry.

Steve Stahl became a longtime tenant. Though he lacked much formal education, he had good sense and an uncanny ability to remember Baltimore Orioles statistics, birthdays, and when each member first began attending Faith. Recognizing Steve's quiet but consistent efforts to help others, the church elected him one of our first deacons. He distributed food and money to people in crisis situations, and proved faithful.

Steve often joined us for dinner. He would arrive freshly showered after his workday, bearing his contribution—an aluminum pot of canned mixed vegetables or peas floating in gray water. While many of our members were huggers, wrapping their arms around each other to say hello or goodbye, Steve was more reserved, rarely initiating full-body contact. But before returning to his apartment, he would seek me out, thank me, and pat me gently on the shoulder, a touching, almost paternal gesture. I would reach up to hug his lanky, six-foot frame. When we celebrated his birthday every year, Steve let the candles burn down until they extinguished themselves in the homemade cake. "Makes the birthday last longer," he said.

Young men and women flowed through the house for the next several years. In the early 1980s, Allen Schmidt and Kelly Simpkins arrived on our doorstep after graduating from Covenant College in Chattanooga. When Allen couldn't find work due to the slumping economy, Craig's dad made room for him in his plumbing company. Allen—who would later become a doctor— cleaned out sewers, dug ditches, and laid pipe. After work and on weekends, Allen and Kelly played basketball with teens and held weekly 'rap sessions' where they discussed everything from the latest movies to a Biblical perspective on sex and dating. Other volunteers ran children's Bible clubs.

With the support of these strong believers, we were able to provide radical hospitality. We opened our apartments to men just released from prison, those struggling with drug addiction and dysfunctional families, a woman with serious mental illness, and another fleeing an abusive husband. We created a regimen of care, support, and accountability. C.U.D. residents, including Allen and Kelly, helped them find counseling and job skills training, tutored men who needed to pass their G.E.D. (high school equivalency diploma), took them to Alcoholics Anonymous or Narcotics Anonymous, and provided spiritual mentoring.

Robby, one of our young residents, had spent most of his life in institutions. He had never experienced the unconditional love or socialization of a healthy family. His alcoholic parents had lost custody to the state when he was four years old. Robby had frequently fled foster homes to find his mother, but she always returned him to the authorities. Eventually, the court sent him to a state hospital that doubled as an orphanage and a home for emotionally disturbed children. He lived there for nine years. When the authorities released him at the age of fifteen, Robby was functionally illiterate. He found his mother, moved in with her, and shoplifted out of necessity. This moved Robby's case from social services to juvenile justice. After a stint in the Maryland Training School for Boys, he lived on the street for several years, occasionally languished in jail, and rarely worked. When his mother died, a bereft Robby attempted suicide.

In 1982, while incarcerated at the city jail, Robby met Arlette, a physician assistant there. Arlette talked with him about Jesus, and Robby eventually gave his life to Christ. In keeping with the Scriptural call to "Remember those in prison as if you were their fellow prisoners," the church sought to provide a context for Robby outside of prison.

At Robby's parole hearing, elder Bob Jenkins presented the judge with an alternative to prison. The church would assist Robby with housing, meals, employment, life skills, remedial reading, and counseling.

The judge was flabbergasted.

"What kind of church is this?" he asked. "In my many years on the bench, I've never seen anything so comprehensive." He released Robby on parole.

Robby moved in with Gil and we helped him find a job at a car wash. Robby had difficulty navigating the structure and demands of the real world: alarm clocks, time clocks, money management, delayed gratification. His first impulse was to immediately spend his paycheck without any thought of rent, food, or other living expenses. We tried to teach him how to budget his money, but he bristled at this. We helped him into a G.E.D. program to get a high school diploma, but he stopped attending. For Robby, attending church and household dinners also became optional.

"Do we keep drawing a line in the sand and then erasing it?" we wondered. "How much do we bend or accommodate to make allowances for his past? And at what point are we enabling his immature behavior?"

One day, Robby brought home a bicycle that he insisted someone had given to him. Later we learned it was stolen. Money disappeared from Gil's apartment, and then the church offering disappeared from Arlette's dresser drawer. When confronted, Robby admitted that he had stolen it. When Arlette reluctantly informed his parole officer, he was stunned. He turned to Robby. "You stole from a church? From a church?" he kept saying.

We asked Robby to leave, and he moved in with a girlfriend nearby. Had all our prayers, all our efforts been for nothing? We wondered.

Arlette kept in touch with him off and on for many years. One day, the receptionist buzzed Arlette, saying, "Your son is here to see you."

"My *son?*" Arlette wondered. She entered the waiting room to find Robby, grinning at his "mother." He expressed appreciation for the help Arlette and the church had offered him and was eager to tell her about his modest successes. He was in an adult assistance program, had a job, and was studying for his G.E.D. "I'm really trying to turn things around in my life," he told her.

Some large suburban churches, having little experience with people like Robby, referred their hard cases to us. A few years after Robby left, a sister church in the county sent us eighteen-year-old Greg. The oldest of five children of a black father and white mother, Greg grew up in a home plagued with domestic violence. He had a long drug history and was on parole. He had fathered two children but was separated from his young wife. He moved into the one-bedroom apartment Kelly Simpkins shared with Marc Fuller, an African American who also volunteered in ministry. Greg attended vocational school, and Kelly worked with him on life skills, Bible study, and G.E.D. homework. He encouraged Greg's attendance at Narcotics Anonymous meetings, but Greg could not stay drug-free. He also had a little trouble understanding the concept of personal property—other people's personal property. Money, cameras, and other small valuables kept disappearing. I had borrowed a thousand dollars—to us a very large sum—from my older brother to buy a sound system for a music ministry I was trying to get off the ground, and was squirreling away fives and tens to pay him back. One day, Greg saw me tuck some money in a drawer. When I opened the drawer a few days later, the money was gone. After several other incidents like this, we again wrestled with the fine line between assisting and enabling. Reluctantly, we asked him to move out.

After Greg left, we found several of our missing items in boxes he had left behind. I also found a tattered photo that Craig had taken of me sitting on the beach, smiling, embracing our tow-headed daughter. Lying in bed that night, Craig and I discussed it.

"That really creeps me out," I told Craig. "He went through our drawers to find that. Or he took it out of the photo album." I hadn't recovered from the fact that he had rifled my drawers and stolen my money—but a photo of me as well? In a bathing suit?

Craig sighed. "I don't think it's sexual. I think it's family. We're the closest thing he has to a family. He's seen the love of Christ through Kelly...and Marc... and us... and part of him can't let that go. And deep down, God is still pursuing him."

I rolled over and went to sleep.

CHAPTER 11

Allen Schmidt and Bill Bolling

CRAIG AND THE PAGANS

WE learned everything, it seemed, the hard way. As churches kept referring their hard cases to us, we got smarter—but once, our inexperience nearly proved fatal to Craig and Allen. One night as I cooked supper for the C.U.D. household, the phone rang. Craig took it.

"That was the secretary at a sister church," he said, hanging up. "Their counseling center got a call from a guy in the city who's suicidal. I'm going to go talk with him."

As darkness fell, Craig and Allen drove to a seedy neighborhood in east Baltimore. Several hours later, as the other house residents finished dessert and Becky smeared food into her high chair tray, Craig and Allen returned looking drained. They plopped down at the table. I passed them a chicken casserole.

"How did it go?" I asked.

Allen kept shaking his head, looking down at his plate. "I'm just really glad to be here," he said quietly. "Really glad."

"What do you mean?" I looked back and forth between the two men. "Craig?"

"It wasn't what we expected," he hedged.

That didn't tell me a whole lot. "Craig?"

Slowly, he opened up. "We drove through some of the most abandoned streets I've ever seen. It looked like something out of a movie. All the buildings had those roll-down security grates over them…"

I waited through his pauses.

"This guy was waiting outside. Frisco. A white guy, maybe twenty-five or thirty, hard to say. Weathered-looking. Lives in an apartment over a closed-up hardware store, behind one of those metal grates. He opened a little door in the grate, nodded us in, and then locked it behind us. His apartment door had four or five locks… I've never seen anything like that room. Drug paraphernalia all over the place. Candles. Pistols. He showed us some of the pictures he had drawn. Tombstones, gun, devils, needles. Scary stuff…"

Allen picked up the narrative. "Frisco was completely erratic. One minute he starts crying, saying he wants to kick his heroin habit, get out of the Pagans."

"The motorcycle gang?" I interjected.

"Yeah," Craig said. "He's afraid if he tries to get out, they'll kill him. They did that to one guy who left—stuffed him in a fifty-five gallon drum, shot it full of holes, dumped it in the Chesapeake. So one minute he's weeping, the next minute he's cursing at God, out of control. Then he started trying to pick a fight with Allen."

I glanced at Allen, who was tall and broad-shouldered. Months of plumbing and ditch digging had built up his upper body.

"He thought I was Craig's bodyguard," Allen shrugged. "There were just two chairs. Frisco in one, Craig in the other. So I was standing next to Craig like this." He folded his arms across his chest. "Frisco kept taunting, 'You're his bodyguard, aren't you? You want to fight me, don't you?' I just kept looking down, saying 'No, sir. I don't want to fight you.'"

The other residents of the house—who included Gil, Arlette, Steve, and Cindy, a young teacher,—listened without moving. I eased into a chair.

"He had guns and weapons all over the place," Allen repeated.

"The most wicked-looking weapon I've seen in my life," Craig elaborated slowly. He grabbed a napkin and sketched a long, sickle-like instrument. "It had a curved blade, like this. But on the other side, a straight blade sticking out. You could do incredible damage with that thing." He thrust his right arm forward and twisted, holding the invisible knife.

I closed my eyes, not wanting to imagine my husband on the other end of this. Our second child was already on the way, and I shuddered to think of myself as a widow raising two children under age two.

"I tried to talk to him about the Lord. I'd read something out of the Bible, he'd calm down a minute, then it would start up again."

"Why didn't you just get out?" I asked.

"Well, we tried. You couldn't reason with him. I told him if he wants to talk to call me. If he does, I'll meet him at McDonalds."

"Yeah, that would be a little safer," Steve interjected.

"So we got up to leave," Allen continued, "and that didn't make him happy."

"Oh, great! So how did you get out?" I asked.

"Eventually he unlocked the door, but he followed us all the way to the street," Craig said. "I got in the car, but Allen was caught on the sidewalk because Frisco was still trying to pick a fight with him."

Allen added, "Then the Honda wouldn't start."

"Wouldn't start!" I was horrified. The car was old, but it usually ran.

"No, not at first," said Allen. "So here's Craig half-breaking the key off in the ignition while I'm backing away from Godzilla-on-heroin, saying, 'No, sir, I don't want to fight you.'"

"It was like a bad dream, where you can't move or get away," Craig put in. "But finally, the engine turned over. Allen jumped in and we beat it out of there. Left him standing in the street."

We all sat for a minute.

Craig shook his head. "I never should have gone to his apartment. I should have met him on neutral ground... like a McDonalds."

We prayed for Frisco. I put dinner away, and Craig played with Becky. As we lay in bed that night, I ran my hand across his broad chest, thankful to feel his breath still moving in and out.

CHAPTER 12

FCF building

MANNA IN PEN LUCY

BY 1982, our curious congregation of whites and blacks, the unemployed, the under-employed, and the financially comfortable had grown to about thirty, including children. Few were "pew-warmers" who sat on the sidelines. The church tended to attract either new believers battling a host of problems and hungry to change, or mature Christians eager to put feet on their faith in the city.

Our worship wanderings had been solved—at least temporarily—when we rented space on Sunday mornings at a local hospital. But after six months, the doctors wanted their meeting room back. As the date of our rental termination drew near, our prayers became more desperate. The hospital agreed to extend our stay by two weeks. "But only two weeks," the administrator cautioned.

Craig started working the phones again. He found favor from the Waverly United Methodist Church, which agreed to let us use its auditorium and an adjacent classroom on Sunday mornings. This largely white, elderly congregation was encouraged to see a group with so many young people, and they welcomed us warmly. They even allowed us to meet at the same hour as they did. But tensions arose. The quiet retirees had perhaps not envisioned Larry and company, nor counted on our troop of boisterous neighborhood children. The final straw was probably our visiting trumpet soloist; we had no idea a trumpet could reverberate so loudly.

After a year with the Methodists, we had fifty members (including children, and probably dogs, cats, and guinea pigs, too). Our average weekly offering hovered under $400. We wanted to purchase a modest building—this would demonstrate purpose, permanence, and commitment to the community in addition to good stewardship. Perhaps, we dreamed, God would help us buy a storefront? We prayed and fasted, seeking God's will.

For the next several months, Craig, Bob Jenkins, and Bill Bolling toured an array of rundown buildings. Tolstoy's adage that "Happy families are all alike; every unhappy family is unhappy in its own way" applies to buildings as well. Happy buildings have solid foundations, firm walls, and functional plumbing. Unhappy buildings can be poorly designed, shoddily renovated, or unsuitably located. They can be under contract, overpriced, or no longer on the market. Craig saw them all. Intellectually, I knew that God would provide, and yet I sometimes felt we had slipped his mind altogether. I read my Bible and wrote encouraging Scriptures in my journal, trying to bring my emotions in line with my faith. "God is able to do immeasurably more than all we ask or imagine." "Wait on the Lord."

So we waited.

Sometimes, God speaks in a whisper. But sometimes, you hear a sonic boom. Our sonic boom was a phone call: Craig learned that the Boundary United Methodist Church on Forty-second Street—in the adjacent Pen Lucy community—was for sale. Its primarily white, elderly congregation had dwindled as the neighborhood had changed, and they could no longer afford the building's upkeep. They had already sold the three-story Victorian manse next door, and had decided to merge with another congregation a mile away. Even though the building was worth far more, they listed it for $240,000. This was a massive sum for us; our annual congregational budget hovered at $22,000, half of which was Craig's salary.

Although the facility needed major renovation, it brimmed with possibilities: a full basement, classrooms on two floors, a parlor, office space, and a sanctuary ringed with beautiful stained glass. In January, 1983, we began renting the church with an option to buy. But buy with what?

Pen Lucy, located just north of Waverly, took its name from a school founded there by a wealthy nineteenth-century philanthropist in honor of his daughter. But the school was long gone, with no philanthropists in sight. After Baltimore's 1968 race riots, whites fled Pen Lucy and many other urban neighborhoods, and investors snatched up homes to rent to low income, minority tenants. Pen Lucy was even poorer than Waverly, and half of the residents lived at or below the poverty level. Single women headed half of the households. Neighborhood schools were among the lowest-achieving in the city, and only about half of residents over age twenty-five had completed high school.

Just one block east and south of the church, the blighted Old York Road commercial strip cut through the heart of Pen Lucy. With a mismatch of liquor and convenience stores, a dry cleaner, and boarded up storefronts, this strip was as well-known to Baltimore police as lame excuses at a traffic stop. Even with periodic drug sweeps and lockups, a seemingly endless supply of young men loitered on the corner, periodically dashing into nearby row houses to retrieve nickel bags or vials of crack cocaine. Sometimes gunfire erupted.

On the Old York Road strip, possibilities had been snuffed out, sucked out like air from a vacuum-packed jar. The sense of expectation, of limitlessness, of dreams within their grasp felt by drivers whirling up the expressway a mile to the west were absent on the strip. This corner of Baltimore was about making do, about surviving.

As the drug trade seduced and enslaved their young, terrorized their elderly, and proved fatal to scores, many Pen Lucy residents fought back. One resident created a memorial garden that featured a banner listing the names of a dozen young neighborhood men cut down by drug-related violence. Others volunteered in the community association and in the elementary school. Some organized crime walks and block watch programs—and would pay a price for standing up to drug dealers.

We felt God was leading us to plant ourselves in Pen Lucy, and target our Christian community development efforts there. Craig and the elders outlined Faith's vision for a multiethnic church committed to justice ministries in the community, and offered to buy the building for $180,000. Even though another group offered substantially more, the Methodists accepted our proposal. Settlement would take place in six months. But where would we get the money?

More prayer and fasting. Craig and the elders drew up a fund-raising proposal and distributed it to members, friends, and anyone remotely interested in Faith's ministry. Though many people gave sacrificially, we still struggled to come up with the required amount. The Methodists agreed to postpone our settlement date. Then they postponed it again. Finally, we raised $80,000 through the sale of bonds, secured a $40,000 no-interest loan from the denomination, and borrowed the remaining $60,000 from a bank. But as the day of settlement approached, the church still lacked $5,000 for settlement costs.

Craig, Bob Jenkins, and Bill Bolling personally signed an IOU, which the Methodists agreed to accept.

As the day to redeem the IOU—Easter Sunday—drew near, we felt anxious. Although the church had grown to sixty members, we did not have the promised $5,000.

On Good Friday, one of the Methodist trustees called and asked to meet with Craig and the elders after Easter services. With heavy hearts, Craig, Bill, and Bob drove the long mile to the meeting. As they sat around a long table, the Methodist pastor slid a piece of paper over to Craig. It was the IOU. The word "Forgiven" was scrawled across it. "In light of the resurrection of Jesus Christ and His grace, we have forgiven this debt," he told them.

We were overwhelmed at this generosity across denominational lines. But God wasn't through yet. One month later, deacon Steve Stahl pulled Craig into a back room after the Sunday service, and took a slip of paper from the offering plate. "There must be something wrong with this check," Steve said, handing it to Craig. "There are too many zeroes."

Craig held a check for $30,000, signed by an out-of-town friend of the ministry. A few days later, Craig talked to the donor by phone. The man dismissed Craig's profuse thanks and asked about the church's purchase of the building. Craig explained that the donor's gift would be used to pay off half the $60,000 commercial loan.

"I have a philosophical problem with an inner-city church being strapped with a high-interest mortgage," the donor said. "At times a debt is necessary to further the work of the church, but I believe it should be retired as quickly as possible, so that funds can be used for ministry."

"I certainly agree," Craig replied.

"I'm going to send another check for $30,000 so you can retire the debt."

Craig was stunned. Through this generosity, God had enabled us to pay off the entire commercial loan in a matter of weeks. In less than ten years, the remaining bonds were paid off, leaving the building entirely debt-free. Through the prayers and sacrificial giving of committed believers in Baltimore and friends around the country, God had provided a ministry base for Faith. God had given us permanence in Pen Lucy as miraculously as manna in the desert.

Safely grounded in the community, our small congregation expanded and threw itself into action. Nearly all of our new members and visitors came from word-of-mouth referrals, and some specifically wanted the cross-cultural, urban experiences Faith offered. We established a crisis food bank, a second-hand clothes store, a thriving youth ministry, a counseling center, and a legal clinic. Though some ministries—such as the second-hand clothes store and a part-time legal clinic—only lasted a short season, others continue today.

Even though it was still a small church, Faith became a sending church, seeing members leave for missions around the globe. One year, our congregation of less than seventy sent out three young people to teach, work in medicine, and do crisis relief in developing nations. Faith also began to attract international students from Johns Hopkins, Morgan State University, and other schools. Over the years, members served God in the Philippines, Turkey, China, Bangladesh, Bolivia, Thailand, Togo, Niger, Kenya, Uganda, and other nations.

After two years of commuting, Craig finally finished his Master of Divinity degree at Westminster Seminary in Philadelphia. At his ordination examination—the oral equivalent of a lawyer's bar exam—the denomination's pastors and elders from a three-state region would grill him on doctrine, church history, and his life and beliefs. But—with impeccable timing—my labor pains began the night before the presbytery exam. We assumed that Craig would miss his big test. But Melissa Joy, a flawless, blue-eyed beauty with wisps of dark blonde hair, obliged us with a short labor, arriving at 7:30 a.m.

After seeing me into the recovery room, Craig raced to the D.C. church hosting the presbytery meeting. At 9:15, he ran down the aisle, still tying his necktie. For his trial sermon, he preached from Acts 6, where the early church faced a crisis distributing food to Greek and Hebraic widows. He stressed that a ministry of mercy and justice was essential in proclaiming the gospel. If the church tolerated injustice, he charged, we could not expect the Kingdom of God to move forward.

The presbytery examination is the theological equivalent of undressing in the junior high locker room—except you're the only one who's naked. If there is any flaw, any theological blemish, any whiff of straying from the truth, the presbyters consider it their bounden duty to find it. If you don't measure up, you're sent back for further study and some overworked pastor will meet with you until you get your doctrine straight.

An elder asked Craig about personal evangelism.

"I don't think evangelism is relegated only to verbal proclamation," Craig said. "It also must be a lifestyle, where believers live out the Gospel." He shared how he was striving to live out his faith in a community of need.

Something about Craig's response set off alarms in a few men. In some denominations, serving the poor had gone hand-in-hand with doctrinal free-falls where the authority of Scripture had become as outdated as wooden dentures. Was Craig espousing a merely social gospel, where good deeds replace a sound theological focus on Jesus? In his sermon, had he *isegeted* the text—read his own interpretations into it—rather than *exegeting*, or drawing truth out of it?

Craig was dismissed, and a heated discussion ensued. Exhausted from sleeplessness and running on adrenaline, he paced the hall, wondering if his ministry was history.

Finally, a venerated minister who had known Craig for years and had supervised his internship rose. Only the appearance of the Apostle Paul would have carried more weight. "I can vouch for his doctrinal soundness, and his character," he said. Craig's cousin, also a pastor, spoke for him as well. The vote was taken, and Craig passed. Now he was legit. A few days later, he was officially ordained.

CHAPTER 13

Mud play

RAISING CITY KIDS

JUGGLING a pair of babies under age two while married to the spiritual equivalent of a battlefield medic proved challenging. I found similarities between caring for a young church and raising small children. Both could expand to fill all available time, and people had absolutely no *idea* what you did all day. Both required firmness. ("You need to take a nap!" "You need to leave that abusive boyfriend!") Both required flexibility ("Yes, we can go to the park again!" "I can meet you whenever you're available.") Both required juggling the next crisis. ("How did Becky get into the Crisco?" "Guess who's down at Central Booking?") In both settings, temper tantrums erupted from time to time. Both involved keeping people fed, growing, and moving in the right direction. Both presented unexpected challenges. ("Guess what, Craig? I'm pregnant again." "Craig, Larry called. He's being evicted again.")

I hosted weekly dinners and Bible studies, wrote a newsletter we sent to people who supported the church, typed Craig's papers and church communications, and played guitar at services. Everywhere I looked I saw overwhelming needs. I wanted to do more and more. Our phone rang constantly, and became the lifeline of a few emotionally starved parishioners. One journal entry summarized my general pace.

> *I feel burned out, frustrated. I need some time alone instead of serving others. Becky is sick, very cranky. I took Pat G. grocery shopping yesterday from 4:00-6:30. I was exhausted physically, emotionally, and spiritually. I rushed home, put away food, made dinner, cleaned up, took care of girls, and almost immediately started typing for Craig. I typed till 12:30 a.m. Becky was up at 6:30. I rushed out today to run off bulletins, cooked lunch, did Bible study lesson, paid bills, wrote ministry letters. I also washed diapers and a load of laundry and folded it. Emptied dishwasher. Tidied! Not feeling well either.*

Even our house wasn't a place of respite. Our bedroom was neither private nor restful, as it was the running path to the communal laundry room and the girls' room. During the summer, our only relief from the heat was to throw our mattress into the girls' small bedroom, the only corner of the house with an air conditioner.

I was committed to being home with my children, even though we could have sorely used a second income. Working—for money, anyway—even part time was impractical on several levels. My heart was in the ministry, Craig worked long hours, and I hated the idea of day care. Besides, what part-time job would pay an English major enough to even cover the cost of a babysitter? I wrote *poetry*, which for centuries has doomed its impoverished practitioners to a lifetime of scribbling in unheated garrets. "Why," I asked God more than once, "didn't you send me to *nursing* school?" Now *there* was reasonable part-time work!

While we did collect some income from the house, these modest rents were plowed back into building materials. Craig spent his few non-pastoring hours trying to make up for the previous owner's neglect. He built closets, hung sheetrock, fixed plumbing, and replaced the crumbling back stairs with a large deck.

As the girls grew, our apartment shrank. To provide more space, Craig fenced our small back yard, ending its previous existence as a parking lot. He built bunk beds, a rope swing, and hand-over-hand bars in their bedroom. But even with Craig's masterful use of space, our apartment felt more and more cramped. I began to look longingly at single-family homes "Do you think we could move, maybe into a little house in Pen Lucy?"

"But this house has so much potential for ministry, living in community like this. I don't think we should move," Craig said. "But we do need more space."

When it comes to renovations, structural possibilities and impossibilities, I trust Craig completely. But when he announced that we could add onto the house, I couldn't figure it out. After all, we lived on the second floor.

In an estimate that lives on in our family annals of optimism, he calculated that, with an additional worker or two, he could rip off the roof and extend the third floor the entire length of the house during his three-week vacation. Using his architectural training, Craig drew plans to add a master bedroom, bath, and two small bedrooms. We would move in temporarily with Arlette and her roommate Donna Cahan, who had bought a modest row house a few blocks away.

Craig received a low-interest loan from the city, submitted plans, and discussed the project with his father. But the materials cost more than expected, and he soon realized he couldn't afford to hire a carpentry firm. Deflated, he put his head in his hands and prayed.

"Lord, I have no idea how to get the help I need for this project. Can you show me what to do?"

That afternoon, a slender, scruffy man in his thirties with long, brown hair in a ponytail appeared on the church steps. John was a carpenter, and needed a job and a place to live. He had vague references from another church. We brought him home, and he moved in with an easygoing young man downstairs.

John proved to be an excellent carpenter. As the skeleton for the new floor rose, he shimmied up support beams and straddled rafters with the sure-footedness of a cat. But he had a serious drinking problem, and his frequent absences slowed down the project. He developed other quirks as well. He decided he no longer would share the apartment with his roommate. Granting the other fellow the living room, kitchen and bathroom, John put locks on the door and sequestered himself in the bedroom. He used a five-gallon bucket for a toilet. He stuffed his apartment and a broken-down van he parked behind our house with boxes of books and old *National Geographic* magazines.

The three-week project stretched into three months. We celebrated Thanksgiving with our new housemates Arlette and Donna. And Christmas. And New Year's Day. And Valentine's Day.

When Craig told John we could no longer afford to hire him, he was furious. "You promised me a job," John charged.

"I did give you a job for several months." Craig reasoned with him. "But I'm out of money. I can't afford to pay you anymore." Irrational and angry, John argued with him at every opportunity. Craig remained patient and calm. I found the conflict unnerving. While John wasn't angry at me, I was, after all, married to the Antichrist.

When he finally left a month after we moved back home, I breathed a sigh of relief. And not a moment too soon. Shortly after unpacking, I felt the familiar nausea again—our third child was on the way. I was still nursing Melissa, who was just short of her first birthday. Becky was not yet three. Three pregnancies in four years of marriage; just imagine if we *hadn't* tried to avoid pregnancy! Craig obviously needed some other recreational activity. My neighbor the roofer had taken to greeting me with a smirky "So! When's the next one due?" What we lacked in money, we were making up for in offspring.

To counter the fatigue of pregnancy, I weaned Melissa and grudgingly joined the girls for afternoon naps, giving up the only free moments I could snatch for Bible study, prayer, reading or getting anything done. Craig was sympathetic. He drew a sign for me to put on the apartment door to alert the other tenants— "Sssh! Maria is sleeping! Her body is busy making a baby."

Becky was so active that I consulted books about hyperactivity. "Is this *normal*?" I wondered. Before her first birthday, she not only walked but climbed anything that offered higher vistas—tables, chairs, and countertops. Our day went better if we spent the morning burning off energy at the park. Unfortunately, only one of us had energy to burn.

In my fourth month of pregnancy, premature contractions started. Panicked, I called Craig. "Something's wrong."

He rushed me to the birthing center. I lay trembling on the examining table, willing my body to relax, to stop expelling this tiny life. The midwife gently placed her hand on my knee. "I think you'd better prepare yourself emotionally to lose this baby."

Tears spilled down my face. I nodded dumbly. But inside, a small voice fought back, urging me to pray.

"Of course," she said, "there's still a chance the labor could stop and you could carry to term. I'll give you something that might help."

I gulped down a Tylenol with codeine. Craig took me home and put me to bed. We waited, and I slept. The labor stopped.

I slept most of the following week, and Craig's mom, Cleo, helped care for the kids until my strength returned. Eighteen weeks later, God gave us Caroline.

Caroline was quiet, sweet-natured, and easygoing. Even in her birth she was downright thoughtful—the labor was brief. Craig and I listened to a tape of favorite songs during labor. I remember hearing the "Chariots of Fire" theme song over and over. Caroline must have heard it too, because under all her sweetness and sensitivity beats a determined little heart.

Adding a third child demanded all the strength and creativity I could muster. Fortunately, the city provided a useful range of shops where I could gather the necessary materials. Dress-up clothes came from the thrift store and books from the library and Goodwill. Reams of scrap paper came from the church office. Museum "free days" provided fodder for the imagination—even if the sight of multiple preschoolers did make the security guards break out in a sweat. Craft supplies, homemade Play-Doh, and buckets of crayons kept them busy. The girls also spent hours riding Big Wheels on the deck, splashing in a plastic wading pool, making mud pies and mud soup, digging for worms, and consulting on their discoveries. We hung sheets from their bedroom monkey bars to create forts and hammocks. I wanted to create a cocoon, an oasis, a magical childhood against the callousness and danger they would soon see outside.

In the quest for new activities and safe, clean playgrounds, I put Caroline in the backpack and pushed my double stroller farther and farther. After extensive lobbying with the city parks department, a nearby community association received a new playground. My daughters loved the brightly colored tunnel, the yellow slide, and the suspended tire swing. The adjacent basketball court had actual nets hanging from the basket rims, a rarity in city parks. It was a wonderful place.

But one day at the park, two teenage boys started to fight under the hoops, cursing and shoving. Becky and Melissa stopped their play and watched, transfixed. One boy picked up a bottle, smashed it over the other boy's head, then ran away. I tried to help the wounded boy, but he staggered home, blood dribbling down his face, vowing revenge with his uncle's gun. I tucked Becky and Melissa back in the stroller and headed home. Becky looked up at me soberly. "I don't want to go back to that playground, Mommy." We didn't.

On another day, as I drove down Greenmount Avenue, two young men began to brawl in the middle of the street. Cars slowly veered around them. One of the men flailed away with a bat while the other threw trashcans, sticks, rocks, and finally a bicycle. I leaned on the horn, horrified, trying to shock them out of their rage. The children sat in awestruck silence. Throwing bicycles went way beyond the rules they knew—rules against calling your sister names or telling her to "shut up." I wanted to protect them from seeing more of this. But I couldn't.

We struggled over how to educate our children. Standardized test scores from our neighborhood schools sank like an anvil tossed overboard. Few students passed state proficiency exams. I objected to the city schools' approach to reading, which had abandoned phonics. We wanted to identify with the lives of neighborhood people as much as possible, but refused to jeopardize our children's future. How could we subject them to the kind of "learning" the local schools really offered, which had little to do with books?

With no money for private school tuition, and convinced from research that my tiny budget and lack of training in pedagogy were not fatal flaws, I began home schooling Becky. To help launch our home school, Craig hung shelving and built a long desk from an old door and scraps of lumber. Now Becky and I could sit side by side for her lessons. But how do you tutor one child while amusing two preschoolers? Juggling three weed whackers is no louder or messier, and the weed whackers run out of gas sooner.

In the mid 1980s, homeschooling was still largely unknown or considered peculiar or even potentially damaging. I faced constant questions when we ventured out in public during the day. Many state courts still argued over the rights of parents to teach their children at home, and the city school system was trying to figure out what to do with us. They demanded that twice a year I bring my curriculum, attendance records, and samples of the children's work downtown to the school system headquarters for an evaluation. I practically needed a hand truck to haul my supplies. The children and I would perch, dressed as if for church, in the same office where truant teens in torn jeans and t-shirts slouched with their overwrought mothers.

Both sets of grandparents worried about homeschooling; good public school systems had educated their children. Craig's mother lived close enough to see the pressure we were under. "Maybe you should raise your children, then move back to the city," Cleo suggested. She quizzed Becky on letters and numbers when I walked out of the room.

"I think it's too much on you," my mother fretted. Over the years, my parents had made gentle inquiries about Craig's availability for other pastorates. Home schooling only heightened their concerns. "I notice there are several churches in your denomination in Orlando," my father said. "Do you think any of them might be looking for a pastor?" When they realized that Craig did not feel called to suburban ministry, they took another tack. "There's a rescue mission here in Melbourne that does wonderful work. Might Craig want to look into it?" More than once, my father said, "Craig's so youthful and energetic. He'd be wonderful in a college ministry." I didn't blame them. As much as I loved Faith, if Craig had announced that God was urging him elsewhere—say... to a suburban ministry in a warmer climate with a bigger salary—I would have started packing. Both of us were running full tilt, in crisis mode almost all the time.

Two months into homeschooling, I panicked. Could these few hours of teaching be enough, or would Becky be stunted by my sincere but floundering efforts? Was I ruining my child for life? I walked the five or six blocks to upscale Guilford, to a large stone church with a new educational wing nestled among old oaks and maples. There I had seen smiling parents leading backpack-toting children out through shiny, glass doors, their Volvo station wagons idling in the pickup lane. I wanted my child to belong there, to know this normalcy of small classes and cheerful teachers, recess and lunchboxes. I approached one of the teachers. "Do you have any openings for kindergarten?"

She smiled at beautiful, blonde Becky, saw the preschooler and toddler in my double stroller. "You mean for next year, don't you?"

"Actually, I was considering this year," I stammered. "I know the school year has already started, but her present school situation...may not work out."

She looked at me, caught off guard.

She thinks I'm an idiot, I thought.

"Oh, we're full for this year. With a waiting list. Perhaps for next year?" She fetched a brochure from the office. I thanked her, turned away, felt her eyes on me, berated myself for not knowing these private schools fill long before September. At home, I scanned the brochure, saw the tuition costs and threw it away.

I redoubled my efforts. Becky learned to read, haltingly at first, but with increasing skill and confidence. We walked to the library often, returning with twenty or thirty books. I spent hours curled up on the couch with the children, reading until my speech slurred and my eyes closed and I begged for a ten-minute nap.

Becky became an avid reader. Fueled by a mix of adventure, history, and nature stories, she announced that she wanted to be "a missionary doctor mountain climber." I told her that sounded great.

CHAPTER 14

1987

LEARNING FROM THE OLD SCHOOL

I would not have survived the first ten years without three older women: my mother-in-law Cleo, Jean Jenkins, and Catherine Watson. As I raised three small children, home schooled, and volunteered fifteen to twenty hours a week, they were islands of sanity in a sea of chaos.

Jean Jenkins was intimately aware of all the issues swirling through Faith. Though I did not call her often to complain or ask advice, I knew she would drop everything if I needed her. This was a stress release, a valve to let the steam out of the pressure cooker, even if I didn't use it.

One summer afternoon, I needed to talk. I sat in her kitchen, where there were no dishes in the sink, no broken faucets or unpainted walls. A clock ticked, and birds chirped in the woods behind the patio.

"I don't know how you do it," she said, bringing me a glass of ice tea. "I don't know how you and Craig put up with the lot of us. And I don't know how you're feeding all those children on Craig's salary."

I shrugged. "I'm careful, I guess. I make everything from scratch."

"I have two nightmares," she confessed. "One is that I'll have to cook for a living. The other is that I'll have to watch small children." She eyed me warily. "Just what is your weekly food budget?"

I named a figure, and she gasped. "You can't live on that! Why, Robert and I spend more than that, and there are only two of us!"

Jean began to slip me a little money every month. "Find someone to come in and help you for a few hours," she said. "You can't possibly get anything done with all those children underfoot."

She was right. The children could stickify, soil, spill on, or otherwise mess up a morning's scrubbing in minutes. Even my perpetual motion was no match for them. The second law of thermodynamics—which postulates that everything moves from order to disorder—is never so obvious as in a home with several small children.

A friend recommended Catherine Watson, who cleaned her husband's office. Catherine began to create order—or at least cleanliness—out of my domestic chaos several mornings a month.

In my misguided perfectionism, I struggled with hiring help, even with donated funds. My mother had set a standard for impeccable housekeeping— but I had temporarily forgotten that she, too, when raising five small children, had briefly hired help. And my mother had not been living in a construction site, or felt compelled to save the world in her spare time! But I felt most squeamish because hiring an African American housecleaner dredged up images of hundreds of years of domestic servitude and racism. How can I be committed to racial reconciliation and have a black woman cleaning my house? But the only white housecleaner I knew was of dubious mental health.

Catherine was the kind of woman who is the backbone of any community. She had wrestled with urban Baltimore for half a century, and prevailed. As we cleaned together she mentored me. My favorite conversations often began with her saying, "Now, I'm not trying to get in your business, but—" followed by her pointed advice. Catherine was "old school," full of common sense, generosity, and a steely work ethic.

"I been working like a man since I was a child," Catherine said. "Down North Carolina, up with the chickens. I was running a hotel when I was just a girl. My parents, God rest their souls, they made a woman out of me. I know how to work, you hear me?"

I heard her. Although sixty years old, she still worked several days a week and took her elderly neighbors shopping. Her only son had drowned as a young man, and she had raised her nieces and nephews after her sister "passed." Sometimes her conversation crossed into a preaching style, using the rising and falling inflections of the black church—strong, lyrical, powerful. She loved the Lord, sang in the choir at Southern Baptist, and fed scores of friends at her tidy corner row house on Sunday afternoons: cornbread, chicken, collards, green beans. When her church needed money for the mortgage, Catherine organized the church ladies to cook and sell Saturday suppers. They paid off a thirty-year mortgage in five years. Catherine gave her whole heart to those she loved. But she tolerated no nonsense. She kept a shotgun in the hall closet.

After using the key she kept on her ring to unlock my door, Catherine would call, "Where are my children?" They would run from the corners of the apartment to present themselves. "You been good? Or does 'Lil Mama need to get a switch?" The children would hug her and wait shyly for the four peppermint candies she doled out. We came to love her deeply. In a rare moment of peace and quiet, I tried to capture her in a poem.

Catherine

The boys, eyes wide as horses',
bolted down narrow streets
leaving a trail of water
like blood.

They pounded on Catherine's door,
wailing. Her son,
her only son had disappeared
under the water at the reservoir.

At the city morgue
they pulled back the sheet.
Catherine saw dark skin bleached white.
She saw her mother's wide forehead,
her dead husband's eyes.
She caressed the boy who would never
shave, know the fire of women,
bring her grandchildren.

That day, her menses stopped
though it was not her time.

She buried her son
wrapping the resurrection around herself
like a woolen shawl.
It held.

That was twenty-five years ago.
Today, at sixty-eight
Catherine works and rests
and sings like the Second Coming.
"I been through some changes," she declares.

When death reaches in my window
to snatch my son, my daughters,
my husband,
lock the door against morticians,
neighbors, mourners.

Bring me Catherine.

A city building inspector, Mr. Berkowitz, dogged us, showing up every few months for several years to unearth a new code violation. He gave us thirty days to fix violations; after that, the city would levy fines of five hundred dollars a day with the possibility of imprisonment. The initial list of deficiencies seemed endless: wood rot on the front porch; rotten back deck; improper smoke detectors; no railing on the front steps, and more.

We had a little dance: Mr. Berkowitz showed up and found a problem to cite. We fixed it, and he returned thirty days later to inspect. All around us, the neighborhood was falling apart, substandard housing spreading unchecked. We felt unfairly singled out. We suspected we made Mr. Berkowitz look good: twenty citations given, twenty violations fixed. Exasperated with the constant onslaught of citations, Craig questioned him one day. "Why weren't these things addressed over the last fifteen years when Continental Realty owned the house? You know we're fixing it up ourselves and can't afford to do everything at once."

Mr. Berkowitz brought his face close to Craig's. "You stick to your business, and I'll stick to mine."

One encounter with Mr. Berkowitz left me in tears. Craig had missed the deadline to replace the smoke detectors, and the inspector scolded me, dangling the specter of fines. He returned a few days later and berated Craig. "And you're a man of the cloth! You promised to fix these, and you haven't."

"I'm sorry," Craig said, honestly contrite. "I've been busy."

"If you don't replace these by next week, you'll be fined five hundred dollars a day."

If we didn't have money to pay someone else to renovate, we certainly didn't have five hundred dollars a day to fill city coffers. And Craig wasn't planning on starting a jail ministry from the inside. He put up new detectors, and Mr. Berkowitz signed off on the inspection. We continued our dance.

But finally, something happened to change the dance steps. On his next visit, instead of the docile, submissive housefrau, Mr. Berkowitz encountered Catherine. She peered through the glass sidelights, refusing to open the door.

"Building inspector. Is Mrs. Garriott home?"

"No. I'm sorry she's not," Catherine said sweetly.

"I'm the building inspector. I'd like to come in and inspect the property." He showed his clipboard and badge. She was not impressed. "You'll have to come back when Miz Garriott is here," she told him.

Mr. Berkowitz didn't want to come back later. He waved his clipboard and official photo ID "I was here last week, and I need to check on a code violation."

His persistence raised her hackles. "Any joker can go down here to Sunny's Surplus and get a badge and ID card. That don't mean nothing," she declared. "You don't never know what these jokers are carrying these days. I know how they do."

Mr. Berkowitz, unaccustomed to rejections of his authority, didn't want to back down either. "Mrs. Garriott knows I'm coming to inspect."

"I don't know you from Adam," she snorted. "You just wait one minute." She marched to my kitchen and returned brandishing a butcher's knife. "Let me school you. I been around, and I know what's what. Don't nobody fool with me, you hear me?"

Mr. Berkowitz decided to come back another day. When he returned, he was meek, tame.

CHAPTER 15

Carl Ellis and Calvin

RACE, REPENTANCE, AND RECONCILIATION

ALTHOUGH having a church building provided permanence, nurturing our diverse congregation was slow, laborious work. Craig's peers who had started churches in the suburbs had one or two hundred parishioners, but after five years, we had barely crossed the seventy barrier. Our group was like an updated, multiethnic version of a Mother Goose rhyme—with a butcher, baker, candlestick maker, and all the offspring of the Old Woman who lived in a shoe. And maybe Craig and I were Jack and Jill, always tumbling down the hill and breaking our crowns. We needed to figure out a better way to fetch that living water.

Craig wondered: am I a missionary or a pastor? We lived and ministered in a culture not our own, yet had no preparation, no warning of the toll of culture shock, no furlough to catch our breath. While missionaries in foreign cultures receive denominational support such as pre-deployment training, furloughs, and teachers for their children, we fell into a shadow category marked "other." Urban ministries were new to the denomination. I suspect that denominational officials didn't know what to do with us.

Craig struggled to formulate a philosophy of ministry. While John Perkins' three Rs of community development—reconciliation, relocation, and redistribution—had provided an initial framework, we had more questions than answers. How much should we depend on outside funding? Should the church encourage members to relocate into Pen Lucy? Must the elders live in the community? How can we help our largely white denomination reach the African American community? How can we best develop spiritual leadership from within the neighborhood?

But year after year, the question that dogged Craig most was how could he—a boy from the country, a member of the race that had enslaved African Americans, a pastor in a denomination with a poor track record in the African American community—reach the urban community? God wants to reach all people with the Gospel—not just the white middle class. Many of the nation's largest cities, including Baltimore and Washington, had majority African American populations; how could the denomination reach them?

Racial sensitivities are felt most keenly in areas such as inner cities, where they also intersect with class. Many African Americans, who experience the sting of racism day in and day out on their jobs, are not interested in attending a church with a white pastor. In mixed settings, whites can dominate or be insensitive without realizing it. The black church historically has had enormous social, cultural, and spiritual significance, the only place where African Americans could gather, develop and recognize leaders, organize, celebrate, and worship free from white domination. For a historically white denomination and a white pastor, building credibility in an African American neighborhood could take a decade or more.

Our Presbyterian heritage included men like Elijah Lovejoy, a minister killed by a proslavery mob when he refused to silence his abolitionist press in the 1830s. But it also included some shameful counter-examples. In the 1860s, some prominent southern Presbyterian theologians enslaved African Americans. When the Presbyterian Church voted to refuse communion to slaveholders, the church split north and south. Even during the Civil Rights movement, some southern churches had guards-at-arms to turn away potential black worshipers. Many congregations moved out of cities when racial demographics changed, unable or unwilling to adapt. In the mid-1980s, the denomination had only one ordained African American pastor—Carl Ellis in Chattanooga.

Craig was sitting with Carl at the annual gathering of pastors from the P.C.A. in 1984 in Baton Rouge when several events occurred which illustrated what Carl calls the "trauma factor" experienced by minorities in white-dominant institutions. In a large conference center, a thousand pastors watched a stirring video underscoring the need to plant churches among the diverse ethnic groups in the United States. It painted a mosaic of the many people groups now populating our cities—Hispanics, Koreans, Hmong, others—but ignored African Americans—-America's largest minority. Carl was outraged.

"I've had it," he said, walking out in protest. "The only time African Americans were even mentioned was in relation to Hispanics being the second largest minority group after blacks! Talk about marginalization. That presentation ignored four hundred years of African American history."

Craig followed him, urging him to persevere. They eventually returned to the assembly, where a recommendation was proposed that the assembly pray for "our ministry to that flood of people from other nations who now live among us, that we may evangelize and build the church with 'living stones' from these language and ethnic groups." Craig stood.

"I suggest that after 'evangelize,' we add 'be reconciled with.' Even though we have some churches in key urban areas, we are still an almost exclusively white church. Alienation and broken relationships exist between the black and white communities." Craig had been studying, and knew his statistics. "Baltimore is fifty-five percent African American; St. Louis and New Orleans about fifty percent; Atlanta is seventy percent black, and so is Washington, D.C. We are not reaching the black community. We need to acknowledge the need for reconciliation." He sat down. There was a moment of silence as men digested his remark.

Another presbyter stood. "I'm against using the language 'reconciled' because it implies an offense that needs to be removed."

He doesn't get it, Craig thought. After further discussion, the moderator called for a decision. Craig's amendment was voted down. Carl, experiencing his second trauma of the day, again walked out. Craig followed.

After talking with Carl for fifteen or twenty minutes, Craig walked back into the assembly. To his surprise, a heated discussion was still taking place over his failed amendment. Presbyters lined up at two microphones, awaiting their turn to speak.

"I'm concerned that our denomination will go on record as being against reconciliation," one man was saying. Finally, someone offered a substitute amendment stating, "seeking to build good relations with and good will toward." Although the language sidestepped acknowledging a breach that required reconciliation, or sin requiring repentance, it recognized a problem that required a remedy. It was a start. Fifteen years later, the denomination would revisit this issue, and overwhelmingly pass a resolution expressing repentance for historical racism. For Craig, Carl, and others, this was a watershed event.

While our elder Bill Bolling provided critical lay leadership at Faith and other African American members played prominent roles, Craig wondered if the white solo-pastor model would work in an urban context. Day after day, he processed intense ministry issues with no other staff.

"I need an African American co-pastor," Craig said over and over. "I wonder if it's even possible for Faith to reach African Americans in this community with me as the pastor."

When a black church, New Life Evangelical Baptist, began using our facility on Sunday afternoons, Craig sensed an opportunity. He befriended the pastor, Milton Williams, and the two churches held several joint worship services. Craig, always an optimist, pushed the edges.

"Maybe the two churches could merge," he said. "Milton and I could share the pulpit, and we have a great facility. I think our people would be up for it."

"But Craig, they are *Baptist*. We are *Presbyterian*."

"I know," Craig said. "Milton is a careful thinker committed to Scripture. Maybe over time he could be persuaded to accept Presbyterian distinctives. Though infant baptism would be a stretch," he admitted.

In a crisis, fine gradations of theology and lesser denominational distinctions fade away. Martyrs die for the authority of Scripture and the deity of Christ. Not for infant baptism versus believer's baptism. The crisis mode of thinking that would mark the first twenty years of our ministry had already taken root. Craig was just trying to survive.

"What I have now isn't working," he said bluntly.

Milton graciously considered Craig's offer, and both congregations discussed it. Craig and Milton traveled to the denomination's assessment center in Birmingham to evaluate compatibility, doctrinal issues, and potential hurdles. But both men and their congregations decided this was not what God was calling them to do.

Craig's search for an African American co-pastor—or at least a mentor—led him to meetings of Baltimore's Black Evangelical Ministers Alliance. He became the only white attendee. At one meeting in a storefront church in West Baltimore, a compactly-built man in a blue suit stuck out his hand. With characteristic humility, Pastor Tony Dorsey introduced himself as "just a little hoodlum from West Baltimore, saved by grace."

Craig grinned. "I'm a white boy from the country, living on Greenmount Avenue and trying to pastor a church by grace."

Pastor Dorsey slapped him on the back. "Well, God bless you, brother!"

Pastor Dorsey had grown up in Sandtown, a depressed area of West Baltimore, and had been drawn into the drug trade as a teenager. These activities eventually caught up with him, and he went to prison. After he got out, he resumed his work on the streets. When he went to a prominent black church to meet a fellow dealer for a drug trade, he ended up giving his life to Christ instead. As he matured in the faith, he felt God was calling him to the ministry.

Like most urban pastors, his preparation for the ministry centered more on mentorship than full-time academic study. He took Bible classes at night, and an older pastor discipled him. God led him to the small, struggling First Baptist Church of Pimlico, which met in a converted house not far from the racetrack. Pastor Dorsey began preaching and teaching there in addition to his day job. When the church asked him to be its full-time pastor, he took the position even though the salary was significantly less than his day job and offered no stability. Under the leadership of Pastor Dorsey and his wife Joann, the church grew significantly. The congregation decided not to leave its distressed neighborhood, and built a large, new facility where families are strengthened, leaders developed, and youths nurtured in their faith.

Pastor Dorsey became a close friend and mentor to Craig, a ready source of advice and encouragement. He would need that support. Over the next few years, crises lined up like waves to pummel our fragile efforts.

CHAPTER 16

Kelly Simpkins and Gary Tibbles

HARD KNOCKS

EVERYWHERE we turned we saw needs: children lacking supervision and healthy activities after school; youths standing idle for want of jobs and job training; dropouts needing tutoring and G.E.D. classes; teenage mothers desperate for mentoring to break the cycle of poverty; drug addicts waiting months for scarce treatment slots.

Members responded by giving generously of their time, talents, and money. Some moved into the neighborhood to be part of an intentional effort to share Christ in the community. Others volunteered to work with youth, teach adult education classes, or assist in our food pantry. Whenever people learned of a need—a single mother's car broke down, our boiler needed replacing, a family faced daunting medical bills—they opened their wallets or purses.

One year, Craig did the math and realized that Faith's average member gave thirty-three percent more money than the average member of our denomination. Statistics show that lower-income people tend to give proportionally more than the middle-class or wealthy. Faith may also have attracted more committed givers than the average church. But we saw a third reason as well: our economically diverse church offered a chance to step outside one's own culture or background, and therefore evaluate it more clearly. Missionaries have known this for years. Do I really need a new SUV, a spare bedroom, another pair of shoes? God's value system is far different from America's consumer culture. At Faith, economic hardship had a name and face. Confronting the gap between the haves and the have-nots either made people uncomfortable enough to leave, or deepened their commitment to Christ and the church's mission.

The church grappled with whether or not we should solicit outside money to address some of the needs we saw in the community. Some inner city churches start large development efforts that depend on outside resources. Others depend primarily on what members put in the offering plate, and their development services—such as housing renovation, job assistance, youth clubs, or drug treatment programs—expand more slowly. While each design has pitfalls and advantages, we believed ministry should flow out of and be owned by the church community. The church provides the surest foundation for all change and growth, whether the issue is drug addiction, emotional healing, or poverty.

Although most of our budget came from people in the pews, several outside churches and individuals did help fund our outreach and evangelism ministries. In 1984, a generous donor gave $15,000 to allow members Kelly Simpkins and Gary Tibbles to work full-time with youth. They bought a run-down house in the neighborhood and began a thriving youth ministry, reaching young men who never would have walked through the doors of a church. But when the money ran out two years later, Faith could not afford to pay Gary and Kelly's modest salaries. Craig offered to give up half his salary and take a part-time job, but the elders did not want his energies divided. Without financial support, both men eventually moved on to other opportunities. Kelly and several other members helped found New Song Community Church, also based on John Perkins' community development principles, in a depressed neighborhood in west Baltimore.

While Faith attracted the highly committed, it also drew the dysfunctional. The latter craved the attention and care that a small church offers. A handful of needy individuals struggling with mental illness, abusive backgrounds, and deeply entrenched emotional problems monopolized the time and resources of a caring but inexperienced pastor and church. Over time, we became more adept at bringing the healing touch of Jesus without burning out, of extending grace balanced with tough love. But gathering that wisdom took many years.

A single white mother and her six children began attending our church. She confided that she was dying of an inoperable brain tumor. The church rallied behind her, and an elder and his wife—who already had four young children—took in her three youngest children with an eye to permanent adoption. The stress of raising and home schooling seven children under age ten sent Sherry, the elder's hardy wife, to the doctor with an ulcer. We learned a month later that the entire story was a fabrication. The mother retrieved her children and disappeared.

A mentally ill woman in the church moved into one of our apartments. We hoped that the stability and care from our family and Stella and Miguel DeAngulo, who also lived in the house, would help Sharon. Miguel, a physician from Colombia, had training in counseling and was studying for a Master's in Public Health at Johns Hopkins in order to deliver health care to the poor in South America. Stella and I had become close friends and our children played together like siblings. But when Sharon joined the household, in addition to my three toddlers I daily faced an adult capable of Terrible Twos tantrums. Sharon's demands for time and attention soon overwhelmed me.

One day, when Miguel and Craig gently confronted her about a self-destructive behavior, she screamed at them for a full forty minutes. Stella and I stood transfixed, cringing in the hallway between the two apartments. Craig and Miguel's soft replies floated through the thin walls.

"Yes, Sharon," they said calmly. "I'm sorry you feel that way." She resumed her tirade, and only after she had vomited out all her rage was she able to hear their quiet reasoning. While Miguel and Craig could endure her screaming, such encounters left me shaken and depleted.

Even our church services were not immune from drama. Though most of our members were stable, working adults, occasionally odd events occurred. Once, a man walked in off the street, marched up to Bill Bolling at the podium, and told him to take up a collection. "I need $136 for rent," he said. Another time, a burly, deranged attendee took a swing at one of our elders, sending him crashing into the pew. Another woman, whose childhood had been particularly traumatic, sometimes erupted during services, screaming, weeping, and threatening suicide. After a while, we could anticipate which topics, Scripture passages, or offhand comments would trigger an outburst. Jean Jenkins, myself, or another woman would take her aside and talk her down. I tried to capture one stressful week in a poem.

Revisions

Willy came twice this morning
circling, seeking food, money, an ear.
He snatches our offerings,

scavenging Protestant, Catholic, Jew
for anything religion extends.
His wife squirrels flotsam and jetsam,
packing the walls until her husband explodes
and beats her.

Ronald called;
he wants to kill his wife.
The pastor nods, probes.
"What does God want you to do?"
"God wants me to kill my wife."

Sunday, during the sermon
on unconditional love,
Phyllis wadded bulletins,
hurled them at the wall, hissing,
"I hate her. I hate her."
For Phyllis, this is actually
quite healthy.

And I
am rewriting my speech
on urban ministry.
"It's too heavy," my husband contends.
I erase
the pedophile who asks for my daughter,
red-eyed men drinking from brown bags,
the splintered lock on my door.

The page fills with whiteness.

Aware that the urban crucible was taking its toll—especially on members from suburban backgrounds—Craig started a small group ministry. A few leaders were designated, and people chose which group to attend. But to our dismay, the groups self-segregated according to race, revealing that true friendship and reconciliation were occurring only at a superficial level. To build community and relationships across race and class, small groups were reorganized.

Urban realities began to crush many of Faith's folks. As our single adults moved into their late twenties and early thirties, they felt the absence of potential marriage partners. Many left for larger suburban churches. Married members who had relocated into the community faced stark choices as their children reached school age; they felt they must pay expensive private school tuitions or homeschool. The preschool son of one elder tested positive for exposure to tuberculosis—an epidemic in Baltimore in the mid-eighties—and faced a long course of treatment.

In one excruciating year, half of our members left. Two of our elders, concerned about the effects of the city on their children, moved to the suburbs. Miguel DeAngulo finished his master's in public health, and he and Stella returned to South America. Stella and those elders' wives had been my closest friends, my main source of emotional support while navigating the hazardous terrain of small children, needy church members, ministry hardships, and urban stress. I grieved the loss of these feminine soul mates.

Letter to Stella

I think of you every season:
Summer: you arrived, pregnant,
holding the wobbly banister as you climbed
to my second floor apartment.

Fall: bulk apples shared like secrets,
the aroma of our friendship
assuaging our hardships.

Winter: my health broke,
and you nursed my children with your own.

In spring, tulips at Sherwood Gardens,
hope that our own silent bulbs
would bloom.

You were more than a grace note:
counterpoint, two melodies twined together.

When you left, my woman-soul
returned to me, alone,
like Noah's first dove.
There was no land.

There is no land.
I content myself with footings:

a pebble, earth that holds no weight,
quicksand to smother me.

I miss being safe.
I can accept your absence
but not the loss
of every Eden,
all sanctuary.

With the addition in 1988 of our fourth child, Calvin, I struggled against sleep deprivation, exhaustion, and emotional and spiritual depletion. Part of this was due to my conflicting, unrealistic expectations. I couldn't decide if I wanted to be Maria von Trapp in *The Sound of Music,* and have ten children and teach them all to sing, or a married version of Mother Theresa, serving the poor but wearing makeup. Or maybe Emily Dickinson, a recluse scribbling in her bedroom.

I pushed myself relentlessly, listening more to my own perfectionism than Jesus' quiet voice. My times of prayer and personal Bible study were constantly derailed until I became spiritually anorexic, subsisting on minimal spiritual intake while trying to do strenuous spiritual lifting. I was driven by an earnest desire to help those around me who were drowning and an irrational conviction that I could do more if I organized my time better. Even when I wanted to slow down, I couldn't. There were lessons to teach, dishes to wash, diapers to change, ministry commitments to fulfill. Many people have it worse, I told myself: at least I have a husband, a steady income, a car, a roof over my head, stable and supportive parents and in-laws.

Craig was consumed with one crisis after another. Even brief times away served only as opportunities to problem-solve the latest church issues. Once, as we prepared to visit friends for a couple of days, I begged him with tears. "Please! Can we *not* spend the entire two days discussing the ministry? Can we not spend all our time rehashing the issues of the neighborhood?"

When we returned home to the phone calls in the middle of the night, to the drug dealers on the corner, the cluttered apartment and its unpainted walls, I cried and lashed out at the toys sprawled over the floor.

My dreams were full of calamity: tornadoes, floods, rapists chasing me as I fled barefoot through a field of thorns. Often, disaster was paired with shepherding small children. In one nightmare, I herded several children into a closet, where we survived a tornado, only to be run over by laughing rednecks in a rock-filled pickup truck. In another, flames shot out of my house, and no one would help me save the children, so I rushed in, alone.

I struggled to know acceptable boundaries, to find time to be alone with God or myself, to read a book, to pray. Recognizing my need, I bought Richard Foster's *A Celebration of Discipline*, and vowed to embrace disciplines of prayer, solitude, and meditation. But there was no time, no respite. In frustration over constant interruptions from the children, I threw the book across the room. I developed chest pains, a feeling that a cinderblock rested on my rib cage. Strep throat dogged me, returning after two, or even three, courses of antibiotics. The stress of pastoring, writing a sermon, and preaching every week sent Craig to the doctor with stomach problems.

The book of Galatians urges us not to grow weary in well-doing, and promises that, at the proper time, we will reap a harvest if we don't give up. But at what point do you say, "Enough!"? Should Craig resign? Should we join the continuing exodus of white and black middle-class residents fleeing Baltimore city? Should we provide a safer, less stressful environment for our family, or stand with a community of need, working with others to bring restoration? Had we done all we could for Faith? Was God still calling us here?

CHAPTER 17

With Stella, Miguel, and Steve

LOSING STEVE, KEEPING FAITH

ONE afternoon in 1988, I heard a knock at my front door. I scooped up Calvin and walked downstairs, trailed by three curious little girls. Two policemen stood on my front porch.

"Is this the residence of Steven Stahl?" one asked. He held a small plastic card in his hands. A driver's license. Steve's license.

"Well, it was...but he moved a few months ago. He lived with us for several years...until he..." I chose my words carefully. "Until he got sick."

Their presence alarmed me. What was going on? Steve would never break the law. I used the official title that gives legitimacy to the deep affection we felt for Steve: "My husband is his pastor. Is Steve all right?"

"There's been an accident." Few words, dreadful words, police words in passive voice, telling me nothing, suggesting everything.

"Riding his bike?" I groped. "Is he O.K.?"

"His bike was involved." The officer looked at my children, peeking out from behind the door. "Can you tell me how to reach your husband?"

I stammered the number, and peppered him with questions. His evasiveness only raised my fears. Scribbling down the address and phone number of the church, he turned and left. My heart fluttered. I herded the children back into our apartment, pulled out paints and paper, and urged them on the girls. Should I call the hospitals, try to find out more?

Several months before, Steve had begun a slow, initially imperceptible decline. He had injured his back several times, and had been unable to work for longer and longer periods. He had withdrawn, spending more and more time alone. He had struggled with his singleness, becoming romantically interested in beautiful, college-educated young women in the church who could only return an *agape* love, not the romantic *eros* love he sought. His face had taken on a grieved, tormented look.

In hindsight, after we recognized that Steve had become ill, after a diagnosis of schizophrenia and depression, after he became unable to care for himself, we could trace the danger signs that marked his downward trajectory. But at the time, we didn't know.

One summer afternoon a year earlier, Steve knocked on our apartment door. Craig was away at church, but Steve sat in our living room and unburdened himself. As baby Calvin played at my feet, I watched a dear brother disintegrate before my eyes. With tears, he tried to put words to the pain that was eating him alive.

"I've been with the Lord six years, and it's been good, but I'm going to leave the church, move out of this apartment, and go back to my old friends. I'll make an announcement Sunday." He ran his hand through his thinning, sandy hair, and tried to compose himself.

"I just can't take it anymore. I want a woman to love me, to hold me. I just want to be loved." He hung his head and bent over, tears splashing onto his bony knees. "I know that some people in the church like me. But maybe others think I'm strange, or weird.

"I'm stupid. I wish I were smarter. I just cut grass and paint. I'm in a rut. I appreciate the jobs people have given me but I'm sick of living alone, watching television, the same old thing."

His mental state alarmed me. I tried to reason with him, assured him of our love, his worth to us, his worth to God. After he left, I called Craig, full of fear.

Steve began seeing a psychiatrist and a counselor. With Steve's permission, Craig consulted with the counselor about how to be supportive. We tried to provide a family, regular meals and social interaction, but Steve continued to deteriorate, to withdraw and waste away. He began to hear voices urging him to kill himself. When he reached the point where he spent most of the day in bed, emerging only to walk to the store to buy a half gallon of ice cream, then return to eat it alone, we knew he needed more help than we could give.

We helped him move into a structured group home nearby. Just a week before the policeman knocked on our door, Bill Bolling had taken him to Washington, D.C., where they visited museums and indulged their mutual love of history.

Craig arrived home mid-afternoon, and lay heavily on the bed.

"Steve's dead. He committed suicide. I had to identify the body." He covered his eyes with his forearm, trying to block out the image of Steve's mangled body sprawled on the pebbled railroad bed under the 41st Street bridge. Steve's glassy, empty eyes stared up to a heaven he had longed for, had sought, had pursued when this world had become dry and grating like two bones rubbing together. His tortured mind had succumbed to the voices urging him to jump, jump, *jump*, and he had thrown first one long leg, then the other over the railing.

We were crushed. Why didn't we see this coming? Maybe if we had done more...We berated ourselves. Craig called Steve's counselor. "Don't blame yourselves. You could have rented that apartment out to someone else," he said. "Steve knew you loved him. He just couldn't fight the demons of mental illness anymore."

We held a memorial service. There was no body—his brother had him cremated—so we displayed artifacts of Steve's life on a small table: his dog-eared Bible, Orioles memorabilia, photographs, his worn baseball glove. His brother choked up, shook Craig's hand, left. We learned several months later that he had not told their father, who lived in another part of town, of the service.

Steve's death hit Craig especially hard. Steve had been a tangible sign that our presence, our hardship, had made a difference. In low moments, Craig saw Steve's transformation as a validation of his ministry. Now, he saw Steve's lifeless body in his mind's eye, and anguished before God, "Is this it? Is this what You've brought me here for?"

We were still reeling from Steve's death when a new crisis threatened to split Faith. Two teenage girls from the neighborhood accused a church leader of improperly groping them, and the police filed charges. Fred denied the accusations, and we desperately wanted to believe him. While one of the girls came from a troubled home and was known to act up, the other lived with a loving and attentive grandmother, had attended for years, and was so responsible that I occasionally hired her to baby-sit. She had much to lose by making such a charge. Could she have misinterpreted something innocent? Or could Fred have somehow "snapped" in a weak moment, and run his hand across her breasts? And if so, could he have repressed this?

Craig agonized over what to do, and how to be fair to all parties involved. Night after night, he woke up to pray. He consulted two mental health professionals for advice. The urban, African American psychiatrist said that when girls grow up in a sexually explicit context or have suffered abuse, they might misread events or even fabricate stories. The white, suburban psychologist was blunt: "Kids don't lie about things like this."

Fred firmly maintained his innocence. When the elders reluctantly removed him from active ministry until the issue was resolved, his wife felt betrayed and angry. While most church members avoided gossip, extended love to all parties involved, and withheld judgment, a few people were upset that we would not dismiss the girls' claims outright. I felt the currents of sadness and anger that traveled through the congregation. It was like seeing my family torn apart.

In the midst of this crisis, on a rare weekend away, we attended a seminar on urban ministry. We were tight, on edge, and desperate for guidance and resolution. In gentle, professorial tones, with dry humor, Professor Harvie Conn of Westminster Seminary in Philadelphia spoke about the culture shock many people feel when they move to the city. He talked about the strain of cross cultural ministry: the constant sense of walking on eggshells, of never fully fitting in or understanding the rules. In urban environments, he confirmed, the possibility of violence always lurks just under the surface. He told of walking into a 7-11 just a few nights before to pick up a gallon of milk. As he waited in line, the two men in line in front of him began brawling. They pushed Harvie, and his milk flew up into the air and exploded on the floor. He wondered if someone would pull a gun. In some city neighborhoods, he said, this chaos is normal.

Yes! my heart leapt. I began to cry, full of relief at this naming, full of exhaustion and loneliness—-and I couldn't stop crying. I was ashamed to be weeping in public, and struggled to control myself all weekend, to stop this endless falling, but I couldn't. In a darkened Motel Six room, I fell apart completely. "I can't keep living like this," I sobbed. "Look at me! I can't stop crying. This is not normal. This is not me."

Craig sat down next to me on the bed, rubbing my back. He looked stricken.

"I feel like I'm drowning, like I'm being sucked dry. It's too much!" I sobbed. "You're consumed with the church. Even when you're home, you're not really there. The lights are on, but nobody's home. You don't even sleep at night!"

Craig hung his head. "I know," he said softly. "Things are really hard right now, with these allegations, and trying to hold the church together—"

"No!" I exploded. "It's always hard! It's been hard from day one! This is the worst, no doubt about that! But there's always a crisis! One right after another! Can't you see that?"

Craig didn't speak for a minute. Outside our window, we heard the rumble of eighteen wheelers and the hiss of their air brakes. "Yes," he admitted. "You're right. There's always a crisis." He looked utterly beaten. He had no idea how to fix this. "I'm sorry. I'll do better. I'll be home more, be less preoccupied," he promised. He began to pace the room. I knew he was mentally readjusting his schedule, trying to pencil in more family time, developing a four-point plan, looking at systems and structures like an engineer.

"You've said that before," I accused. "This is not a new conversation."

"I know," he sighed. "I want to do better."

"I know you do," I said softly. "You want to do the right thing. I've always known that about you. But you get derailed by everybody else's needs! There's nothing left of you by the time you come home. Why should I believe you when you promise things will be different?"

He looked out the window, not seeing. He returned to me, embraced me. "I want to change."

I tried to breathe normally, to stop the heaving that wanted to erupt again. We had jumped into the crucible of urban ministry just weeks after our marriage, when the concrete of our relationship was still wet.

Had Craig not been such an attentive suitor during our courtship, not wooed me so completely, and had I not remained utterly convinced that he wanted to follow Jesus above all, that he wanted to love me, wanted me to feel loved, and that Jesus could intervene, could change us—our marriage would not have survived. Leaving him—breaking my marriage vows, depriving my children of their father, dishonoring the name of Christ—was not an option. But my heart was ragged.

I thought of the box of yellowing letters on my closet shelf, each paper full of his neat, square architectural printing, so full of faith and desire. I thought of his arm, reaching for me even as he slept.

"Can you believe I can change?"

I shrugged.

"Or can you believe God can change me?"

I believed.

Several months later the police dropped charges against Fred, and the situation was resolved at some level. However, the fallout lingered under the surface for years, and later resulted in the departure of not only Fred and his wife, but several other families.

Our old friend Larry, who had wandered in and out of Faith's orbit since our earliest days, struggled with more health problems as he entered his fifties. A lifetime of poor nutrition, heavy smoking, and a lack of exercise caught up with him. Finally, depressed and exhausted from mental illness and intermittent hospital stays, he took his life.

We looked for signs of grace to bloom like the scraggly flowers our neighbors planted in vacant lots. We both saw a Christian counselor to deal with stress. Craig decided he needed more training and mentoring, and enrolled in Westminster Seminary's urban missions doctoral program in Philadelphia. Working during brief sabbaticals, evenings, and vacations, it would take him six full years to complete the doctorate. But from Professors Harvie Conn, Manny Ortiz, and others, he learned how to pastor whites and blacks, Latinos and Asians and internationals; how to join graduate students from Johns Hopkins with streetwise dropouts from Baltimore City public schools, to pastor Volvo-driving professionals and bus-riding single moms living from paycheck to paycheck

God did not abandon us. Day after day, He sustained us in a thousand resurrections as we read, prayed, and wrote in our journals. We felt acutely the words of the Apostle Paul: "But we have this treasure in jars of clay to show that this all-surpassing power is from God and not from us. We are hard pressed on every side, but not crushed; perplexed, but not in despair; persecuted, but not abandoned; struck down, but not destroyed."

God brought new believers. Bert and Nancy Williams moved into the neighborhood with their two children. Bert became an elder, and Nancy volunteered twenty hours a week, taking our crisis food ministry to a far more organized and extensive level. Sandy Clark, an engineer, and his wife Laura, who worked with AIDS patients, also joined. They moved into the community and volunteered for several years with our youth ministry, teaching kids the Bible and taking them on camping trips. Sandy served as deacon, treasurer, and head usher—sometimes simultaneously. Laura's quiet, gracious spirit was an asset in many ministries.

Another young couple arrived from the Dakotas one Sunday morning in 1988, their Honda Civic hatchback crammed with their worldly goods. Joe Brandli was scheduled to start work at a Baltimore architecture firm the following day, and Mary Ann hoped to find work as a music teacher. That morning, their credit card had reached its limit. They checked out of their hotel, knowing they had nowhere to sleep until their apartment became available on Monday. They prayed about their homeless status, and decided not to tell anyone and to see how God would work.

They had planned to attend a P.C.A. church in the suburbs, but got lost. They had almost given up when Mary Ann saw Faith's large, stone building. "Wait, Joe, there's a P.C.A. church right near here!"

They found Faith to be a small, diverse, and welcoming congregation. Coming from homogeneous South Dakota, they naively assumed that all churches in the diverse east were multicultural. They soon learned otherwise. After the service, another young couple introduced themselves. Roy Chisholm was a surgical resident at a Baltimore hospital, and his petite wife Cindy a nurse. After chatting briefly, Cindy felt led to make a generous offer to these strangers.

"I don't know what your situation is," she began, "but if you need a place to stay, we have a guest room and you're welcome to stay with us."

Joe and Mary Ann's mouths dropped open. Somewhat sheepishly, they admitted they didn't have a place to stay the night.

Joe and Mary Ann began attending Faith, and the following year, they bought a small row house near the church. They joined the choir led by elder and music minister Andrew Talley. Mary Ann co-led our Summer Youth Ministry day camp with Andrew for six weeks, and that fall, when our part-time church secretary quit, she filled in for several months. When Andrew resigned as music minister a few years later, she stepped into that role. She learned to play gospel piano and blended contemporary, classical, and gospel styles in one service. Joe became a deacon, a multi-faceted role at Faith involving not just budgets and buildings but extensive mercy ministry. Over the years, they have labored long, often to the point of exhaustion.

But God wasn't finished sending additional warriors to join the fray. In 1989, our friend Bruce Gustafsen called. Bruce, an elder in the church Craig had attended while in seminary, had been involved in urban ministry since the mid 1950s. I had lived with them after Craig and I got engaged, and they provided some of our earliest exposure to urban ministry. A few years earlier, Bruce had left his job as CFO of a Fortune 300 company to work for a California urban ministry.

Bruce told Craig he had resigned from the California ministry, and they were praying about moving back east to be near their daughter in Maryland.

"Why not Baltimore?" Craig urged. "We could really use your leadership and wisdom at Faith."

Bruce's son-in-law Gary Herwig and daughter Krista had also resigned from the California ministry. Along with Joan Nelson, another former employee, they drove across the country to Baltimore. They volunteered with Faith's youth, molding and guiding a diverse group of teens that included our daughter Becky and many neighborhood youths. One unforgettable summer, Gary taught all the summer camp kids kayaking. They bought and renovated a house near the church. Joan ran our Summer Youth Ministry and worked part-time in the church office. Bruce became an elder, taught Sunday School, assisted with pastoral counseling, and helped guide our small group ministry. He also encouraged Craig to stop tempting fate by walking back and forth to church in the middle of the night. Marlene volunteered in our crisis relief food pantry, in counseling and teaching women, and other activities. In a church absent of other gray-headed saints—with the notable exception of Bob and Jean Jenkins—they served as surrogate parents and wise counselors to many. For seven years, they provided strategic leadership before retiring to Maryland's Eastern Shore. But perhaps the bucolic life there was too peaceful, too bland, too uneventful: several years later, they returned. We didn't mind at all.

CHAPTER 18

Graffiti on Old York Road

THE GIRL NEXT DOOR

SOME people argue that drug addicts should be locked up, that treatment programs don't work. Some argue that prostitution is a victimless crime, that there is nothing sordid or wrong in women selling sex to strangers. They argue that there is nothing wrong with young women gyrating before leering men on The Block. I won't buy it. I will never buy it. I will always see Lindi, who took up this line of work to feed her drug habit and had to be high to do it. I will always see Lindi, who wanted a husband and a baby but signed away the child she had carried, the child she loved.

Lindi, a dark-haired beauty in her early twenties, lived with my neighbor Tom, a man more than twice her age. I saw them come and go, saw him kiss her in a way that let me know he was not her father. One spring day, as I played with my children in our tiny back yard, I introduced myself. We became friends, sort of.

She was sweet, almost child-like, and related sordid tales of hardship with more surprise than bitterness. She was kind to my children even if she couldn't quite focus on them, or on me, for more than a minute.

She did not have a job or go to school. She did not cook or keep house. "I'm not going to do his *laundry*," she scoffed one day as I gave her a lift to the dry cleaners, where she dropped off several baskets of their clothes. She provided other services. She and Tom played a little game with me; they pretended he was a platonic friend, a sexless father figure. The ruse wore a little thin when I arrived mid-morning to take her job hunting and found her naked in Tom's bed.

"She's still asleep," Tom drawled, nodding towards his bedroom. "She just crawls in there after I get up."

I let it pass, thinking, "Tom, I'm not that stupid."

Tom later told me he found her working on The Block, Baltimore's infamous red light district. He took her home, he said, because he was worried about her.

Tom did not want her to use drugs, but she did. She started getting high in middle school after her parents divorced. She regretted starting on drugs, was always trying to stop using, or to at least stop using bad drugs. She loved them more than anything else, more than Tom, more than the boyfriend she saw on the side, more than herself. She took them because she had to, because she wanted to be somewhere other than inside her own body. She took them because her father had left and she didn't see him for years and when she finally found him, he propositioned her. She thought she had seen all the depravity men can dish out, yet this still galled her. "My own father, Maria! My own father! You can't sleep with your *father*!"

One summer morning, she banged frantically on my screen door.

"Maria! I can't hear!" she said, gesturing wildly at her ears.

"What do you mean, you can't hear?" I shouted.

"I woke up this morning and I couldn't hear. It sounds like airplanes taking off and landing in my head."

I tried to calm her down. I prayed with her in my living room with my four little children running about, and offered to take her to the emergency room. I was wildly naïve as to the extent of her drug problem.

"So you woke up this morning and you couldn't hear?" I asked.

"O.K., well, I took some drugs. My friends gave them to me at a party. I don't know what I took, and I passed out. They just left me there, just *left* me there. I could have died! When I woke up, my ears were like this."

I left the children with Craig and drove her to Union Memorial Hospital, where nurses whisked her away. Nearly an hour dragged by. Finally, I asked to see her. She wore a thin hospital gown and was propped up in bed with an i.v. line running to her chest.

"Oh, my God," she told me. "They couldn't find a vein and I had to sign some stupid form. The nurse was jabbing me all over and had to put a line into my *heart*."

I imagined nurses standing over her, seeing the tracks on her arms, the useless veins, jabbing between her toes and giving up, settling on her chest as the last hope.

Outside her room, nurses in pastel medical smocks moved through the corridor. I pulled one of them aside.

"Is she going to be all right?"

"And you are?" the nurse asked, sizing me up. I got this look whenever I appeared with Lindi in public, at hospitals, in prisons, at court appearances. Officials sized me up, tried to figure out how I fit into this picture, tried to pigeonhole me. I saw the wheels turning in their heads: *Funny, she doesn't look like...* "I am her friend," I would tell them. "Her neighbor." I would still see the questions. Sometimes, I would add that my husband was a pastor, and the suspicion would melt away.

I didn't tell her that I was probably the only person Lindi knew who did not get high, who did not want to use Lindi's body, gobble it like a McValue Meal and leave the scraps for someone else to throw away.

The nurse looked at me. "It's a good thing you brought her in. She's in renal failure."

"Renal failure?" I parroted numbly. I was still thinking about her hearing, and now we were dealing with another critical body part?

"Whatever she took shut down her kidneys," the nurse said. A clinician with professional detachment, she saw the ravages of drug use regularly.

Her kidneys returned to life several days later. When Lindi was released, she got a hearing aid that she hated and lost frequently. The constant roaring in her ears drove her to distraction—or more drugs. She vanished for weeks at a time.

Tom told me he found her working at The Jewel Box again, a strip club on The Block. "I happened to be drivin' by late one night aftah work, and there she was," he said.

He cared about Lindi, wanted the comfort and sex and beauty she provided, wanted her to stay away from her loser old boyfriend. But she never did. She was drawn to defective men, locking onto them like a heat-seeking missile. Tom took her back again and again, but eventually his patience would wear thin.

One afternoon, I received the first of many collect calls.

"You have received a collect call from…." the mechanical voice paused. I heard Lindi's sweet tone inserting her name. The computer resumed its instructions: "Say 'yes' to accept this call."

"Yes," I said, and in a moment we were connected. I heard a din in the background, an acoustic onslaught of yelling and metal clanging echoing off concrete walls and floors.

"Maria, I'm in jail," she said.

"Jail? Why? What happened?" I imagined possibilities, but wanted to know what we were dealing with this time. She paused, reluctant.

"I don't want to tell you," she said. "But Tom won't bail me out. He says he's through with me. Maria, can you come see me, bring me some clothes? I don't have anything here."

"Yes, of course," I told her. She gave me a list of things she wanted and told me the visiting hours.

"I have to go," she said. "Someone's waiting to use the phone." She paused. "Maria," she added, almost as a postscript. "Solicitation. I was arrested for solicitation."

"I'm so sorry," I told her. "I love you. I'll see you Saturday."

I know prostitution is mostly addiction-driven, but it pained me to think of Lindi turning lovemaking into a commercial transaction, servicing random strangers like a cheap drive-through. I ached at the inevitable scarring and scabbing of her soul each time a man zipped up his pants, threw crumpled bills at her, and walked away.

Tom bailed her out a few days later, and they resumed their relationship. She attended NA meetings for a while, and proudly showed off her different-colored NA key fobs: one day clean, one week, one month. Not long after, however, she left.

"She's off with her drugging friends," Tom told me in his soft Southern drawl, stroking his neat salt-and-pepper beard. He is not a bad sort, I thought. He might be a decent boyfriend—but for a thirty-five or forty-year-old woman, not a twenty-three-year-old who's developmentally about fourteen.

"I tried to help her out," he said. "Told her I'd pay if she wants to go back to school, get her GED and go to community college. But she won't stay away from the drugs."

She eventually bounced back to Tom, and when he bought a house in the suburbs, she moved with him. One day, she invited me to bring my children to swim in their backyard pool. The children rarely had a chance to swim, so this was a big treat. I had managed to shield them from any knowledge of Lindi's problems.

I lost touch with her for several months, but one fall afternoon, she called collect from jail. "It's a misunderstanding," she said. "I was in the wrong place at the wrong time." She told a convoluted story about snorting coke with a stranger on the Amtrak and police busting him and sweeping her up in the dragnet. The quantity of drugs was large enough that she was slapped with charges of distributing. She faced the possibility of several years in prison.

She had no one to put up money for her bail—not Tom, not any of her drugging buddies, not her mother or sister. She did not ask me, perhaps knowing we couldn't. Or wouldn't. So she languished in jail awaiting her trial. I visited her there.

To house the swelling tide of Baltimore's drug-related offenders, the city bulldozed nearby low-income housing to create a sprawling, block-long penal purgatory—the Maryland State Penitentiary and the Baltimore City Jail. Faceless, five-story concrete rectangles with tiny, block-glass windows squat next to the Jail's nineteenth-century blackened granite walls and towers. All grass, all trees, all dirt were plowed under, covered over, banished. The architectural effect is Charles Dickens meets Karl Marx.

I tucked my old Honda into a parking space a few blocks away and walked past blighted row houses and barbed wire. Outside the jail entrance, hardscrabble men and women in jeans and sweatpants smoked cigarettes and well-coiffed lawyers cradled cell phones. When visiting hours began, we shut our purses and wallets in little lockers and endured a long wait before signing our names and passing through metal detectors and a series of locked doors.

To reach the women's division, I had to pass through a courtyard. Behind rows of windows several stories high, men waited, had been waiting, peering out tiny grills to watch the visitors walk this gauntlet. To avoid attention, I had dressed conservatively: long coat, long denim jumper. It didn't matter. One or two yelled and soon a cacophony swelled, bouncing off the concrete quadrangle. These were not catcalls but verbal assaults, men suggesting and demanding sex as though I hawked it in a G-string. I put my head down and kept moving.

The guards searched the bag I brought Lindi: transistor radio and headset still in original packaging, underwear, slippers, toiletries. I threw in a Bible—I was always throwing in a Bible— and they flipped through the pages, making sure I hadn't slipped little tabs of acid or who knows what in there. They peered through the windows of their elevated cubicle at me, down to the Bible in their hands, then back at me, down to the Bible. I felt like a bug pinned to a specimen board.

"Hope she reads it," one guard said, the frozen veneer thawing for a moment. I nodded. I had prayed for Lindi, and believed God could make her clean, could fill her with a contentment she couldn't find inside a needle or vial. I had told her Jesus is the only man who will never let her down. But she demurred, put him aside.

I filed into a sterile, dingy room with other visitors. Guards stood behind us, legs slightly apart, arms folded across their chests. We sat in front of double-paned glass windows with sound vents through which we simultaneously yelled private conversations at our loved ones.

When Lindi was convicted and transferred to the state prison at Jessup, Tom washed his hands of her. He brought me several Hefty bags of her clothes: leather jackets, designer jeans, boutique t-shirts, lacy underwear. But she never bothered to get them back from me.

After several months, Lindi was released on probation. Though we had corresponded, she did not contact me when she got out. By then, I had known Lindi for almost two years; I was accustomed to her long silences. I knew this meant she was using. I wondered when—and if—I would ever see her again.

"I want what you have," she told me once. "I want a husband who loves me, children, a house." So simple. So elusive.

Then one winter day, after a silence of many months, my mailbox held a letter from Lindi, four pages of her life on yellow legal paper. I noticed the return address in Lindi's artistic, feminine script: Jessup, Women's Division. Her name was followed by her prison ID number.

> *Yes Maria I violated my probation and the Judge gave me the whole 3 years! Well Maria a lots happened since we last saw one another. I had a little baby girl. her name is Tiffany, Maria she is so precious.*

Maria I want my baby more than any thing. And Mom and Tom think I'm being selfish they tell me I can't give my baby what she needs and she deserves a better life with a good family. Maria I got a lot of love to offer my baby.

Lindi wrote that after giving birth to Tiffany, she entered a methadone treatment program. After several months of methadone, Lindi wanted off. She found a treatment program that would take her, but had no one to care for the baby.

Maria I really have no friends that I would trust to watch my baby for 4 days. The only friend I would ever trust is you but I didn't want to bother you with this problem and you got to many to keep your eyes on now you didn't need another one.

Lindi asked Child Protective Services to take Tiffany for the four days. "What I didn't know is that I wasn't getting her back when I completed my Detox! When I got out, I called to pick her up and they told me I would have to wait for a court date which was 2 months away."

When she tried to visit Tiffany in foster care, the social worker was "extremely rude she would cut me down every time I would come up there then she started changing Tiffany's visit days. It was a mess. I ended up going back to Tiffany's father (who by the way is no better than that Billy I use to go with!) and got back on the drugs and now I'm here."

Lindi persuaded her mother, who lived out of state, to take Tiffany. But at the last minute, when she learned Tiffany was biracial, she backed out. "Maria that hurts. I tried to call Tiffany's father but he wants no responsibility for Tiffany he's no good."

Social Services wanted to terminate parental rights, but Lindi resisted.

I want my daughter but then again maybe my mother is right... I plan on getting my life together for me and Tiffany. Mom says who ever adopts Tiffany will give her a better life and provide for Tiffany and give her more than what I have to offer. Maria I just can't do it I can't. I Love my baby and will do my best for her and I will try to be the best Mother I can possibly be for her. I really want your honest opinion, do you think I'm being selfish? I am putting every thing in the Lords hands. When I go to court on Jan 22 I know the Lord will do whats right for my Tiffany.

I'm sorry I never made it over your house I got real mad at the guy Tiffany and I was staying with and we went to the Salvation

Army. Maria we've been thru a lot. What I want more than any-thing is for the Lord to watch over Tiffany and me and for a new happy Life with her she is so precious and I Love her so very much.

I wrote her a long letter with assurances of my love and prayers. Two days before the custody hearing, her public defender called me. He was cobbling together a case, and I was, apparently, his best shot: a mother of four, a pastor's wife who had known the defendant for several years. He milked me for any positive statements.

"She's very sweet, very fond of my children," I told him. "She says she wants to get into a program, get clean and raise the baby." I sighed. "Who knows, maybe she'll make it this time, now that she's got a baby."

"So you'll testify on Lindi's behalf?"

"I can testify," I told him. "But I'm going to tell the truth."

The night before the trial, I composed a statement. I racked my brain for positive memories, any show of responsibility on Lindi's part. No job. No education. No stable address. I couldn't imagine being separated from my children, much less terminating parental rights. But I knew what it took to raise children, the endless putting aside of personal desires, the careful tending. The need for stability and focus and self-control.

Outside the courtroom, I showed the lawyer my statement. With a pencil, he crossed through large swaths of my honest but ultimately negative assessment.

"Can't you just leave this part out?" he said.

"No." I looked in his eyes. "Do you have children?"

He didn't answer. He handed me my statement, marked up like an errant student's paper.

A sheriff's deputy led Lindi in, handcuffed. She was effusively happy to see me. I was the only person here for Lindi who was not on a payroll; she had social workers, caseworkers, a public defender, and one friend. My stomach was knotted and twisted like a macramé key chain.

The judge called the lawyers to the bench. After a brief conference, he announced a recess and the lawyers and Lindi filed into the judge's chambers. A few minutes later, her lawyer retrieved me from the courtroom, ushering me into a spacious room lined with finely crafted bookshelves. At a large, polished wooden table, Lindi sat with lawyers, social workers, and the judge. She smiled brightly when I entered and motioned me to sit next to her.

"The paternal grandmother, who has been providing foster care for almost two years, has offered to adopt," her lawyer told me. "Lindi is going to voluntarily terminate her rights."

Lindi turned to me. "Do you think this is the loving thing to do?"

I nodded and took her hand. This was a better outcome than I could have imagined. I started to cry with relief and loss. She comforted me.

"It's best for Tiffany. I'm doing it because I love her. Don't you think this is an unselfish thing to do?" I pictured Solomon judging between two pleading women, a soldier with a drawn sword, baby dangling by its heel.

"Yes," I told her. "It's a very unselfish thing to do." With shackled hands, she picked up a pen and signed away her child. She returned to her cell at Jessup, and I returned home to my children.

When Lindi was released a year or so later, I picked her up. Guards with automatic weapons watched from towers as Lindi left a squat, drab building with a paper sack of her possessions. A guard escorted her though the final, massive chain link fence topped with rolled barbed wire. I embraced her, gave her a bouquet, its reds and yellows and greens extravagant against the gray setting. I couldn't imagine what she had been through, what she had lost. Later, she confided that she had been raped in prison.

I dreamed her future: *You can get your GED*, I told her, *figure out what you want to do, get a job. We can look at the want ads, I'll take you to fill out applications.* She was twenty-six now, and had never had a real job unless you counted dancing on The Block. *I can teach you how to cook a little, how to budget your money. We'll help you get your own apartment. You can buy a car!*

The next day, Sunday, I brought her to church. People embraced her, remembered her from previous scattered visits, loved her, never condemned. She said she liked church and that she really needed to get right with God.

"I'm going out for a walk," she announced airily twenty-four hours later. I felt a vague sense of unease, of dread, but what could I do? She strolled out of my house, leaving my dreams for her, the affection of my children, and the clean sheets on Caroline's single bed. Her clothes remained neatly folded in Caroline's white dresser drawers. After a few days, I packed up her things and stored them in the basement. I tried to explain to the children.

For months afterward, when rain or cold buffeted my house, I thought of her, a little electric current of worry and loss running through me. I would wake up at night sensing I had lost something, left something valuable and precious outside, uncovered in the rain. I prayed for her, wondered where she was, whether she was warm and safe. I thought not. I have never seen her again.

I offered Lindi friendship, but she wasn't able to take it. Experts say that addicts don't have friends; they have colleagues in addiction, or hostages, or enablers. Experts would say she was not "ready" to get clean, that she hadn't hit bottom. This is true. But it is also true that Lindi was never too far gone for God to reach.

CHAPTER 19

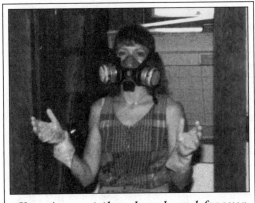

Cleaning out the abandoned freezer

A HOME IN THE 'HOOD

FOR several years, we toyed with leaving our apartment house and moving to Pen Lucy. Though our house was only three blocks outside the neighborhood's official boundary, we wanted to be more involved in Faith's outreach there. Putting down roots in Pen Lucy would send a message.

Craig and I divided the labor of owning an apartment house: he handled all repairs, and I screened and managed tenants. Sometimes I made mistakes, wanting to extend grace, swayed by hard-luck stories. The occasional bad tenant pushed me to the edge—if not over it.

I allowed one couple to move in without a security deposit because the woman's mother was an acquaintance who lived near the church. Even though she had a job—and her husband Joe was "looking" for work—once they moved in, they never paid any rent. After two months of broken promises, I began my first eviction. I learned that the process would take at least a month, possibly two. Eviction is stressful enough—but living directly upstairs from your evictee ratchets the stress level to an unbearable level. Joe, a well-built, thirty-something unemployed laborer, watched TV most of the day. He became hostile once he learned his free rent would end.

One afternoon, the children informed me that a rat had gotten into Joe's trash.

"We see needles, Mommy," they announced, wide-eyed. We sometimes saw needles scattered around the neighborhood, and I had put the fear of God into them about touching them.

I cleaned up the trash carefully, and called Craig. "He's using needles. Or she's using needles! No wonder there's no money for rent."

He sighed. "That explains a lot. Where are we in the eviction process?"

"It will take several more weeks. Do you think Bess knows her daughter and her husband are into drugs?"

"Probably not. But it's not our place to tell her. 'Course that would explain why we're evicting them," he said dryly.

"I wonder what he's using? How dangerous is he? He's already angry at me about the eviction. The children run in and out all day, and the door's always unlocked. What if he decides to hurt one of the kids to get back at us?"

"I don't think he'll go that far," Craig assured me. "But I don't want you or the children having any contact with him."

We gave the children strict instructions to keep away from Joe, and I kept them inside or stayed with them outside. I wanted to be free from tenants— or, if this was financially unfeasible, at least free from living with them. My own house no longer felt safe

Evicting Joe and his wife sealed our desire to find a single-family home in Pen Lucy. Craig scoured the neighborhood for available properties. The housing was almost equally divided between brick row houses and older wooden frame houses. Many residents lacked the money or skills to maintain their homes. Hardware stores had fled the area—the closest was a twenty-minute drive away. Landlords were notorious for failing to keep up properties or doing the bare minimum.

Because of Craig's experience, we could consider houses needing extensive repair. We looked into several properties: a small house on a quiet side street; a vacant lot where we could bring in a modular home; and a renovated, end-of-group three-story row house. But each time, after several months of progress, the possibility evaporated. The asking prices were too high. An owner changed his mind about selling. Banks refused to lend us money to rehabilitate or build in a depressed community. Though red-lining is illegal, one loan officer leveled with us. "We can lend you the amount of money you are asking for, but not in that neighborhood."

Months stretched into a year, then two years. Four active children age six and under had too much energy for our close quarters. We wondered: Why is the Lord making it so hard for us to move?

Craig roamed Pen Lucy, looking for a house and praying. "Lord, you know my family needs more space. We believe you have called us to this neighborhood. We believe it is your will that we move into Pen Lucy. Please provide us with a house."

An abandoned, three-story Victorian on Springfield Avenue, just two blocks from the church, caught his eye. He squeezed through its locked gate and crawled through an open window. Its three stories contained six bedrooms, two bathrooms, two old gas fireplaces, and a gutted kitchen. Ancient wallpaper and thick strips of lead paint peeled off the walls, and many of the rooms were lined with dark, 1970s paneling. Several feet of water had flooded and frozen solid in the basement. Trash and dead rat carcasses lay embedded in the ice. Frozen clumps of tall grass and weeds, which grew several feet high in the summer, filled the large yard. The house was filled with trash, old mattresses, and broken furniture.

"Lord, is this the house you have for us?" Craig asked. Through the mess, Craig's experienced eye recognized underlying qualities: spacious rooms, a large dining room separated from the living room by twelve-foot pocket doors, ten-foot ceilings on the first floor, ornate millwork in the foyer, a stained glass window in the front room, and starburst glass in the front door. His eye settled on a small, framed picture of Jesus—a tacky, white Jesus in the Garden of Gethsemane. It provided all the encouragement he needed.

From city records we learned that a developer had recently bid on the property for back taxes. If the owner failed to pay his $3,500 tax bill within a few months, the deed would transfer to the developer. Craig tracked down the owner, who had inherited the house from his mother and lived in California. We offered to buy it.

"Call back next week," he told us. When we called back, his wife claimed he was not home. We called again and again. The owner refused to return our calls.

"If the tax bill isn't paid, your husband will lose his inheritance," we reminded his wife. "We'd like to buy it."

Finally, we sent a blank contract. "Fill it in," we urged him. "We'll pay what is reasonable."

He refused to sell, and lost his inheritance. The developer was all too happy to make a quick sale—for a price as high as the market would bear, considering the extensive renovation needed. But then, sensing our eagerness, he raised his price by a third. The house needed new plumbing, electrical systems, a kitchen, bathrooms, front and back porches, painting, and siding—the cost of which would leave the home over-improved for the neighborhood. Yet we believed God would provide. Hadn't he already given us far more than we could afford based on our modest income? We remembered the gift of our Greenmount house, the miraculous church building, the car he had provided when our old Honda wore out. The children never lacked food, clothing, or even toys.

Scripture says God is able to supply our need above and beyond what we can ask or imagine, and this proved true in our Springfield Avenue home. The house was more spacious than I had ever dreamed of owning, with turn-of-the century charm (admittedly a bit buried at present!). Although we hired out much of the work, Craig and I attacked the house's many deficiencies. We hauled more than a dozen old mattresses out of the house and hacked down the tiny trees and weeds that filled the yard. A large chest freezer was full of food that had liquefied. I donned gloves and a lead paint mask to diminish the odor and emptied the putrid, black sludge. Craig, Bruce, and Marlene laid tile in the kitchen, and Gary Herwig installed cabinets.

As we worked outside in the yard, men often stopped by. "I'm looking for work—carpentry, painting, anything. Are you hiring?" We regretted that we usually had no jobs to offer. But the steady flow of willing and available men spoke volumes about the high rate of unemployment all too typical in urban neighborhoods.

Neighbors stopped by frequently with another question. "When will the apartments be ready?" The sight of a young white couple seemed to indicate that this house, like many of the larger old homes in the neighborhood, would be broken into apartments.

"There aren't going to be any apartments," I answered. "We're going to live here."

"You are? No kidding!" Their faces registered surprise, skepticism, and sometimes approval. "Do you think the neighborhood is on the upswing?" a few asked. In general, our neighbors in Pen Lucy were far more open-minded about Caucasians integrating their street than the white inspectors and contractors we met. "Well, good luck," one tradesman snorted. "I wouldn't do it."

Several neighbors were especially helpful. The Purdies allowed us to snake an extension cord between our properties, providing electricity to power our tools. When Craig offered them a check, they refused it. The Grays helped us locate a relative of the house's original owner, to whom we gave the family photos we found inside. The Winklers gave small gifts to our children. Miss June Randall, a cheerful grandmother who monitored the neighborhood from the porch of the row house she and her husband had rented for over twenty years, frequently invited me to visit her on her stoop.

In the fall of 1989, overwhelmed with trying to homeschool three grades while supervising a toddler, we enrolled Becky in a nearby Lutheran school. I dropped Becky off in the morning, home schooled Melissa and Caroline, and brought the three younger children to Springfield to play in the afternoons while I painted and cleaned. I packed snacks and toys, spread them out on a blanket, and let the children play in the house and yard. Little did I know that I was exposing them to an invisible danger.

Lead poisoning was off our radar screen, but public health attention later exploded around this issue in Baltimore. A month or two before our move, I began to read articles about it and immediately took the children to the pediatrician for blood tests. Calvin, at three, had the highest levels, followed by Caroline and Melissa. Becky, who had spent less time at the house, had the lowest. While the children did not require drastic intervention, such as hospitalization, all exposure had to stop.

That night, I sat in our rocking chair, pouring out my soul on the phone to Jean Jenkins. "How could I have been so stupid? Will the children be permanently damaged because of my carelessness?" I cried, utterly unhinged.

Jean comforted me. "I'm sure they'll be fine. You've caught it in time. You just have to get rid of all the lead paint in the house."

"Do you know how much that will cost? We're already over budget," I wailed. "We have to hire someone to repaint all the wood trim with encapsulating paint, AND buy replacement windows. That house will never be worth what we've paid to live in it."

"I know," she soothed. "The Lord has provided for you all these years. I don't know how, but He has. He'll make a way somehow."

Craig's father ordered replacement windows and spent several days helping Craig install them. The bill for the windows never appeared in our mailbox. Pete and Cleo paid it.

Further blood tests revealed that the lead levels had dropped, and the children suffered no lingering effects. In February of 1991, assisted by the strong backs of members of Faith, we moved into the house God had provided.

CHAPTER 20

Caroline in homemade swing

LIVING ON SPRINGFIELD

A FTER years of sharing an apartment house on a busy street, we had landed in a real neighborhood. Our large Victorian with its welcoming front porch and mature magnolia and maple trees looked like an idyllic hamlet, especially compared to some of the rundown rental units on our block.

Life on Springfield Avenue was a paradox. Sometimes I felt so different I must be neon. We were the only whites on our street, one of a handful of non-African Americans in Pen Lucy. Craig and I were college graduates in a neighborhood where more than half didn't finish high school, homeowners where two-thirds of the houses were rentals. Our old television boasted only a bent coat hanger antenna, while cable television snaked into homes up and down the street. Our daughter (and eventually her siblings) rode in our clunker cars to a private school. While some neighbors had newer cars, most kids walked to our under-funded neighborhood schools. Some of my neighbors toiled day after day at low-wage, repetitive jobs with little hope of advancement; for over ten years I was a home schooling, non-employed, stay-at-home mom. Every day, I wore the twin issues of race and class like an out-of-season coat.

Who was I to most neighbors? I wondered. *The white lady?* Or a slight step up in the identity game, *the minister's wife? Melissa's mother?* Was I Maria to anyone?

Building friendships across class and race took time and effort on both sides. After moving in, we decided to host an open house. We knew people were curious to see how the newcomers had fixed up one of Pen Lucy's eyesores. I dropped invitations in my neighbors' mailboxes, whipped up food, vacuumed, and waited. No one came. After an hour, Barbara, with whom I shared a back fence, walked over and pushed the door bell. The three of us perched on the living room sofa, chatting and nibbling—enjoyable, but hardly the houseful I had hoped for.

Afterwards, I tried to figure out what went wrong. "Maybe open house parties aren't really done around here," I ventured to Craig. "Should I have called it something else? Or is it just too odd because we're white?"

"Maybe when the weather breaks we can have a cookout," Craig offered. "Maybe that won't be so weird."

Other times—talking over the fence with Barbara, visiting Miss June on her stoop, watching children climb our trees or shriek with delight on our tire swing, or attending a neighborhood child's birthday party—I felt connected to the neighborhood. I belonged. Some mornings, as I jogged or walked our streets, crossed into Guilford and then back again, I felt immensely grateful to live on the Pen Lucy side. I knew I was richer for seeing life through the eyes of my neighbors. Pen Lucy was teaching me to be less selfish, and to focus on God's value system, not the one that bombarded me every day in the newspaper and on television. Pen Lucy reminded me that I am weak. It forced me to depend on God's provision rather than my own competence, to be broken before God, to see with spiritual eyes. Joy came from investing in an eternal kingdom, not a hammer-and-nails one.

"This is so lovely. Maybe I'm exaggerating the problems of Pen Lucy," I thought sometimes. But in the next block, homes stood crumbling and condemned. Most houses our size had been chopped up into apartments. We had landed in a real neighborhood, all right, but one that was more troubled than Waverly.

The city's high unemployment rate and estimated sixty thousand drug addicts spawned a host of social ills. Petty theft plagued us like a chronic pulled muscle. Anything left outside was liable to disappear—bikes, ladders, potted plants, door wreaths. One morning, I awoke to find someone had stolen the twelve tiny azaleas I had planted the day before. Another afternoon, I came home to find the plastic, faux stone planter at the base of our porch missing, a pile of dirt in its place.

Whenever we returned from vacations I held my breath. Even with an alarm system and friends checking on the house periodically, break-ins were frequent.

"Your alarm went off, but I didn't see anything missing," our friend Joan told us one year. "Maybe the cat set it off." Closer investigation revealed bits of insulation and sheetrock on our basement stairs. Someone had smashed the basement window, climbed the stairs, but had failed to break through the latched, solid wood door to the first floor. So he had tunneled through the sheetrock behind the refrigerator. In the kitchen, his movement had set off the alarm.

Occasionally, while I played with the children outside or tended my scraggly garden, a police car raced by. Once, several officers with drawn weapons chased a man across our yard. Several times, SWAT teams swarmed onto a neighbor's front and back porches. Especially on summer nights, violence would spill onto our block and police helicopters hovered overhead, shining their spotlight through our back yard. I always prayed that no gunfire would disrupt my parents' infrequent visits. While I took every precaution to protect the children, I knew their safety ultimately depended on God. Trusting Jesus with my children required that I exercise more vigorous faith. I would later learn just how much I would have to trust him.

Crossfire Children

"Our children are being damaged in ways we don't even know about yet. In my own community, I see more helicopters flying around with searchlights than I ever saw in Vietnam."

George Buntin, Executive Director, Baltimore NAACP, 1993

Again,
I lie awake.

Outside,
I hear loud voices,
gunshots, screams.
Men run through the alley, laughing.
Another pursues, cursing.

Fools, I fume.
They play, but

life is snatched away,
DNA returning to dust
with the hot boring of a bullet.

I circle through the bedrooms
touching each child

pulling flimsy covers
over fragile limbs

remembering the God of Daniel
in the lion's den.

Sundays, I sat near the front of the church with my four squirming children and watched Craig preach with passion to members who had been kicked around all week, or clocked in at menial jobs, or were trying to heal from childhood trauma or sexual abuse or drug addiction. He looked so dear to me. I sometimes feared a deranged man or woman would come in off the street or jump from a pew with a handgun to execute the preacher. Or this: as Craig walked through dark streets on Sunday morning after working half the night on his sermon, some young hood would kill him for his wallet. Tears would fill my eyes and in the space of ten seconds, I was choosing pallbearers and funeral hymns. Then I would shake myself back to reality, back to faith, back to trust.

But living in Pen Lucy gave my children heroes willing to step out in faith. Some, like Robert and Earline Nowlin, risked the anger of gang members and drug dealers. When the Nowlins bought a renovated row house on Cator Avenue, they didn't realize they had settled onto one of Pen Lucy's most notorious streets. They soon learned.

For Earline to catch a bus to her 11 p.m. – 7 a.m. nursing shift, Robert had to escort his frightened wife through a gauntlet of armed dealers. "I wanted to move. This block was so ugly," she said. But rather than running, she told Robert, "The Lord sent us here to clean it up."

Robert began lobbying for greater police protection and became active in the community association. As chairman of its crime committee and later president, he helped established block watch programs, held crime walks, and encouraged the use of police hotlines to report drug transactions and suspicious activity. Dealers began to feel the heat. One afternoon, police arrested several neighborhood dealers, and the enraged, handcuffed men threatened

Robert. That night, as the Nowlins slept, a car jerked to a stop in front of their row house. Staccato bursts of automatic gunfire ripped through the house, smashing windows and passing through several interior walls.

"I didn't believe anyone could be so cold. We have four children; one of them could have been coming downstairs to get water and been killed," Robert later told me.

Faith enabled Robert to overcome his outrage and fear. "There was anger—but peace, too, in my heart that everything was going to be OK. That's because of the Lord," He said. Robert stuck a three-foot white cross on his small front lawn. It read, "Father, forgive them for they know not what they do."

"The Lord is with me no matter what," says Robert, who worships at nearby Blessed Sacrament Church. "No matter what happens here, I'm determined to see it through." For the last fifteen years, Robert has remained faithful to Pen Lucy. He has a vision for his community. He sees not what is, but what could be. And this is all the more remarkable because Robert is blind.

CHAPTER 21

Playing beauty shop

SPRINGFIELD'S CHILDREN

CHILDREN quickly learned they were welcome in our spacious yard. They marveled at the things they saw in our house: a guitar, a dishwasher, a pantry stuffed with food. They taught me about their world. Some of them stole my heart.

Four-year-old Jackie, a petite, mischievous girl, lived in one of the row houses on my block. One afternoon, as I doled out bananas to my children, she stopped me. "What's that? What are they eating?"

I was taken aback. Is it possible she didn't know? Or was she just yanking my chain, finding a creative way to ask for a snack? "It's a banana. A fruit. Do you want one?"

"Yeah," she nodded, and ate it happily.

Another day, as I planted marigolds along my front porch, Jackie sidled up to me, wanting to help. I let her poke the small plants out of the gray plastic flat and place them in the dirt. She started talking, almost to herself.

"White people be bad," she said. "Cain't trust no white people. Cain't be talking to no white people."

I assumed she had heard this at home. "Oh," I said. "All white people? Are all white people bad?" She looked at me, a little shock of realization and fear crossing her face. I let it drop.

A few minutes later, we heard several shots nearby. She put down her spade and looked at me soberly. "I have to go home now."

"Yes, run home," I told her. I knew her mother would be worried, had taught Jackie this lesson as surely as she had taught her to brush her teeth. "Go inside and see your mama." I watched as she scampered up the street and slipped behind her chipped front door.

Sometimes, the class distinctions between children in my neighborhood and adjacent Guilford (similar to my relatively privileged upbringing) felt especially stark. Even a simple holiday celebration struck me.

The Costume of Their Native Country

On Halloween, the children arrive in rivulets:
store-bought Barbie, Barney, vampires with bad teeth.
Some have no costumes
and thrust open backpacks or blue plastic bags toward me.
Teenage girls leave strollers at the bottom of my porch
and ring the bell for candy.

Dion wears a mask and street clothes. He cries
as his siblings scamper down my steps, orphaning him.
His brother turns from my gate
to gently retrieve him.

Bobby points proudly to his faded wrestling shirt. "I'm
Stone Cold Steve Austin," he announces. "Do you still have
the—the piano?" He edges into my foyer.
"The girl let me play it one time," he pleads.
He sits on our faded bench, rapturously
striking random notes with small fingers.

It is not quite dark. I walk several blocks,
cross into Guilford.
A mother holds the hand of a Renaissance princess;
two sisters wear hand-painted signboards, the Queens

of Hearts and Spades. A father
holds the paw of a tiger with a wire-strutted tail,
gently shows him how to ring the doorbell, but only once.

A woman and her daughter drift by,
wearing the flowing costumes
of their native country. I remember my mother,
the homemade kimono, the pilgrim costume,
the year my brother and I were a pair of dice.
I remember Bobby and turn homeward, weeping.

When Becky was in middle school, she became best friends with Tamika, who lived nearby. Tamika's mother, Betty, worked long hours in a university cafeteria and attended another church. Her father did not go to church. Craig invited him to church events like the Pen Lucy breakfasts and Superbowl parties, and he showed a mild interest. I felt comfortable letting Becky visit and even sleep over at Tamika's. Until one day, when Betty confided with frustration that her husband "spent his whole paycheck on drugs."

While I wanted to be supportive of Betty and her family, I felt it unwise to let Becky sleep at a home where one member of the family was addicted to drugs. What drugs was he taking? How did he behave when high? Did he get high in front of the children? What if he couldn't pay his supplier? Craig shared my concerns, and we agreed that Becky could no longer spend the night at Tamika's. We did, however, continue to allow her to visit there during the day—a compromise.

Craig and I had not had a chance to discuss our concerns with Becky when she asked, "Mom, can I spend the night at Tamika's?" I was cooking dinner, Craig was at church, and the younger children and assorted friends were running through the house. It was not, in short, an opportune time to discuss a sensitive matter with a twelve-year-old.

"No, not tonight."

"But why? We can walk to church in the morning." She held the phone against her chest. Tamika awaited her answer.

"No. You can't spend the night at Tamika's."

"What do you mean?"

I sighed. "Tell Tamika you'll call her back in a minute."

"Uh, Tamika, let me call you back." She hung up and looked at me, waiting.

"You can't spend the night at Tamika's anymore."

Becky's mouth dropped open. "Why?"

"Becky, this isn't the time to discuss it. But Tamika's mom told me that Tamika's dad is addicted to drugs. We don't want you sleeping there."

"But Mr. Michael never bothers us."

"So you knew about his drug problem? And you didn't tell us? What is he using?"

"Well...I don't know...." she said evasively. "I know he uses...but he doesn't bother us."

"Just tell Tamika it's not going to work out this weekend. We'll talk about it later, when your dad gets home."

Becky, hurt and disappointed, shared our entire conversation with Tamika. Tamika, in turn, reported it to her mother. The next afternoon, an irate Betty, Tamika, and her thirteen-year-old sister appeared on my front porch. This other daughter, a bright but saucy girl, had recently taken to hanging out with me after her periodic shouting matches with her mother. I invited them in, but Betty refused. She stood on my porch, hands on her hips, seething.

"I can't believe how unchristian you and your husband are being. Here I tell you something and you use it against me and Tamika! If I weren't a Christian, I don't know what I'd do."

"Betty, I'm sorry, I—"

"I would never act like that, because I *am* a Christian! And your husband being a pastor! I just don't know what to say." Betty didn't seem to mind taking me down a few notches in front of her other daughter.

"Betty, I'm sorry. I should have spoken to you first. I'm not saying the girls can't play together, or that Becky can't visit. I'm just not comfortable having her spend the night because of Michael's drug problem."

Betty dismissed my concerns. To her credit, she did not play the race card. But race was an obvious subtext, the proverbial elephant stomping around the living room. After a few more minutes, she stormed away, leaving me in tears. An important community relationship we had tried to nurture lay in tatters.

Craig arranged a meeting with Betty, and she arrived a few days later. She brought Tamika, her son, her other daughter, her grandbaby, and a preschool cousin who was spending the weekend at the home. Every member of her household was present except for Michael. While Becky and Tamika tended the younger children, the adults hashed out the issue.

Betty and her family vented for an hour and a half. Craig listened in his most patient, long-suffering, pastoral manner, looking down at the floor periodically, nodding his head, asking follow-up questions. He has a seemingly inexhaustible ability to listen to irate people without striking back. We apologized profusely for not discussing our decision with Betty before telling Becky, and emphasized that we wanted the girls' relationship to continue. We detailed the many positive character traits we saw in Tamika, and our admiration for how hard Betty worked for her family. But we refused to back down and resume sleepovers.

I thought Michael's absence highly significant. Many families with drug or alcohol problems try to protect the addict or guard family secrets but end up further enabling the addictive behavior. "Maybe Michael should have come today," I suggested. "After all, it's his behavior that is negatively impacting the family."

"Oh, no," Betty shook her head. "He has just started attending those Saturday community breakfasts at church. If he knew you were acting like this, he would never set foot in those doors again."

Our refusal to back down felt like a slap to Betty. Our daughters' relationship continued—teenagers are used to thinking their parents are ridiculous. I deeply regretted causing Betty pain, and felt her anger and wounded pride whenever I ran into her for several years afterward. I continued to complement her on Tamika's achievements, and her resentment dissipated somewhat. I don't know if Michael continues to use drugs.

Neighborhood kids came often to play with my children, borrow bikes or skates, or get sympathy and Band-Aids for minor scrapes. One afternoon, a frantic pounding made me leap to my front door.

"Miss Maria! Miss Maria! He's gonna kill me!" Ten-year old Daisy screamed in terror. She clutched the doorframe with both hands while her fourteen-year old brother Derrick yelled and tried to pry her off. In a few brief seconds, Derrick threw her to the ground and began dragging her off by one arm. They were both screaming. He started to kick her.

Craig, who had providentially come home for lunch just minutes before, arrived at the door just one step behind me.

"Hey! Hey! Hold on there!" Craig said sharply. He stepped directly in front of Derrick, holding his arms up, palms out. Derrick stopped kicking, but still jerked the hand of his prostrate, sobbing sister. "Let her go. Let's just talk about this, man to man."

I wrapped my arms around Daisy and tried to pull her free. She was terrified. Her brother was so volatile, so completely out of control that I knew that touching him — even grabbing his arm to restrain him — would break an urban taboo and invite retaliation. But I was so outraged that I didn't care.

Craig's cooler head prevailed, and he continued to reason with Derrick. After a few tense moments, the boy released his hold. I ushered Daisy inside.

I had often watched Daisy play with Caroline or neighborhood kids in our yard. She was sweet and quick and honest, and sometimes we invited her in to bake cookies. When I hugged her goodbye or patted her back, she smiled shyly, looking down with her enormous, expressive brown eyes and impossibly long lashes. She was very slim, obviously more interested in jumping rope and playing than eating.

While almost always a kind and fair playmate, Daisy could also put her little hands on her hips and dish out a verbal tirade when bigger boys pushed her too far. Once, she lost her temper spectacularly over a minor slight, threatening an older boy with a large, jagged rock. I intervened, and she quickly regained self-control. But I pondered it, wondered what those nine-year-old eyes had already seen.

I didn't know Derrick, but his mother had told me that the school had expelled him and the city now sent a tutor to his home regularly.

Safe on my living room sofa, Daisy trembled and sobbed, her thin shoulders heaving. She wore a little white slip with broken straps tied behind her neck.

"He hurt me, he hurt me," she moaned. Outside, Derrick paced like a caged animal, his voice loud and angry. Craig stood quietly, listening, occasionally speaking softly.

"He's my brother, he shouldn't be hitting on me. He hurt me so bad," she wailed.

After several minutes, Daisy calmed down enough to tell me what happened. Her father was at work and her mother was out job hunting. Derrick was babysitting Daisy and two younger cousins. The girls put on some music and started dancing, and he became angry because he couldn't hear his own stereo. He hit Daisy and chased her around the table. She threw the remote control at him, trying to fend him off, and then ran out of the house, screaming. She ran to a neighbor's house, where Derrick caught her, grabbed her neck, and put his hand over her mouth. The neighbor refused to get involved. Daisy broke his hold and dashed up the street, looking for refuge.

She was ashamed to have run up her street half-clothed. I gave her some of Caroline's clothes, and she slipped into the bathroom to dress.

Craig closed the front door and stood beside me.

"He's promised not to touch her again," he said quietly.

I was skeptical. I wanted to keep Daisy all day, until her mother got home. I wanted to go get the other two cousins and bring them over, too. I was already envisioning a four-point intervention plan: put all three girls in our Summer Youth Ministry camp, where they would be safe, happy, loved, and out of their brother's reach; send Derrick to the counselor who worked at Faith one day a week; provide opportunities for him to be around healthy, self-controlled adult/senior males in our youth group; encourage the parents, whose relationship was volatile, to attend A.A. and get counseling and spiritual nourishment. Calling the police would only escalate matters, and they had been to that home before. They were impotent. Call Social Services? Taking Derrick away from his parents might only further damage him. Many foster or juvenile homes breed worse pathologies.

Half an hour later, Daisy said she would go home.

"Hon, you don't have to go," I told her. "You can play in Caroline's room until she comes back from summer camp, or play in the backyard."

"That's ok," she said softly. I sighed.

"If he touches you again, I want you to run to me, do you hear me?" I said. She nodded quietly. So we let her go. I burst into tears.

Craig and I debated. We knew we needed to talk to the parents, but we weren't sure how to handle this delicate situation. I knew Daisy's mother a little. Should I go alone? Would another mother be less threatening than a pastor? But would a pastor's concern carry more weight? As always, race and class complicated every transaction. Would Daisy's parents take offense or reject our concern because of our whiteness? Would we hear the excuses and put-downs, the wounded pride and pain of prejudice we had heard many times from others? "You don't understand because you're white." "It's a black thing." "You don't know what it's like for working folks in this neighborhood."

We prayed about it and agreed to go after dinner, when both parents might be home. We felt we should get advice from someone with more experience with troubled youth and called a friend, a former social worker. But she wasn't home.

That night, as we finished dinner and debated how to speak to Daisy's parents, the doorbell rang. Our neighbor James Allen, who had attended Faith for several years before leaving for a more traditional black church, stood holding his two daughters' tiny hands in his own meaty ones. We couldn't believe the providential timing: James was a counselor at a juvenile group home for troubled boys.

"I was taking the girls for a little walk after dinner," he grinned. "And I thought, 'Let's stop by and say hello to Pastor Craig.' Is this a bad time?"

Craig and I just looked at each other. "No, this is a great time."

We asked his advice about Daisy and Derrick. He recommended that we both tell the parents what had happened and express our concern. He agreed that if Social Services came and took the boy out of the home, Derrick would become even more troubled.

"That's one of the things we've been concerned about at work," James said. "The longer the kids are out of the home, the more agitated they become. And they don't learn good behavior from one another; they only pick up the bad behavior."

After James left, Craig and I prayed and set off to visit Daisy's parents. As we stepped outside, Daisy's father happened to be walking up the street—another providential coincidence. We greeted him.

"Say, Robert, did Daisy mention anything to you about some trouble with Derrick today?" we asked.

"No," he said, looking at us quizzically. Robert was slender, in his fifties, with salt and pepper hair.

We told him, as non-threateningly as we could, about Derrick's behavior. He looked down at the ground. "I sometimes have .... altercations ... with my woman," Robert said. "But never with the children, I don't allow that," he said firmly. "Some folks say I should beat his butt, but I don't believe in that, either. He don't smoke, or get into any of the trouble some of these other kids get into. He's basically a good boy. He just needs time." He fingered the bottle-shaped brown bag he carried. "But I will talk to him."

Daisy continued to play in our yard, and we chatted briefly with her parents from time to time. One day, Robert asked Craig a favor. "I've started going to AA, and was wondering if you'd be my sponsor," he said. In Alcoholics Anonymous, a sponsor is usually a fellow recovering alcoholic. But Robert felt confident enough of Craig's empathy and concern to ask for his help. Craig was honored, and attended a few meetings with Robert. As they spent time together, Craig learned that Robert, who had fathered Daisy in his later years, was the grandson of a man who had been enslaved as a child. The inhumanity of America's chattel slavery lurked only a few generations in the past.

One day, Daisy knocked on my door. "Miss Maria, I just came to say good-bye," she announced. "We're moving this afternoon."

"Moving? Today? Oh, Daisy!" I was used to neighbors moving frequently, often with little notice. But Daisy had lived on Springfield nearly all her young life. "Where are you moving to?"

"Over the west side. I'll be back sometimes to visit, though," she said bravely.

Daisy's family didn't have a car. Returning to visit old neighbors meant several long bus rides. I doubted I would see her again.

I gently stroked her head. How could I help Daisy make this transition? "We will sure miss you around here. A whole lot!" I blinked back tears. "But I'm sure you'll make many new friends in your new neighborhood."

I wanted to have a going-away party for her, or invite her over for a special dinner, try to bless her one last time before she left, before the streets tried to stake their claim on her. But there was no time. I bent down and hugged her.

"Goodbye, sweetie. You're a precious girl, and Jesus is watching over you. Don't forget that. And if I can ever do anything for you, come see me, O.K.?"

She nodded, turned, and walked down my steps. I've never seen her again.

But I think of her sometimes. I remember Jesus' words, in Matthew's gospel. "See that you do not look down on one of these little ones. For I tell you that their angels in heaven always see the face of my Father in heaven."

I think of all the hazards Daisy will have to navigate—the drugs on the corner, the boys who will want her, the schools that will fail her, and I tell myself, she has an angel. She has a Father.

CHAPTER 22

Miss Evie and BCS choir

BETWEEN EDUCATION AND CATASTROPHE

As a homeschooling mother, I ferried my children all over the city to reproduce what a healthy school and neighborhood provide: co-op learning classes; field trips with the homeschool group; play dates; a baseball league at a Catholic church; ballet lessons at the YMCA; music lessons at a city after-school program.

We thought we should at least investigate the public schools in Pen Lucy, even though statistically they were even worse than Waverly's. I nursed a smoldering anger toward the school system that failed so many of Baltimore's children. I knew several dedicated teachers who dealt with overcrowded classrooms, lack of administrative support, low salaries, and no money for supplies. Maybe, I thought, I'm not being completely objective. We made an appointment to meet with the woman who would be Becky's teacher.

As Craig pulled open the heavy, dented steel door, a large poster of a handgun pointed at us. "Guns don't belong in schools!" it shouted. I wanted to run. Were *elementary* kids packing pistols?

In the tidy classroom with faded beige floor tiles, we squeezed into two of the twenty-five or thirty desks arranged in rows. The teacher was puzzled. Why were we here? What did we want to know? Perhaps few parents in our neighborhood visited the prospective school to check on curriculum and meet the teacher. Or perhaps she couldn't believe that two white parents would enroll their daughter in a school where she might be the only child of her race. But if she thought that two college-educated parents wouldn't send their child to a school where most students failed mandatory state tests, she was right. We wanted more for our children.

By the end of third grade, almost 40% of the students in low-income, minority neighborhoods like Pen Lucy were at least one year behind grade level in reading, and 12% were two or more years behind. This meant that they couldn't decode words, and were doomed to a future of struggling and feeling like dummies. According to a study at The Johns Hopkins University, 76% of Baltimore's black males drop out before graduation.

Why aren't people rioting about this?

We heard firsthand accounts from neighbors and friends. On back-to-school night, a church member whose daughter attended our neighborhood school approached a teacher, her child in tow. The teacher, who had nearly forty children in her sixth-grade class, did not recognize the girl who had sat quietly in her crowded classroom for more than a month. "Are you in my class?" she asked.

In my neighborhood middle school, I visited one teacher who locked her door to prevent wandering students from entering and disrupting her classroom. A student had assaulted her in the classroom. She earned less than her suburban counterparts, yet bought books and materials out of her own modest paycheck because some of her students read only on an early elementary level. While I admired her determination and sacrifice, I was not ready to put my children in her class.

Years later, when Melissa was in eighth grade, I visited our zoned public high school. Only a fraction of its graduates go on to community college or four-year colleges. Other teens in my neighborhood told of insufficient textbooks, no homework, and only half a year of English. The newspapers reported beatings and assaults on school grounds. A male student raped a fourteen-year-old girl in the bathroom.

The mother of one of Melissa's neighborhood friends approached me. Mattie knew that I was teaching Melissa at home and worried about sending her daughter to high school the following year. Private or parochial school was financially out of the question for her.

"Can you teach my daughter?" Mattie pleaded. "I don't want to send her to Northern." She had not allowed her daughter to attend our youth activities or summer camp because Mattie was of another faith, but she was desperate enough to put her child under my tutelage every day.

Another woman, usually a staunch defender of our community, shook her head when I asked about Northern High. "I would climb mountains before I would put my kid in there," she declared. But what other option did she have?

Becky had adjusted well at her small Lutheran school, and I still felt overwhelmed trying to homeschool two grades while watching a busy toddler. So the following year, Melissa joined her. Since we were cash-strapped, the school agreed to give us a tuition discount if I would help out in the classroom regularly. Two years later, when tuition bills rivaled our mortgage payments, we realized that I must work part time or homeschool everyone all the way through high school. Seeking advice, I called Marlene Gustafsen, who hurried over within hours.

"What was I thinking? Why didn't I see this coming?" I lamented. I had come down squarely in the mothers-at-home camp in the Mommie Wars, and now I had to switch sides? "How will I manage it all? And who would hire me?" I felt unprepared to reenter the work force. I hadn't worked since college, and I refused to consider full-time employment. I feared that left me only a bright future bagging groceries at the Giant Foods. "I'll do it," I vowed, "if that's what it takes to help provide for my kids." Marlene wisely suggested that God might provide other job possibilities.

I thought earning a master's degree would better position me for part-time jobs and looked into several evening programs nearby. "This could work," I thought, "*if* I get accepted *and* get a graduate assistantship." Craig and I prayed. I got a graduate assistantship that not only covered my tuition but paid a small stipend. I began working part time and attending school two nights a week, and Caroline and Calvin joined their sisters at the Lutheran school. When I graduated two years later, I got a part time job at a Johns Hopkins University educational research and development center that sought to improve schooling for at-risk students. For years, I had lamented the educational opportunities for at-risk students; now I could help encourage solutions.

Educating our own children was a constant challenge. We searched for the right school to fit each child, and at one point juggled schedules for four children in three different schools. All the income from the apartments, my salary, and part of Craig's went to their education.

In sixth grade, Becky was admitted to an elite private school and offered partial financial aid. Class sizes were one-third those of the public schools. On back-to-school night, we were stunned by the quality, resources, and choices now available to our daughter. But we felt angry and frustrated over what her friends in the neighborhood received. This was the Gourmet Giant of education. Kids in my neighborhood stood in bread lines.

Eighty years ago, H.G. Wells wrote, "Human history becomes more and more a race between education and catastrophe." While I disagree with his premise that education is the answer to humankind's moral and social ills, a lack of it exacerbates societal problems from AIDS to xenophobia. What would Wells say after seeing today's inner city test scores and dropout rates?

We feared for these children. What happens to the two-thirds of the students who don't graduate? Were they headed for lucrative, meaningful McJobs? Would they become statistics in Baltimore's homicide/dropout/teen pregnancy/incarceration rates? We were outraged that the children of Baltimore got the scraps from the educational table or the crumbs from the floor. We were outraged that the least of these got so little.

After years of reading dismal test scores in *The Baltimore Sun* and witnessing the perpetual flight of the urban middle class, we felt compelled to offer an alternative. Faith had provided after school programs, remedial help, and summer reading camps, but these efforts were insufficient. We prayed about starting a school where children would learn to read, be nurtured, and taught about God's love. But how could a church of one hundred and fifty members pull off such a feat? We had few resources, little expertise, and great need.

So God sent people.

With two doctorates, Doug and Martha MacIver could have settled in upper-class Guilford or at least middle-class Northwood, but they bought a duplex in Pen Lucy. They wanted to live as part of an intentional community and serve the neighborhood. Their house sat at the end of one of the most well-preserved streets in the neighborhood, but also bordered the blighted Old York Road strip.

The MacIvers were unable to escape the random shooting from around the corner—even in their own home. One Sunday afternoon, gunfire erupted on the strip, and a shooting victim staggered around the corner and collapsed in front of their steps. In another incident, the MacIvers heard five shots from a semi-automatic weapon just before dawn. They had heard hundreds of bullets fly during their five years in Pen Lucy, but never this loud. A few hours later, they realized why. One bullet had pierced the side of Doug's car. Another had ripped through the dashboard, gouged a hole in their son Peter's car seat, and exited through the trunk. A third bullet had sliced through the sliding board of the play set in their yard. A fourth had passed through the siding of their house and burrowed into the ceiling above the room where their son Daniel slept. It showered plaster dust into his crib, and came to rest somewhere near the foot of Doug and Martha's bed. When Martha discovered the bullet holes so close to the crib, she cried. Doug called the police. And the cops looked at them, looked at the mountains of books piled on their living room shelves and said, "Why do you live here?"

The MacIvers didn't flee. Living in Pen Lucy put names and faces on the statistics Doug and Martha studied every day as educational researchers at the Johns Hopkins Center for Social Organization of Schools, where they focus on at-risk students. As he sifted through data on Baltimore's public schools in the 1980s, Doug saw "an educational famine of biblical proportions…The learning opportunities provided are so deficient that they irreversibly damage the future life chances of most of the children." While a few schools still offered a good education, many zoned high schools would later be labeled "dropout factories." One of their colleagues compared Baltimore's dropout rate to a daily airplane crash. If two 747s took off from Baltimore Washington International Airport every day, loaded with children, and crashed, wouldn't people do something about it?

He chaired a committee at church to pray about starting a school, a committee of housewives and sanitation workers and engineers and lawyers. Was this feasible for a small church like Faith? How would God provide the substantial funds needed? Should we form a partnership with an existing public or Christian school instead?

We prayed and planned. In 1993 we birthed a school, a little enterprise based on a dream that children should receive an excellent education whether their parents are poor or middle class. No child would be turned away for lack of funds. Because the need was greater than one church, we invited other churches to join with us. The First Baptist Church of Pimlico, led by Pastor Tony Dorsey, signed on.

Baltimore Christian School opened with five kindergarten students because God in his sovereignty sent the money and the people. But it happened because Doug and Martha sat up night after night, writing grant proposals, attending meetings, planning curricula, making phone calls, and doing the thousand tedious, unglamorous tasks of starting a school. It happened because at critical junctures, money appeared anonymously in the school's coffers. Cindy Beck Homans, one of the InterVarsity students who had helped launch Faith and had lived in our house, returned to teach kindergarten. Each year, we added another grade level until BCS accommodated students in kindergarten through fifth grade. For almost one hundred students each year, education was no longer a catastrophe.

CHAPTER 23

Craig and Lessie

"AND MAKE 'EM WITH MEAT!"

ORD got around that Craig and I were eager to obey the biblical mandate to feed the hungry. In the Gospels, Jesus equates care for the poor, the sick, and the imprisoned with care for Him. Men and women knocked on the doors of the church, or failing an answer there, knocked on our front door.

"Is the Father home?" some asked, exuding the aroma of a night on the town. The fine points of denominational address—only Catholic and Episcopalian clergy are addressed as "Father"—don't always reach street level.

"If you're a Catholic Father, you're in big trouble," I teased Craig. "Living in sin with me and spawning all these children. I can see the headlines now— *My Priest Fathered All My Children.*"

But how do we separate those in the grip of alcoholism or drug addiction, and those who have lost dignity and subsist on con games and handouts, from those who are down on their luck, unemployed or underemployed, oppressed or abandoned?

Jesus modeled dignity-building charity. He addressed the deeper issues underlying human actions. To blind Bartimaeus, who shouted for Jesus' attention while begging by the side of the road, he asked, "What do you want?" He treated Bartimaeus not as a disability but as an individual able to articulate his own needs. He was not paternalistic but incarnational, entering into human struggle and listening to the individual's heart cry.

Because we lived in the neighborhood, we eventually gained a better sense of who was addicted or alcoholic, and who was unemployed or underemployed. But for many years, until we built up a reservoir of experience, we agonized over how to deal with each case. We asked ourselves, "What would Jesus do?" Is feeding an alcoholic who refuses treatment a loving thing to do? Or are we enabling destructive behavior? We found few easy answers.

A mother of three, whose daughter attended our youth ministry, lost all her possessions and documents in a house fire. Her homeowner's insurance had lapsed, and the family was left with only the clothes on their backs. The church responded with money, household goods, transportation, and emotional and spiritual support. After several months of intervention, we were puzzled by her lack of progress, the missed opportunities, the evasions and half-truths. Further evidence mounted, and we realized she was a heroin addict, and that our efforts only enabled her to continue her addiction. When Craig and others confronted her and offered to help her seek treatment, she denied having a drug problem. When the supply of goods and services from the church dried up, she severed contact.

One middle-aged neighbor regularly approached us for food. He knew we would not give him cash—no matter what desperate or intricate story he unfolded—so he contented himself with free lunches and dinners. Craig and I developed a protocol to keep me from being absorbed in endless requests for food and money. I had to clear all handouts with Craig first. And I would not feed Mr. Jefferson if he was drunk.

One day as Craig walked to church, Mr. Jefferson staggered up to him.

"Can you give me some money for food? I haven't eaten since yesterday."

"I can't help you," Craig said.

"How about a sandwich? Can you give me a sandwich?"

"Can't help you today," Craig said. "You've been drinking. You made a choice to spend your money on booze today rather than food."

Mr. Jefferson tried again.

"Can I get money for some bus fare?"

Craig shook his head.

"Money for my kid's diapers?"

Mr. Jefferson didn't have any little kids.

"Money to get a prescription filled?"

"Can't help you," Craig said.

The previous Sunday afternoon, Mr. Jefferson had come to our house, asking for money for food. I had fixed a bag lunch: sandwich, cookies, soda, a napkin. He returned ten minutes later with an equally disheveled man.

"Can he have a sandwich, too?"

"Fine," I said. "But you ate the last of the ham. Peanut butter ok?"

"What, you don't got no meat?" Mr. Jefferson was stunned and a little miffed. Perhaps he saw us as the SuperFresh supermarket of Springfield Avenue, always open, always well stocked.

"No meat. You ate the last of it. Do you want peanut butter? Or a cheese sandwich?

A few weeks later, he knocked on the door again. When I opened it, I smelled alcohol seeping through his ragged coat.

"Can I get a sandwich?" he asked.

"Mr. Jefferson, I can't feed you right now. You've been drinking." I hated doing this.

"Nah!" he insisted, like this was an outlandish idea. "No, I had a beer *yesterday*, but I haven't been drinking *today*." He smelled like he had fallen into a beer vat.

It was futile, but I tried anyway. "Mr. Jefferson, you're spending your money for alcohol instead of food, and I can't encourage that behavior. It's killing you. If you want to get in a program, we'll help you."

He looked disgusted. "No, I haven't been drinking! Honest!"

His vehement denials irritated me. I knew it was pointless to argue, but couldn't stop myself. "Mr. Jefferson, I can *smell* it." I folded my arms across my chest and looked at him evenly.

"Well, a buddy gave me a few sips of his beer, but you can't punish a guy for that, can you? It wasn't even my beer, I swear." He held up his hand as if swearing before a judge. Worn down, I capitulated.

"Just a minute," I sighed. "I have to call Craig first, see if it's ok with him."

"Yeah, I know your husband," Mr. Jefferson assured me, like this was new information. "I see him up to the church. He helps me all the time."

I called Craig's cell phone, but he didn't answer. The children were pulling on me, and a friend stood in my living room, waiting to resume our interrupted visit. I felt harassed. I prayed silently. *God, forgive me for doing the easy thing, not the right thing.*

"O.K., Mr. Jefferson," I sighed. "One sandwich or two?"

"Two. Please."

As I turned for the kitchen, he called after me. "And make 'em with meat!"

And there were always those quick with a story, men like Bernard.

Bernard appeared at the church door one afternoon. A trim, white man in his thirties, Bernard had recently moved to Baltimore. Back home in South Carolina, he said, the trailer he shared with his wife and two children had caught fire. They lost everything. His brother-in-law offered them a place to stay in Baltimore and a job.

"But when I got here, I found out my brother-in-law was a drug dealer. He wanted me to look after his money," Bernard said. "I would earn a thousand dollars a week. But me and my wife are Christians, and to do such a thing would be like turning our backs on salvation. I wouldn't do it," Bernard insisted.

Bernard said he had moved his family into a cheap hotel, but their money had run out. His job with a contractor wouldn't start until next week.

"We had to move out of the hotel, and now we're homeless." Bernard began to cry. "I can't bear to see my kids go hungry."

The story sounded moderately plausible to Craig, but he had been hoodwinked so many times before that he kept probing.

"Do you have family who can help?"

"My wife's parents are dead. She had an aunt in Greenville, but she's a Jehovah's Witness, and she's been shunning my wife since we don't go to the Kingdom Hall anymore. My only relative is in Pennsylvania."

"Have you looked into the Salvation Army? The Helping Up Mission?"

"They are all filled." He ticked off a list of the city's homeless shelters. He obviously knew the system.

Bernard picked up steam, unfolding trials to rival Job's. The tears that began to roll down his cheeks only heightened Craig's suspicions.

"My wife has MS. She is losing all muscle control. Sometimes even her bladder. She has to walk with a cane. The medication has side effects. It throws her tongue into flipping convulsions." He took a deep breath. Craig tried not to imagine what "flipping convulsions" looked like.

"My son has seizures and has to take medication four times a day. But we don't have money for the medicine anymore. The kids are asking why God is doing this. But I tell them that the Bible says God works all things together for good."

When Bernard's knowledge of a few Bible verses failed to impress Craig, he plowed on.

"I myself have had three open heart surgeries. The last one was just eight months ago. But I'm doing great, praise the Lord, with no further signs. My wife stood by me, and I have to stand by her."

Craig toyed with the idea of asking to see the scars. "Why don't you give me the name of your employer and the name of the landlord whose house you want to rent," Craig suggested. "If your story checks out, I'll see if the deacons can do anything to help." Even though Bernard gave him some names, Craig doubted the story would check out.

"Can I get some money to stay at the hotel one more night? And money for bus fare to get back and forth to work? I sure hate to see my wife and kids out on the street." Bernard's eyes teared up again.

"It's church policy not to give out cash. I can give you some food and bus tokens, though. And if the deacons can help you with rent, the church will write a check directly to the landlord."

Bernard said he would come back for the food later. Craig said he would check with the deacons, and prayed with him. Later, Craig tried to call the landlord to verify Bernard's story, but the directory listed no such name. When he called the construction company, he learned that Bernard had worked for them for a short time two years before, and recently contacted them to look for work. Bernard, who must have sensed that his elaborate tale would not achieve the desired results, never returned.

Those who came to the church for crisis relief were not the core of the community. The majority of those who struggled did not ask for help outside their extended families. The African American community has a strong heritage of gathering around struggling family members, of enfolding the hurting and of sharing resources even in times of scarcity. Again and again, we saw overextended relatives take in not just one endangered child but two, three, or four. Fifty-year-old grandmothers adopted multiple small grandchildren. Aunts and uncles took in nieces and nephews when their drug-addled parents abused or neglected them. Older brothers raised younger siblings.

But churches—and their leaders—were easy prey for those who wanted anonymity, a handout rather than a hand up. At times, the endless parade of crises and con jobs wore us down. In the midst of preparing weekly sermons and Bible studies, shepherding the congregation, and attending meetings, Craig wearied of endless interruptions—even though we believed on a deeper level that God ordains such interruptions.

One day, while working alone at church, Craig heard the doorbell. "I don't need any more interruptions," he thought. The bell rang again. He sighed, and left his desk.

A frail, elderly woman stood on the church steps. When she saw this young-looking white man, she asked to speak to the pastor. "I'm the pastor," Craig grinned. He invited her in. Because he had never seen her before, he expected she might express some need: rent money? Money for prescriptions? Help with a gas and electric bill?

"I need someplace where I can serve God's people," Lessie Phillips declared. "Where can I serve?"

Lessie began attending Faith. She volunteered in the church's food pantry and second-hand clothing ministry. In spite of the casual dress of most worshippers, Lessie wore hats and white gloves every Sunday.

Lessie had raised several children in spite of poverty, hardship, racism, and her own bout with alcoholism. Hardship had made her gentle, not brittle, other-centered, not self-centered, thankful, not resentful. She was quick to "amen" the preacher or testify of God's goodness and faithfulness, declaring, "Can't nobody do me like Jesus!"

She sang in the gospel choir, a rich alto seasoned with age and struggle emanating from her swaying, diminutive body. Her rendition of "Amazing Grace" squeezed the last possible drop of meaning from every syllable. As the piano played softly in the background, she began, singing half-time, barely moving, chugging slowly up the mountain like the Little Engine That Could.

"Uuuhhh—maaay—zinnng graaace." She stopped to breathe. "How swe—-eeet the souuuund."

"Tell it," a worshipper would call back to her. "It's all right."

"That...saaay—ved uuuuuuuh wretch... li—ike meee—." Sometimes a shudder would travel through Lessie's whole body. After a slow journey through the first verse, the pianist would kick the tempo up, driving through the song like they were on a mission.

"That's all riiight," Bill would say approvingly at the end.

Craig was especially fond of Lessie. When she died, old and full of years, he grieved. On his office wall, he taped a photo of Lessie standing in the church doorway, clad in her favorite pink dress and hat. Underneath, he wrote her birth and death dates and her mantra, "Can't nobody do me like Jesus!"

Sometimes, a modest investment of time, money, and spiritual nurture yields results for generations. Like a mustard seed. Like you've witnessed a resurrection.

A church member from the neighborhood asked Craig to visit his friend Victor in jail. Craig passed through a series of locked doors to meet a wiry man with a medium dark complexion, gold-capped tooth, straight nose, and a long, thin braid.

Victor Mitchell had grown up near the Lexington Terrace public housing projects in Baltimore, the son of Lumbee and Cherokee/Blackfoot parents. He had started cutting fish with his father at age thirteen and been active in the Boy Scouts and Boy's Club. But in his teens, Victor followed the lure of the streets. At fifteen, he was expelled, lost his private school scholarship, and landed in the Maryland Training School for Boys. After his release, he continued to travel with the wrong crowd. At twenty, he was arrested for armed robbery. His sentence: twenty years in the State Pen.

After serving five years, Victor was released in 1986. He had some legal problems, and Bob Jenkins made him a deal: "I'll handle your legal business for free," he promised, "if you'll come to church for six months, and not miss a Sunday." Victor agreed, and he and his girlfriend Linille began to attend with their two small daughters. Because Victor and his family had no transportation, Bob Jenkins or Bruce Gustafsen picked them up and brought them to church or Bible study. Week after week, as he heard the preaching of God's Word and met Christians who cared for him, spiritual seeds began to take root. Linille had grown up attending a cultish church ruled by a man that members called "Daddy Faith." The church was long on rules and short on grace. Members believed they must go through Daddy Faith to get to God, and be baptized every year to keep their salvation. At our church, she was experiencing true grace for the first time in her life. Victor recalls that Linille "was using Daddy Faith to get to God. Then she found out it was just Jesus she needed to know. Her whole life changed."

At this time, Victor was working as a "hoagie person," wearing the distinctive orange jumpsuit of city sweepers. In spite of the potentially debilitating effects of his Crohne's disease, Victor also worked several side jobs to make ends meet. Linille received government assistance and was home with their two small daughters.

Eventually, Victor and Linille both committed their lives to Christ. Victor remembers one moment that crystallized that transformation. "I laid my knife on my dresser and picked up my Bible. I had the Bible in my hand and walked up Old York Road. I was scared because I had carried a knife for so many years. I haven't picked it up since."

Now that both Victor and Linille had made solid professions of faith in Christ, they wanted to honor God with their living arrangement. Victor had been briefly married to a drug addict, and was afraid to marry again. Craig insisted they go through premarital counseling, which Victor says "calmed my nerves." Linille began to sing in the choir, volunteer in the nursery, and read her Bible regularly.

For Victor and Linille, marriage would have serious financial repercussions. Linille and the children would lose their government check and health insurance. Victor's job wasn't adequate to support the family. They prayed together, and Victor and Linille decided to honor God and trust him for the results. They had no idea how they would make ends meet.

They married in a joyous celebration held during a regular Sunday morning service. Several church members quietly bought them a used car and a year of auto insurance as a wedding present. This enabled Victor to get to his jobs more easily.

It was a difficult time for the Mitchells financially. Their oil tank leaked, and they faced astronomical heating bills. Victor took on more side jobs: he cleaned the church, swung a hammer, raked leaves, or painted. When their youngest child entered kindergarten at Baltimore Christian School, Linille got her first job.

The church helped them buy and rehabilitate a rowhouse in the neighborhood. Members helped with gutting, plumbing, carpentry, painting, and even decorating the new home. Victor earned a promotion to supervisor. Then he was promoted again. Linille landed a full-time job at the post office, where she also earned promotions.

Victor looks back on the difference Jesus made in his life. "Coming up, you learned how to be a better criminal. When you come home [from prison] you have respect and then you do bigger crimes. You gain respect in the neighborhood for being mean, bad, revengeful. There's lots of fast money, kids making a thousand dollars a week.

"My lifestyle has dramatically changed. I'm a retired hood, a stronger believer, a family man. I never had family values like I have now."

The Mitchell family has been transformed by the Gospel, from incarceration to freedom, from unemployment to supervisory positions, from welfare to productive employment, from renters to homeowners. This transformation continues in their children as well. Both daughters eventually graduated from high school and went on to college. Through Christ, they had risen above the cycle of welfare dependency that had stretched back for two generations.

CHAPTER 24

Yellowstone, 1994

WEST OF BALTIMORE

IN 1995, when Becky was thirteen and Calvin almost seven, we decided our children needed to see more of America than urban Baltimore or Ocean City. Our vacations were generally funded by the extended family: a visit to my parents in Florida, or a week at the beach with Craig's parents and his brother Chuck's family. While we appreciated these times, we rarely seemed able to schedule time away as a family or couple. Lack of money and ministry demands conspired against us.

Yet even a week at the beach set our family apart. Many of the children in the neighborhood had never been out of the city. Once, when our church took the children enrolled in summer camp to Ocean City, a little girl cried when she lost her bathing cap in the surf. But she brightened, saying, "That's o.k. I can get it when they let the water out."

After looking through library books, each of our children picked one National Park and we outlined an ambitious, three-week whirlwind tour: Yellowstone, the Grand Tetons, Mount Rushmore, Mesa Verde, the Grand Canyon and several smaller parks. Our Plymouth Voyager minivan—a gift to us from a missionary family, boasting over 180,000 miles—would make the trek, saddled with a car-top carrier. We already owned most of the camping gear we needed, but Craig splurged on two new four-man tents.

"Why not just one big tent?" I asked.

"I want to sleep with my *wife*," he grinned, eyebrows raised.

"I figured *that*," I rolled my eyes. "But two tents to set up and break down every night? Sounds like a lot of work."

"We'll have a system," he planned with characteristic optimism. "Each child will know what part to play in setting up and breaking down camp. Only take a few minutes."

With so many destinations, and to allow for the daunting drive three quarters of the way across the country and back, we would set up and break camp nearly every night.

Complications arose the week before our departure. Eleven-year-old Melissa picked up a severe case of poison ivy. Strep throat had latched onto me like a pit bull, leaving me weak and retching. My immune system was in outright rebellion, worn out, and the strep returned after the first course of antibiotics. But because we had reservations at several western parks, and Craig had only three weeks off, we were reluctant to postpone our trip. On departure day Melissa's face was still swollen and blotchy, and because of the rash on her torso and underarms, she held one arm out at an awkward angle like a skinny, wire coat hanger.

"Don't touch me!" she pleaded to any who came near. Otherwise, she rarely complained, and was eager to leave.

Craig preached, met with people after church, finished packing, and loaded up the car. He was so exhausted from staying up half the night to finish his sermon that he needed a nap. Finally, armed with the joy of anticipation, a cup of coffee, and a diet Pepsi, we waved goodbye to our neighbors around four o'clock.

We traveled the interstate until one or two in the morning. When we started looking for a cheap hotel, we found nothing within our budget. Even worse, all the hotels had an occupancy cap. With four kids, they demanded we rent two rooms. This seemed like a wanton waste of money, a budget buster for only a few hours of shuteye. By now, the children were asleep in their seats. More out of necessity than sense, we pulled over and slept at a truck stop.

I crawled to the back of the van and lay flat on top of a bumpy pile of camping equipment that stopped just eight inches from the ceiling. Craig stretched his six-foot frame across the front bucket seats. Becky, already five foot five inches, tried to stretch out on the floor but was bent like the meandering

Mississippi. I dozed on and off, periodically jerked awake by the abrupt hiss of air brakes from idling trucks a few dozen feet away. The children took turns waking and groaning, "Where *are* we?"

As dawn broke, Craig slipped out of the car and untied our water container from the roof. I watched him set it up on a picnic table, strip off his shirt, and give himself a sponge bath. He strode back to the car.

"Was that refreshing?" I chuckled.

"Absolutely," he replied.

As the children awoke, they were hard pressed to find vocabulary to express the discomfort of sleeping in the van. "That was the pits," Caroline moaned.

"Calvin kept poking me," Melissa complained.

"Oh! My! Gosh!" Becky burst out, staccato. "I could not sleep on the floor. We won't do that again, will we?"

We assured them that we wouldn't. We took them to IHOP and told them to order anything on the menu. With the money we hadn't spent the previous night, they could at least order a few pancakes.

When we reached the South Dakota Badlands, Becky voiced a concern that had rolled around in her head since leaving Baltimore. "Where are all the black people?"

"Yeah," Melissa chimed in. "Why don't we see any black people?"

They wondered if perhaps there was some conspiracy, if the Midwest was so racist that African Americans stayed away. Living in a predominantly black city, in a nearly entirely black neighborhood, attending a nearly entirely black school, they found all this whiteness odd. I explained about demographics, and about the Great Migration to northern cities. They were relieved.

We pitched our tents in the Badlands, on a bluff providing spectacular views. Ten feet behind our tents, a steep gully dropped twenty-five feet. During the night, the winds picked up with gusts so strong that I feared the entire tent would pitch down the cliff with my children inside. I decided that my weight would provide the ballast to keep the children from hurtling to their deaths, and if not, I would join them in Glory. I picked up my sleeping bag.

"I'm sleeping in the children's tent," I told Craig.

A few minutes later, he wedged in behind me. "If we're going to blow away, at least we'll go together," he said.

The next morning, we took an unpaved road to the Pine Ridge Indian Reservation. I wanted to see Wounded Knee, site of the 1890 massacre, the last major clash in America's decimation of the Indians. We listened to a local radio station, FM KILI, "the voice of the Lakota Nation," featuring native chanting, bells, and drumming interspersed with public service announcements and interviews. A representative from the Native Head Start program urged parents to enroll their children in this free federal program. The microphone scritched as it slid back and forth across the table from host to guest. *Volunteer, come out and show your support, get involved, help our people*, the host cajoled. It reminded me of the city.

We soaked in the American West. The children wrote in the journals I had bought them—at least for a few days. We cooked over the campfire every night, and for lunch, I made sandwiches in the car or passed out yogurts. We discovered that fried chicken from supermarket delis was less expensive than Kentucky Fried Chicken and bought this until they refused to eat it anymore.

Late one afternoon, as we attempted hairpin ascents in the Bighorn Mountains of Wyoming, the engine overheated and shut off—along with our power steering. Visions of plunging down a cliff like a Roadrunner cartoon sprang to mind. We returned to the town of Sheridan, in the foothills, and pulled into a gas station. Closed for the day.

"We'll have to get some repairs here tomorrow morning," Craig said.

"But we have reservations in Yellowstone tonight," I lamented. "And we're supposed to meet Robert and his family tomorrow." My brother Robert, his wife, and daughter had flown out from Florida to meet us at the park. Six-year-old Deanna would be inconsolable at this loss of cousins, even for a day.

"Can't be helped. We'll have to find a campground here in town."

"Well, wherever we stay, it has to have a pool. The kids have been squashed in the car all day and need to burn off some energy."

Becky interrupted our planning. "Mom, I have a sore throat. It started yesterday, and it hurts a lot."

Craig and I found a small health clinic, where Becky was examined for strep and given a prescription. "I should probably just buy penicillin in bulk," I grumped, exiting the clinic's chrome and glass double doors. "Keep it on hand like macaroni."

The campground was conveniently located a stone's throw from the interstate, and cars roared by our heads all night. The next morning, we broke camp and pulled back into the gas station. Craig consulted with the mechanic.

"Yep," the mechanic said, wiping his hands on a filthy rag, "I get several Voyagers a day. I see 'em pull in, I say, 'here comes another one.' They just can't make the climb. Weren't designed for this terrain. But I'll do what I can." He flushed the radiator and cleaned and washed every part anywhere near the radiator to boost efficiency.

"If this doesn't work, he can start replacing parts," Craig informed me. As we attempted the mountain crossing again, the engine temperature needle soon edged into the red zone and steam oozed out from under the hood. We turned back.

I was getting desperate. "Maybe we should buy a newer car, sell this one," I suggested. I envisioned a frenzied stop at Joe's Used Car Lot, a quick flash of the credit card.

Craig rarely criticizes me, even when he has grounds. But now he looked at me like I'd told him I planned on assembling one myself from spare parts. "I think we'll take it back to the mechanic."

Craig dropped us off at the campground and returned to Mr. Fixit. I was beginning to think that we should get a site with a water and electric hookup, since we might have to stay here permanently. Our children would have to live in a tent while their parents did odd jobs. "Lord," I prayed, "I feel like I'm locked in some Twilight Zone. Am I supposed to be learning something here? Can you help us get to Yellowstone?"

Maybe Mr. Fixit got a little divine inspiration. Maybe he and Craig laid hands on the car. But the following morning the van crept over the mountains.

In forming Yellowstone, God had pulled out all the stops. He crammed a hemisphere's worth of beauty into fifty square miles: geysers, boiling mud, hot springs (John Colter, the first white man to explore the area, faced disbelief and ridicule when he described these), waterfalls, mountain lakes, meadows, forests of lodge pole pines, canyons, and the neighboring Tetons. Even the air looked crisper, sharper, and purer.

We packed all our food in the car at night to avoid tempting the bears. But one morning, we found that something had chewed large holes into Melissa's sweater, which hung on our clothesline. Little shudders of fear and excitement rippled through the children as they considered that a *bear* might have been snuffling and gnawing at Melissa's clothes just three feet from their heads.

It rained, and even in early July, the air nipped. My brother and his family were tucked away in a heated inn; we mucked around in the muddy campground. Desperate, we piled our soggy sleeping bags into dryers under signs declaring NO SLEEPING BAGS IN DRYERS.

One night, after dropping Deanna off at my brother's room, I made a wrong turn, and ended up at the Grand Canyon of the Yellowstone. The moonlight shimmered off the layered landscape in surreal hues. I got out of the car,

absorbing the beauty, storing it up to recall the next time my eyes were assaulted by the boarded up commercial strip near my home, or by the endless litter
cluttering potholed and patched streets.

What is it like, I wondered, to live around such beauty all the time? Would
I take it for granted, cease to appreciate it? If I had continued my career in the
Park Service, I could have lived in places like this. People often feel closer to
God in such places. Would I?

I considered the uniqueness of Faith, of a community blending African
Americans, whites, Latinos, and Asians together. I thought about the pain of
race, of class, of feeling both rich and poor in Pen Lucy, of never fitting in and
yet belonging to the church, to the people, deeply and completely. I thought
of the daily little deaths and resurrections that forced me to depend on Jesus,
not myself. I felt certain of God's call, and I had always told Him that if He
wanted us to leave the city, He must tell Craig first. Until then, I would trust
Him to take care of us.

Our next stop was the Grand Canyon. At one o' clock in the morning, as we
drove through the sparsely populated Navajo reservation outside the park, our
radiator overheated again. To cool off the engine, we ran the heater. Full blast.
In the dark, moonlit night, I rolled down the windows to see scraggly pine
trees on my right—and then nothing, a great expanse of nothing, and I knew
that if we took a sharp turn, we would plunge a mile into the Colorado River.

We hiked partway down the canyon, and on the second day, drove to Mesa
Verde, our last stop, to see the Anasazi ruins. After setting up camp, Craig called
the church to check in, as he had done every few days. He returned from the
phone booth looking serious.

"Gene's father died last night. They're making funeral arrangements." Gene
and his wife Janine had attended Faith for years, and our children played
together. His father occasionally attended, and Craig had visited him several
times during his illness.

"When will the funeral be?" I asked.

"Saturday. I've offered to officiate."

I nodded. This cut our vacation short several days, and required a nearly
non-stop race back to Baltimore. "That would mean a lot to Gene and Janine. I
think the kids are ready to head home anyway." We prepared to leave at dawn.
But at five o clock in the morning, I woke with that sharp, familiar sore throat.

My spirits plummeted. Was adding grad school to my schedule wearing me down? I hated thinking of dropping out.

"Craig," I nudged him. He opened his eyes. "The strep is back. I need penicillin."

"Again? Are you sure? What is this, the third time in a row?"

I nodded. "We'll have to find an emergency room. I just hope I can get a prescription without a twenty-four hour strep culture."

We planned our assault on the nearest emergency room, in Durango, Colorado, a town of some 15,000 people. Craig dropped me off and took the kids grocery shopping.

Feeling weaker by the minute, I sat in front of an intake clerk and filled out forms.

"I know my HMO will want me to call first to okay this visit," I said. The clerk pointed me to a bank of pay phones. I dialed the HMO and explained my situation.

"I'm sorry, but you'll have to see a local doctor," the HMO gatekeeper replied. "Since it's not an emergency, we can't authorize an emergency room visit. You'd have to pay the emergency room fee."

My frustration rose. My throat burned, and I felt queasy and dizzy. "I can get crack, heroin, pot, uppers, or who knows what else just one block from my home in Baltimore," I thought, "but I can't get penicillin."

I stumbled back to the front desk. "They say I have to see a local doctor," I choked. I was so angry that my eyes filled with tears. "Oh, that is just terrible," the middle-aged clerk said, pushing a box of tissues across her desk. "Tell you what. Let me make a few calls, see what I can do."

In the city, I was accustomed to long lines, crowded waiting rooms, and detached personnel. This woman's generosity made me want to cry. She leaned into her phone, dialing nearby internists one after the other. I heard snatches of her quiet pleas: "traveling," "strep throat," "HMO," "very upset."

After a few minutes, she hung up the phone. "I found a doctor. He's a pediatrician, but he'll see you right away. His office is in the medical building next door."

I wiped my eyes and blinked back tears. I must have looked like a lost child, because she stood up, took my arm, walked me to the door, and stepped outside with me. She pointed to a brick sidewalk. My own personal Yellow Brick Road to Oz and antibiotics.

"Follow that path until it curves around. His office is on the second floor. Good luck, dear." She patted me on the back. This made me cry again.

When I entered the pediatrician's waiting room, little kids looked at my swollen, blotchy face and scrunched closer to their mothers. I filled out forms, went to the bathroom and splashed water on my face, returned to the waiting area. An overly cheery nurse escorted me to an examining room, where I paced back and forth, trying to distract myself into emotional stability. Photos of a man and woman on a hiking trail with a small child decorated one wall. The doctor, I presumed.

When the doctor entered the room, I recognized that fleeting look of surprise ("Oh! She's been crying!"), but he quickly recovered. I poured out my predicament, my history of unshakable bouts with strep throat, ending in a rush. "...and we have to drive back to Baltimore right away. My husband's a pastor and someone's father died."

He checked my vital signs, examined my throat. He made a little small talk, asking about our vacation. He pulled out a prescription pad.

"Based on the medical history you've just given me, and looking at your throat, I'm giving you the penicillin."

I thanked him profusely, feeling guilty, like I had scored illegal drugs.

He opened the door to leave. "And there's no charge for your visit. Professional courtesy," he said gently.

"Oh! But you don't have to—" I protested. But he smiled and closed the door.

The kindness of Durango, Colorado, completely unglued me. The nurse returned to find me wiping away tears. Some explanation was in order, but nothing I could say would make me sound entirely well balanced, so I exited as gracefully as was possible with a swollen red face and sunglasses.

The trip provided a brief escape, a time when we were together as a family without the demands of the ministry and the neighborhood. We knew that soon, our children would pull away from home for summer jobs and college. Though I hardly realized it, our time to shape their character and fill them with memories of a happy childhood was slipping away.

The children never forgot the trip. Craig had fond memories of his many childhood camping trips, but we had squeezed a lifetime of camping weekends into one three-week marathon. The events we remembered most fondly were the quirks and calamities: sleeping in the van, car trouble, too much fried chicken, the bear that ate Melissa's sweater, too many nights setting up tents. The children laughed, eyes shining, faces glowing with the joy of remembering. They would need to draw on those memories to face the storms ahead.

CHAPTER 25

Old York Road

WOUNDED HEARTS, BATTERED MINDS

BECAUSE the mentally ill often live where cheap rent and public transportation make modest government disability checks stretch farther, we have known many people with schizophrenia or other major mental illnesses.

The mentally ill are our modern lepers, feared, misunderstood, shunned. It is hard to sit in church or in a Bible study next to someone who is fidgeting or erratic or smells bad. They make us uncomfortable. We don't know what to do, how to help.

Joey, a young man in his mid-twenties, began attending our church. He listened carefully and was quick to respond during the Bible study he attended in our living room. Though a bit socially awkward, he had endearing qualities: a kind spirit, a friendly manner, and a spiritually hungry heart. His younger siblings attended our summer camp, but Joey was new to us. Perhaps he had been raised elsewhere. We had seen troubling signs in his mother's home, and eventually Social Services would remove several of his siblings because of abuse and neglect. One summer his five-year-old sister, Tasha, came to summer camp with a high fever. Tasha begged camp director Joan Nelson not to call her mom, to let her sleep on chairs in the upstairs parlor instead. Was her home so comfortless, we wondered, that she rejected it even in sickness?

One winter after church, I joined Tasha, her little brother, and their mother as they walked home from church. The children's jackets were held together with safety pins. Tasha started to wail loudly and tears coursed down her dark cheeks. Her mother ignored her for an uncomfortable length of time, pulling her along by the hand. Alarmed by her mother's lack of concern, I bent down to talk to Tasha, who continued to wail.

"She's really upset about something," I said, looking up at her mother. Tasha's mother bent down to see what was wrong. Tasha pointed to her waist. "It hurts! It hurts!" Her mother lifted her daughter's shirt to find that the large safety pin holding her pants up had burst open and was stabbing the child's soft skin. The mother refastened the pin, patted Tasha on the head, and resumed our conversation. But in their interaction, I saw something was missing.

Joan took pains to invite Tasha and her siblings to summer camp and other youth activities. When discipline problems arose, Joan strategized carefully to avoid suspending or expelling them from the warmth and attention of the camp counselors. But we had no idea of the extent of the problems until we met Joey.

A few weeks after he began attending our home Bible study, Joey's behavior began to concern us. He attached to our family and to this strong, important pastor who would meet with him and listen to him. He stopped by the church or our house frequently to see Craig. He called the house nearly every day. He ate dinner with us several times in two weeks. He began to ask me personal questions. Perhaps he saw me as an older sister figure, but I felt increasingly uncomfortable.

Joey's living situation with his mother fell apart. He claimed that she and her boyfriend had sexually abused the children, and refused to live with her. He said a male relative in the home used drugs and kept a loaded gun.

Craig arranged for Joey to live with several single men in the former manse next door to the church. But a few days later, Joey brandished a knife at one of the other residents, and was asked to leave. A few days later, he called in the middle of the night, agitated. After a short conversation, Craig hung up the phone. He began pulling on a pair of pants.

"He's coming over," he said.

"Now? It can't wait until morning?" I knew Craig was exhausted and faced a full schedule the next day.

"He's really worked up, maybe even delusional. I'm calling the police to take him to the hospital," Craig said. "He may need to be committed."

"How will he take that news?" I feared an outburst, even violence.

"I don't know," Craig said.

I sighed and pulled on my robe, knowing I wouldn't sleep anymore. In another minute, we heard Joey banging on the front door.

"Stay up here," Craig ordered me. "Don't come downstairs."

"Are you kidding? No way am I going downstairs."

My mother-heart wanted Joey to grow spiritually and heal from his scarred past. But now he was in my house, with my husband, just a few steps from where my children slept. I perched at the top of the stairs, hearing Joey's erratic voice and Craig's calm but firm one. Craig offered him food, opened the kitchen cabinets, poured a bowl of cereal. I heard the spoon hit the side of the bowl as Joey ate. Craig's voice was a quiet, steady humming, talking him down.

Suddenly Joey began ranting about his mother. He jumped up, grabbed the phone, dialed her number, and yelled obscene, sexually violent threats. I had never imagined the word pictures described in the brief seconds before Craig grabbed the phone and hung it up. The hair stood up on the back of my neck.

My four children and Caroline's best friend slept in their rooms at the top of the stairs. "Lord, don't let him come up here," I prayed. "But if he comes near these children, I will do whatever it takes." I grabbed a baseball bat from Calvin's room and shut the doors to the children's rooms.

"Joey, sit down," Craig commanded. Joey laughed maniacally, then returned calmly to his cereal, as if nothing had happened. It chilled me. Was this a psychotic break? Demon possession? Schizophrenia? From my perch at the top of the stairs, I continued to pray.

"Oh, God, help. Don't let him freak out. Help. Help Joey. Protect Craig. If he kills Craig and comes up here and threatens the children, help me knock him out. And no matter what happens, don't let the children wake up."

"Joey, I think you need more help than we can give," Craig said carefully. "I've called the police, and they are going to take you to the hospital."

I stopped breathing. None of the mentally ill people we knew wanted a trip to the state hospitals. It frightened them to be locked up with a bunch of crazy people. It shamed them.

Joey remained calm. My prayer monologue continued.

Another knock at the door. I peeked through the banister and saw Craig usher two burly policemen into the foyer. They spoke in low tones. Joey still sat passively in the kitchen.

"Where is he now?" one policeman asked quietly.

"In the kitchen."

The policemen exchanged glances. "Which way?"

Their cautious steps creaked on the old wooden floor, and then their voices floated up.

"Joey, how you doin'?" An officer introduced himself and his partner. I couldn't hear Joey's response. "We're going to take you in to the hospital, see if we can get you some help, maybe some medication. O.K.?"

Joey didn't resist. We later learned that this was not Joey's first trip to a state institution.

"Joey, I need to check your pockets before I take you in, alright? Got anything in there we should know about?" Joey still wore his heavy winter coat, and I heard the cop rustling through its pockets. Silence. The cop spoke again. "Well, now, that's a problem. How about you give that to your pastor here to keep for you, O.K.?"

With a heavy tread, an officer led Joey out the door. His partner stayed behind to talk with Craig, and I raced down the stairs. He tried to gather the sketchy facts we knew of Joey's history.

"When you told us he was in your kitchen, we were really concerned," the cop said.

"I never should have let him into the house," Craig berated himself. "I thought it might calm him down if I fed him."

The cop eyed Craig. "Kitchen is the worst place in the house to take someone like that."

We looked at him dumbly. An awareness dawned.

"I've seen them go for knives many a time," the cop said.

"I won't make that mistake again," Craig said, shaking his head and looking at the floor.

After the policeman left, Craig pulled something from his pocket. "Look at this." He showed me Joey's confiscated knife, a martial arts weapon with a six-inch blade. "He's not getting this back." He dropped it in his cluttered desk drawer.

A few days later, the hospital discharged Joey for non-cooperation. Because the doctors did not consider him a danger to himself or to society, he could not be held against his will. Joey stopped by to see Craig and ate dinner with us. He seemed rational but deflated. Craig spent the following day—theoretically his day off—helping Joey, who refused to return to his mother's house and was now homeless. Joey showered and washed his laundry at our house, and then Craig took him to a homeless shelter. But late that night, the shelter ejected him for erratic behavior.

The next morning, a Sunday, Joey knocked on our front door at 8:30. Craig had been gone since seven, and I didn't want to let him in. I awkwardly yelled through the locked door. "Craig's up at church already."

"Can I come in? Can I get some breakfast?"

Which Joey was on the other side: The sane one? The psychotic one? The gentle one? The one who threatened violence against his mother with a switchblade? I prayed: "Jesus, what am I supposed to do here? Am I doing the right thing? Help me. Protect my kids." Then I did something that makes my skin crawl every time I think of it. I let him in.

There is an intersection between faith and foolishness, a fine line between trust and presumption. I suspected then, and know now, that I crossed that line. Compassion offers oneself to another; presumption takes unnecessary risks. I keep replaying that moment, wishing I had sent him away.

He followed me around the kitchen like a disturbed cat. I slipped upstairs and told the children to stay there until Joey left. I tried to get rid of him. "Joey, why don't you go up to church? Craig is there, and maybe Bill Bolling, too. They can let you in."

He started babbling about psychic powers. Do you have them? he asked. Do you believe in them? Sometimes he has them, he said. He fixated on objects in my kitchen, fingering a basket of fruit as though it were miraculous. He said he wanted to wash up, make sure he looked good. "There are girls in church," he said happily.

Every few minutes, he laughed eerily, throwing back his head and booming an open-mouthed, guttural bellow. It unnerved me. My emotions always march across my face like a St. Patrick's Day parade, and he chided me for looking anxious. I called Craig.

"Joey is here," I announced, trying to sound nonchalant. "He wants to see you."

"He's there?" Craig sounded stunned. "In the house?" I put Joey on the phone, and Craig told him to come up to the church. But Joey felt no hurry to leave his sanctuary. After a few gentle reminders that Craig was waiting for him, I realized he wouldn't leave of his own free will. Though it was still early, I grabbed my guitar and led him toward the front door.

"Let's go to church, Joey." He followed me without incident.

During church, he fidgeted and emptied out his pockets, fingering a pen, coins, hard candies. He passed me a note, a few scrawled words about the service. My nerves were so electrified I couldn't concentrate. Numbly, I played guitar with the other musicians, keeping an eye on Joey, who sat next to my children. When he walked out halfway through the service, the tension in my neck and shoulders started to ease.

That afternoon, as we slept the heavy sleep of the exhausted, Joey knocked on our door. I jumped up.

"Just ignore it," Craig said.

"What do you mean?"

"I can't do anything more for him. Just ignore it."

Joey's pounding continued. I was frantic. "You can't just ignore him. He won't go away."

The children appeared in our bedroom doorway. "Joey's banging on the door," Melissa said.

"We're not answering it. Don't answer it. Don't go downstairs," Craig instructed her. Melissa was wide-eyed.

Craig went downstairs and spoke to Joey through the closed door. Joey refused to leave. He curled in a fetal position inside our storm door like a still-born child, half his body hanging out the entryway onto the porch. An hour passed. Two hours. I paced upstairs like a nervous cat, refusing to let the children downstairs.

Craig called the police. After what felt like hours, two sirens screamed up the street and stopped in front of our house. Two officers approached the porch.

"Joey, you need to get up now. You can't stay here," the officers ordered.

"I live here."

"No, you don't. You're trespassing."

"Pastor Craig and Maria are sent by God to be my mommy and daddy."

My heart ached. I saw not a twenty-five year old man, but a boy of five or six, desperate for the stability and tenderness inside my home. I saw a little dark-haired boy whose mother couldn't take care of him, who did or allowed unspeakable things to be done to him. Joey, I am so sorry.

When he refused to get up, the police dragged him away from the door by his feet. He held onto the doorframe. The officers grunted as they tried to pick him up, then lowered him back down to the porch. They handcuffed him and shackled his feet. Joey was passive, neither kicking nor helping. Finally they pulled him to his feet and led him away from the house. Later, we saw that he had peed on the porch, like a dog or tiger marking his territory.

Several neighbors watched the drama unfolding on our porch. Little boys clustered together on the sidewalk, alternately full of bravado and caution. Joey laughed loudly, but as they put him into the paddy wagon, he turned ugly. "F—- you! F—- you, Pastor Craig and your wife, too!" He repeated this over and over. I wanted to put my hands over my ears, cover my eyes, but I would still see and hear him.

We saw Joey once or twice after his release from the hospital, but he floated out of our orbit. He moved in with a cousin, a Jehovah's Witness who demanded he attend the Kingdom Hall. I hope he has stabilized and is living a productive life. I hope his wounds are healing.

Will Joey get the mental health care he needs? Pharmacology for the mentally ill is like a warehouse of mix and match clothes patients try on and discard again and again, looking for a decent fit. Lithium? Prozac? Zyprexa? Abilify? Haloperidol? Will he take his medication, which may have unpleasant side effects, or will he throw it away, arguing that God has healed him?

Will he get the spiritual care he needs? In the church, Joey could be infused, week by week, with the means of grace—worship, preaching, teaching, communion, encouragement from fellow believers. He could grasp the supernatural call of Jesus to forgive those who abused him. He could apply the balm of the Gospel to his battered soul.

CHAPTER 26

Kevin Good

HOOP DREAMS, HARD REALITIES, AND HOPE

CRAIG finally took our basketball hoop down.

We had seen it coming for a long time. The neighborhood boys kept hanging on the rim, bending the metal until the backboard tilted precariously and threatened to fall on their heads. We asked them repeatedly not to hang on the rim, told them rim-hangers would be kicked off the court, that the backboard would eventually break and then no one would be able to play anymore. But they didn't listen, couldn't or wouldn't control themselves. Their heroes, Shaq and Magic, hung on the rim like happy toddlers on a swing set.

Perhaps it was doomed from the start. Recreational space is scarce in the city, and broken milk crates are nailed to telephone poles and above doors in tiny alleys to provide makeshift hoops. Craig often took a vanload of youths to a gym several miles away to build relationships and invest in young men with the hope that some would be encouraged in the right direction.

"We really need a gym," he had said almost every week. He toyed with thoughts of building an inexpensive corrugated shell on one of the vacant lots near the church. He had the necessary construction experience, and the degree in architecture and building construction. He could act as contractor, he said, voice rising in excitement. But our church did not have the resources.

So we built a half court in our back yard. My vague uneasiness was no match for his enthusiasm. We bought a dump truck load of concrete, and Craig laid out the court, measuring and digging and laying lines of metal reinforcing rods, called rebar. Workers dumped the concrete in wheelbarrows and trundled it into the back yard, and a skilled neighbor smoothed it carefully. Craig put up an adjustable backboard so that Calvin and other small boys could know the thrill of making baskets.

There were problems from the start. We looked outside and saw ten or fifteen unfamiliar older guys playing while the younger boys sat on the picnic table. They left candy wrappers and soda cans in the grass, trampled the few lonely flowers I had planted, perched on the picnic table until it listed like a pitched roof. Careless, but not malicious.

Someone broke the sump pump line that juts out of our basement, jumping up and down on the PVC pipe until it shattered. Twice. Craig spent two Saturday mornings fixing it. The boys were loud and boisterous, and our neighbors protested. We shut the gate to the backyard but they climbed over it. We bought a lock and chained the gate shut but they ran through the neighbors' yard and climbed over the fence. I returned from work every afternoon to the endless slapping of leather on concrete, of leather banging against the rim.

We posted hours: "Basketball from 4:00 to 6:00" read the hand-lettered signs. They were torn down and everyone professed ignorance. Craig built a new gate, wooden planks eight feet high, with no latch on the outside. Boys jumped from the porch to the fence, climbed over it, and unlocked it. When confronted, the story was always the same: "We didn't open it. There was guys already here when we came."

I constantly had to stick my head out the back door, asking the boys to keep the noise down, to stop the trash talk and cussing. Occasionally, arguments erupted and I had to referee. After one scuffle, I expelled all players. "You know the rules," I said. "No fighting. Come back tomorrow."

They grumbled resentfully. "Why am I always the enemy?" I wondered. I stood at the open kitchen window, watching sullen boys shuffle slowly out. One boy mouthed off. "I ain't listenin' to no white bitch," he bragged.

"Well, yes you are," I said, sticking my head out the open window. He whirled around, saw me, and his false bravado landed at his feet. His buddies hooted.

To protect me from the stress of endless refereeing, we tried to arrange for men from the church to play during the posted hours. Our good friend Dexter Jenkins, a bright, soft-spoken African American from the Eastern Shore of Maryland who had worshipped with us for years, was always a welcome sight. Craig played sometimes, too. But the trash talk—and the noise that bothered our neighbors—seemed part and parcel of the game. We fluctuated between frustration, anger, resentment, resignation, and hope. One neighborhood teen stopped playing ball and fell in with the drug dealers who occupied the corner house. Carl sat on his porch, front door open and stereo blasting, getting high. "Carl, come play some ball," I called. He nodded, but didn't leave his post.

The inconvenience, the noise, and the anger of my neighbors seemed negligible alongside the chance that Carl or his friends might be influenced for good. We thought of young men in our church youth group who had spent hours playing ball with Gary Tibbles and Kelly Simpkins, earlier youth group leaders. Several became Christians, graduated from high school, got jobs, and became husbands and fathers even though they hadn't known their own fathers. It was worth it to see just one boy go right.

Our basketballs kept disappearing. The rim started hanging, and one day, we saw it propped up with a long board the kids had scavenged from behind the house.

"Carl was hanging on the rim and broke it," the younger boys said. Carl maintained his ignorance. "The little boys did it," he said.

"Well, it's done now," I told him. "Now no one can play." His blank face feigned indifference.

That evening, Craig dragged out the ladder and took the ailing backboard off. The pole remained, jutting out of a sea of concrete like an impotent mast. The back yard was quiet.

An hour later, we heard gunshots from the corner. The children called from their beds. Eight-year-old Calvin left his room and swaddled in blankets on the floor near Caroline's bed. He grumped: "We hear gunshots almost every night. And the police never come." But the police did come, and red lights flashed rhythmically against our neighbor's row house.

I thought about our basketball court. Maybe if there were more recreational areas where boys could work off steam. Maybe if there were more fathers, like our neighbor Cornell, who came occasionally with his boys to play. His sons were respectful, polite, the fruit of a strong father's investment. Maybe if our church had more money to hire youth workers to spend time with vulnerable kids.

"Lord," I prayed. "I can't quit my job to supervise the basketball court. You know basketball is a great way to build bridges with guys from the neighborhood. Send us some men to provide more after school activities and discipleship for these guys."

And in His time, God sent men.

In 1994, Thurman Williams, a YoungLife leader in Baltimore County, began to consider urban ministry. Thurman had been sharing Christ with suburban high school teens for eight years, but felt God tugging him in a new direction. He had read books about urban ministry: John Perkins, Bill Pannell (*The Coming Race War*) and Spencer Perkins and Chris Rice (*More Than Equals*). He wanted to serve in the city, and in a church rather than a parachurch ministry. Although he had no clear idea of the next step, he resigned from YoungLife.

Craig's dad, Pete, had served on the YoungLife committee since his own children had made commitments to the Lord through its ministry thirty years before. He wanted to talk to Thurman about his resignation. They met for an early breakfast at a Friendly's restaurant. Pete also invited Craig.

"You should come to Faith," Craig urged. A mature African American leader like Thurman would be a tremendous asset at Faith. "It sounds like we're doing the type of ministry you want to do." He offered Thurman, who had no prior urban experience, an opportunity to serve at Faith on a trial basis.

Thurman visited Faith the following Sunday. Sandy Clark invited him to a home Bible study, where he could learn more about Faith and begin to build relationships. A few months later, Thurman moved into the former manse next door to the church, where four or five other young men lived.

Thurman enrolled in Chesapeake Seminary part-time and took a job in a warehouse to pay his bills. He began volunteering with Faith's youth group, teaching youth Sunday School, and doing outreach basketball one night a week. In 1995, he joined Faith's staff as Minister of Youth and Outreach. He also attended seminary and preached once a month. He built relationships with neighborhood kids and built a bustling youth ministry. As an added bonus, he met and married his dynamic and deeply committed wife, Evie, who had replaced Cindy Beck Homans as kindergarten teacher at BCS.

At Faith, Thurman honed his preaching, teaching, and pastoral leadership skills in an urban context. Craig looked forward to the day Thurman would finish his seminary degree and share even more of the preaching and pastoral load. But God had other plans for him.

In 1998, Kevin Good approached Craig about forming recreation leagues for city children. Kevin, a former professional soccer player in Charlotte, North Carolina, had started an after-school sports program at his church, but wanted to do this work full-time. Craig caught Kevin's spark like a pile of gasoline-soaked rags. Could this be an answer to our prayers? It sounded great, Craig said, but the church had no money to pay an additional staff person. Faith could no more pay his salary than the mayor's.

"But what if money wasn't an issue?" Kevin pressed.

"Then we would love to have you come on a trial basis," Craig told him. "Just see how the Lord leads. We can provide the structure, oversight, encouragement, and all the kids you can handle."

So Kevin raised his own support, cobbling together a modest salary package. Kevin and his wife Anissa bought a renovated Victorian in Pen Lucy. After surveying the neighborhood to take stock of what was already available, he decided to focus on youth education and athletics. He formed the Pen Lucy Youth Partnership (PLYP), which started with one basketball league and an evening tutoring program.

Within a few years, Kevin established year-round sports programs that taught four hundred players a year about sportsmanship, teamwork, and self-discipline—and about Jesus, too. The tutoring program grew into an after-school learning center that offered one-on-one tutoring four nights a week in math, reading, music composition and computer technology. One hundred students participated each semester, with a waiting list for more. One full-time staff person, eight part-time staff, and dozens of volunteer tutors and coaches, including our daughter Caroline, served in PLYP's ministries.

God had answered our prayers—and the prayers of many others—more spectacularly than we could have anticipated. One lonely net rising out of a half-size backyard basketball court couldn't begin to reach neighborhood kids. But God resurrected our hoop dreams, creating a sports program serving hundreds of kids each year.

CHAPTER 27

Caroline, Juliana, and Melissa, 1998

A DESIRED BABY

ONE summer day, when Becky was sixteen, Melissa fourteen, Caroline twelve, and Calvin ten, I felt a vague nausea sweep over me. A queasiness formed and dissipated like patches of morning fog.

"I must have a touch of something," I thought offhandedly. My mind was as cluttered as a city alley on trash day. I was juggling church activities and a part-time job, transporting Becky and Melissa to their summer jobs, and organizing activities for Calvin and Caroline.

But the queasiness persisted the next day. Something I ate? I skipped a meal, but my stomach still felt like a rolling ship at sea. Little alarm bells went off inside my head, distant memories crowding in from the antechambers of my befuddled brain. I am rarely nauseated—except when I'm pregnant. When I'm pregnant, I'm always nauseated. Nausea equals pregnancy.

I was thirty-nine. I had been out of the diapering business for over eight years.

"Can't be. Naah," I thought. But as the day wore on, a sneaky certainty grew like chips in front of a winning poker player. By the third day, I was counting days backwards and forwards on the calendar. Just how late *am* I? Nine months from now would be when?

I will be the oldest woman in the maternity ward, I thought. Everyone will laugh. Our teenagers will be mortified. People will call this poor baby a caboose, an accident, an afterthought her whole life. Will our parents chide us for being irresponsible? Will people think that we can't figure out where babies come from? If it is a boy, we'll have to call him Isaac, which means laughter, because everyone will be hooting, and because I felt like Sarah, too old to be traipsing around in maternity clothes.

I could hardly trust my instincts. I snuck off to the doctor's office for a blood test. As if I needed it. This was like Noah turning on the Weather Channel to check the forecast.

The next day, I called for results.

"Your blood test was positive," the nurse said with no emotion. She sounded like she was reading a call script. "Date of last menstrual cycle?"

I fumbled around in my memory and gave her the dates.

"Is this a desired pregnancy?"

Did she say *planned* or *desired*? I was barely adjusting to the idea of pregnancy and she was asking if I wanted an abortion? A wave of protectiveness swept over me. "Yes," I told her. "It's a desired pregnancy."

For Craig, as for many pastors, when the week marches ever-onward toward Sunday, the sermon looms like an unfinished term paper, like a final oral exam given before two hundred people. Sermon preparation sucks up all available mental energy, and even some energy needed for bodily functions like eating and sleeping. Absorbing a Major Life Issue like midlife pregnancy— and oh, by the way, you'll be sixty-one when she graduates from high school— is like trying to suck up a wet bath towel with a Dustbuster. All mental processes stop. A pregnancy announcement would bring on the mental equivalent of a fifty-car pileup on the interstate.

So I had mercy on Craig, I had mercy on the church, and I waited until after the sermon. Sunday afternoon I eyed him warily. There wasn't much left. He needed a nap, and would attend prayer meeting that night. This left Monday morning. Any day now, I was going to start my morning by retching violently, and then no words would be needed.

Monday morning, as Craig slogged back and forth on the NordicTrack, I sidled up to him. "So, how're you feeling? You feeling ok?" I probed.

"Fine. A little tired."

"But you're feeling ok?"

"Ye-a—h…" He looked at me strangely.

"Good. Because I've got some news." I took a breath and watched his face. "I'm pregnant."

His eyebrows lifted.

"I even had a blood test, to be sure."

He slogged back and forth, back and forth, absorbing this. Then a smile appeared, a shy, slow dawning at first, then a broad grin. "Wow. Five. We'll have five kids." He thought a moment. "Like both our parents. When?"

"Some time in March."

We discussed the ramifications of this. My salary already funded the children's education—private high school, middle school and elementary school for four—so I wouldn't be able to stay at home full time as I had with our other babies. We decided to ask our friend, Faith member Vernell Lucadamo, to reserve a spot at her Hosanna Christian Family Day Care.

Lying in bed, we prayed that God would give us the energy to do this one more time. We daydreamed about the perfect child, assembled with the assets of each sibling: Becky's artistic gifts and determination, Melissa's social skills and sunny disposition, Caroline's diligence and sensitivity, Calvin's charm and wit. We froze at the possibility of a child who might be an amalgam of each sibling's worst trait.

We decided to tell the children a few days later when we left for Ocean City. I was concerned that they would see me sleeping all day or catch me throwing up and fear I was secretly and stoically dying of cancer. A week at the beach would give them time to adjust. Not content to just blurt out such stunning (or at least family-rearranging) news without fanfare, I devised a word game. Each of the four children and Becky's friend Johanna, who accompanied us, received a slip of paper with several letters on it. They had to collect letters from each player (cooperate!) and unscramble them to fill in the blanks and craft a sentence.

We were barely out of Baltimore when I tried to drum up interest. "Kids, I've got a really neat word game for you to play in the car. Do you want to see it now?"

"No, maybe later."

"No, thanks."

I waited five long minutes before trying again. "Anyone interested in the word game?" I waved slips of paper around. Still no takers. Five minutes later,

I tried again. "You're *really* going to like this game. It's *very* interesting. Come on, it will only take a few minutes."

They rolled their eyes, figuring Mom wouldn't give them any peace until they did the stupid game. I knelt on the front seat, and passed out the little slips of papers. "Here's a big hint. The first word is 'Mom'."

They bent their heads over the task. I craned my neck, checking their progress. Becky had already figured out "MOM IS GOING TO" but couldn't figure out the rest—" _ _ _ _ _ _ _ _ _." But Johanna, quick with a pen, unscrambled the rest: "HAVE A BABY." She nudged Becky, showed it to her. Becky shook her head: no, not that. Too far-fetched. But I saw.

"Yes! Johanna's got it!"

Becky's jaw dropped and her eyes widened. This couldn't be true. Amid cries of "For real?" and "You're kidding, right?" I confirmed the news.

"Caroline, remember last week, on the way home from camp, when you told me you wished we had just one more baby?"

"Yeah, but I didn't think you'd do it!"

"Well, God must have heard your prayers."

Once the initial shock wore off, the children looked forward to welcoming another sibling. My father was soaking in the tub when my mother showed him my email. He sat bolt upright and crowed with delight. Cleo and Pete were just as pleased as they had been with our first pregnancy. Our friends, when they stopped laughing, were also supportive. The women at church threw a surprise baby shower, saying, "We figured you'd given all the baby clothes away." I had.

Pregnancy hadn't gotten any easier. For seven months, I had to eat every three hours to prevent spasms of vomiting. My bones ached. My pelvis and ribs were stretching apart. I could have written an acrostic of my ills:

A is for abdomen, stretched beyond belief

B is for bloated gut and its attendant grief

C is for calcium, leaching from my bones

D is for doctor visits, see how fat I've grown.

I put on so much weight that the doctor grilled me. "What are you eating?"

"Nothing! Just healthy food!"

She looked at me, back at the chart, then at me again. "Are you drinking a lot of juice?"

"No! I can't understand why I'm putting on all this weight. Normally, I'd have to be attached to a trough full of potato chips to put on weight like this."

I started turning my head away when I stepped on the scale at the doctor's office. "Don't tell me. I don't want to know."

The birth was easy, thanks to my first epidural ever. As I held Juliana, our bonus baby, I marveled that God trusts us with these vulnerable, uniquely created newborns. But as my hormones zigzagged like a hyperactive two-year-old, I cried, thinking about raising Juliana amid so much brokenness, enduring the culture shock, the struggle for cultural identity, the lack of educational opportunity, and the dearth of resources. This time, I knew what was ahead, and it scared me. I would have to take this innocent child out into a world where teenage boys had set my elderly neighbor on fire just for fun, dousing him with gasoline and throwing a match as he worked on his old car. A world where one in four girls is sexually assaulted before she reaches the age of eighteen. A world where she would be favored by some because she is white—but at the expense of others, who are not. "Lord, help me," I prayed.

A month later, the pediatrician expressed concerned that Juliana was not gaining enough weight. "But I'm nursing on demand," I insisted.

"Are you under a lot of stress?" she asked.

"Not really. Just the usual."

"You'll need to supplement with formula," she instructed.

It took months for me to admit that my life was so stressful that I couldn't produce enough milk to nourish my baby. I held and rocked her for long hours, tracing the soft skin on her pink face, tickling her chin to make her smile. I rocked her to sleep, watching her slow, drowsy capitulation, seeing her eyelids flutter and finally close. I fell so deeply in love with her that when, at six months, I had to start leaving her with Vernell for six hours a day, it ripped my heart out. Vernell saw my eyes fill up every morning.

"She'll be fine," she soothed, taking Juliana from me. Even her obvious fondness for Juliana failed to completely ease my mind, and at the end of the work day, I begrudged every stoplight, every slow car that kept me from her. She was the child of my middle age, our bonus baby. Our *desired* baby.

CHAPTER 28

Springfield, 1990

AN INCARNATIONAL CHRISTMAS

WE celebrate the incarnation of God at Christmas: Emmanuel, God with us. Angels announced the news not to the powerful and politically well-connected, but to the poor, to outcast shepherds, to men with such diminished social status that their testimony was not admitted in a Jewish court of law. For love, for redemption, Jesus came as a helpless, squalling, mucus-covered infant.

Who would make up such a religion? A young peasant couple endures a scandalous pregnancy, a late-term trek on foot across rugged terrain, and a birth attended not by midwives with competent, gentle hands and female relatives with sympathetic, joy-sharing eyes, but dumb, brooding oxen. A God who condescends, stoops to live in a cave-stable littered with dung and horse-flies. Jesus brings shalom, the peace of God, though we do not deserve it. He forgives, though we have no claim to it. This is grace.

Christmas at our house is low-key. Christmas Eve service: *Silent Night*, short sermons, candles, excited children opening one gift. Christmas morning: bulging, red stockings beside each bed, groggy opening of modest gifts, home-made cinnamon rolls. Christmas afternoon: aunts, uncles, cousins, and presents at the grandparents' house.

When the girls were teenagers, I gave up buying them clothing and tucked a few dollars in their stockings for the after-Christmas sales. One year, I bought three boxes of personalized stationary, pink script swirls of their first names, and Craig bought them study Bibles: adult study bibles for what we hoped would become adult faith. Even toddler Juliana received one, though it stayed in the box on the bottom shelf of her room.

After gift openings and coffee, Craig descended our steep basement stairs to fix a used bike we bought to replace Calvin's, which had been stolen from our front yard a few weeks before. The basement felt unusually cold and drafty.

Because security bars had failed to deter break-ins, Craig had screwed boards to the outside window frame, a solution that plunged our basement into perpetual darkness. No dawn, no dusk, no fresh air. But we hoped no more break-ins. To cut heating costs, he put insulation between the glass and the inside security bars.

Glancing at the boarded-up windows, Craig realized why the basement had been so cold. The glass was broken and the board hung like a dislocated arm. Someone had yanked off the board, broken the window, and kicked through the insulation. But the potential thief couldn't dislodge the metal security bar. The intruder had either been interrupted or given up, thinking it not worth the trouble. No wonder the house had felt so drafty: an open window in sub-freezing weather.

Craig trudged outside, and began screwing the board over the window. As he bent over his task, Lenny entered the yard.

Lenny shivered in his hooded green winter coat. He was thin, ravaged by years of drug addiction and AIDS. He and his wife had recently gone through a detox program, and their daughter attended the PLYP sports program run by Kevin Good. Kevin had helped the family with food and heating bills. He had arranged to study the Bible with Lenny, but when he arrived, he asked Kevin for money. Kevin refused, and Lenny left. We knew Lenny was working the system, trying to get over, get by. We hoped he wasn't getting high, but had our doubts. We kept extending grace. There was a little girl involved, another incentive to make this work.

"Merry Christmas, Pastor Craig."

"Merry Christmas, Lenny," Craig stood to shake his hand, then returned to the broken window.

"Pastor Craig, I was wondering if I could borrow five dollars for bus fare. Maybe shovel some snow."

Bus fare, Craig wondered, on Christmas Day? But he agreed to pay Lenny to shovel the sidewalk.

Lenny bent over our sidewalk, lifting, throwing, lifting, throwing. The shovel made a rhythmic scritch—scritch sound. He worked carefully, making neat lines, clearing the entire walk and not just a narrow pathway. My emotions flitted about: yes, it was compassionate to pay him for what we planned to do ourselves, but I felt guilty about the small amount Lenny had requested, about standing in a warm house with a cup of tea and a new book, while Lenny, impoverished Lenny, chronically-in-crisis Lenny, bent over our shovel on Christmas Day.

We gave him more money than he asked, plus a bag of fruit and some homemade corn muffins. *Our God is gracious and compassionate, slow to anger and abounding in love. His mercies are new every morning.*

A neighborhood boy, Tony, appeared at the door, asking if Pastor Craig could fix his bike. I saw Craig drop his eyes a minute, resisting, struggling: *Where is his father? Why doesn't his father help him fix his bike?* Again he felt the pain and frustration of these boys, sweet boys with winning smiles whose fathers disappeared, whose fathers can't or won't help them fix their bikes and teach them how to be men; fatherless boys who close their hearts after the chambers fill with the pain of it, who push against their tired mothers, boys who ache for mentors and find them on the corner. Tony often borrowed pliers, screwdrivers, and an air pump to fix his bike. Once he asked for a can of paint, but I drew the line at that. "Tell your mother she has to come talk to me about that."

Just the day before, Craig had seen Tony using our sled, a Flexible Flyer we had picked up at the Goodwill that was marked with the previous owner's name. The sled had disappeared from our front yard some weeks before. "Where did you get that sled?" Craig had asked. "It looks just like the one we used to have."

"Miss Lea gave it to me," Tony said.

Craig told Tony that the sled was ours, pointed out the name on the bottom, asked him to return it when he was finished using it. Tony said he would. But he never brought the sled back, and now he stood with his broken bike on Christmas morning. Craig remembered: *A father to the fatherless, a defender of widows is God in His holy dwelling.* He fetched his bucket of tools and stepped outside on the porch. There was grace for Tony.

That afternoon, we visited Craig's parents in their large home in the county, which Pete had designed and built. Under a large spruce in the formal living room, Cleo had placed a gift for each of her five children and twenty-one grand-children. On the kitchen counter, in Christmas china, ham, coleslaw, rolls, salad, and homemade jellies competed for space. On a sideboard, coconut cake, chocolates, and several pies beckoned.

As we prepared to open gifts, Cleo turned to Pete. "Hon, why don't you read everyone that beautiful card you gave me."

"Oh, Cleo, they don't want to hear that."

"I think they would enjoy it," she said, eyes twinkling. Poor Pete was trapped by a chorus of voices urging him to read. He put on his reading glass-es and cleared his throat.

The card featured a long poem rhapsodizing about a lover: the first meet-ing, the first kiss, the marriage, the many years together. The women started to get teary. Finally, he reached the end, and without pause, read the poet's byline: Andrea Fields.

"Andrea Fields! And just who is she?!" Cleo cried in mock jealousy. The room erupted, and we made Pete read the card again, laughing and hooting and gasping for breath.

The phone rang, and Pete answered, expecting a call from Craig's brothers Chuck and Chris, who were pastors in Oklahoma City. "Yes, this is the Garriott residence." He listened for a few seconds, then exclaimed, "Not on Christmas Day!" He slammed down the receiver.

I was stunned. In twenty years of marriage, I had never heard Pete utter an unkind word, never seen him act rudely.

"Dad!" "Pete!" Craig and his mother and sisters burst out, all talking at once. "Who was that!?"

"Fundraising call," Pete answered. "Some Officer Miller from the Northern District Police Department."

Craig and I exchanged glances. "Dad, we live in the Northern District," Craig said.

Pete's children and his wife all spoke at once, trying to find out what the officer had said. But Craig and I already could connect the dots. Pete was saved from further interrogation when Officer Miller called back.

"Yes? Springfield Avenue? That's my son's house....I see." He looked at Craig, nodded. "He'll be right there. And thank you."

We gathered the children and raced home to find the ninety-year-old etched starburst glass from the front door lying in shards on the foyer floor. A brick lay on the broken glass.

My neighbor Gert Winkler, a pretty woman whose house and car were always immaculately kept, ran over. "I heard the alarm going off and stepped outside to see what was happening," Gert said. "I saw a guy in a green coat with a hood, carrying something white, run off your porch and into the alley. I tell you, what people will do. On Christmas Day." She shook her head.

In my mind, I saw the thief break the glass with the brick, then step into the foyer, hoping to score expensive Christmas gifts under the lighted tree. But what disappointment! Bibles, a few books, a calendar, a sweater or two! By now, the alarm was shrieking, the alarm company was dialing the police, and neighbors were peering out their windows. He had raced into the living room, seen a small portable CD player, grabbed it, and fled.

In a perverse way, we felt lucky. He had not seen Craig's laptop computer, buried under a pile of books in his study, or my guitar. We swept up the glass, and Craig nailed a piece of plywood over the gaping wound of our front door. The foyer, once bright and inviting, felt smaller, dingy, besieged.

Later, we realized another loss. Our cat, Prince, was missing. Perhaps traumatized by the break-in, he disappeared. Several times during the night, we opened the front door, called him, but never saw his fat gray body bounding up the steps. We kept hoping we would return home from work or school to find him squatting near the door. After a week, we lost hope. After two weeks, I gently told the children that perhaps we could get another cat in the spring.

We wondered, again, should we continue to live in Pen Lucy, when even Christmas Day is viewed as open season for burglary? When an alarm system fails to deter thieves desperate to get high? Our next-door neighbor, who had fled the civil war in Liberia, had moved out, fed up with the crime and worried for the safety of his adult daughter. How long would God give us grace to live here, we wondered, to participate in this incarnational ministry, to extend grace in His name?

In January, Lenny's wife called Kevin Good, confessing that her husband had broken into the pastor's house on Christmas Day. She was disgusted with her husband. After further investigation, we decided he was probably responsible for the recent spate of smashed car windows and looted vehicles during worship and evening meetings. We did not press charges.

Eventually, Craig replaced the boarded-up window so our front door no longer suggested an abandoned home. The new safety glass lacked the beauty of the old, but was functional.

In a later sermon, Craig told the congregation that the Christmas break-in brought to life the words of Martin Luther's great hymn, "A Mighty Fortress is Our God." "Let goods and kindred go/ This mortal life also/ The body they may kill/ God's truth abideth still/ His kingdom is forever."

Christmas provides a grace so deep that we were able to shrug our shoulders at burglary and lost goods. Christmas is about trusting in the incarnation, in the eternal, in treasures that moth and rust cannot destroy, that thieves cannot steal.

CHAPTER 29

Calvin, age 3

OF MICE, MEN, AND RATS

THREE months later, I returned home from work and found Prince, collar-less and scrawny, waiting by the front door like a resurrection. Prince was a valued member of the household—and not just for affection. He was a soldier in the losing battle we fought against mice and rats for years—a Rodentia Hundred Years' War. Mice skulked about the kitchen at night, and rats gnawed holes in the garbage cans outside. I disliked sharing a house with rodents, but it seemed unavoidable—-mice can squeeze through a dime-sized opening, and a hundred-year-old house has an infinite number of cracks. Traps, paper, poison—each had its drawbacks. Only the addition of a cat helped.

Our cats—useless against burglars but award-winning against rodents— kept us safe. When Calvin was only five, our previous feline, Rascal, provided a story that had nine lives.

One Mother's Day, as I dressed for church, Calvin yelled from the alley.

"Mom! Rascal's got a rat!"

I hurried to finish dressing. *He knows not to go near the cat when it's got a rat*, I assured myself. Suddenly he screamed in terror. I leaped down the stairs and threw myself outside, calling his name. The cornered rat had attacked Calvin, leaping up and latching its long, narrow teeth onto his finger.

For a few agonizing seconds, it hung on, and Calvin shook his arm wildly to dislodge it. He ran to the house wailing hysterically.

I snatched him in my arms and tried to calm him, stroking his straight blond mop of hair. I dressed the wound and called Craig, who was already at church. "Calvin's been bitten by a rat. I've got to take him to the doctor."

"A rat? Where?" He was incredulous. While rats were plentiful in the neighborhood, they weren't usually aggressive. "How did this happen?"

"Rascal had it cornered in the alley, and Calvin got too close."

"I'll be right there."

Craig marched home, followed by Bill Bolling, who knows something about rats. By this time, Calvin had composed himself. He soberly took his father to the site of The Attack. Somehow, Rascal still guarded the miscreant beast, trapping him under debris in the alley. Craig killed it with the back of a shovel and put the body in an empty gallon jar in case it needed to be tested for rabies.

I called the doctor's office. Because it was a Sunday morning, the physician answering service picked up. "My son was just bitten by a rat," I began.

I heard a gasp, a female voice recoiling. She expected ear infections, maybe, or high fevers. "A rat?! I'll have the doctor call you right away."

A few minutes later, the doctor called. "Rats don't carry rabies, so you don't have to worry about that," he assured me. "But they do carry other diseases, so it would be best if you bring him in for a shot of an antibiotic."

By this time, Calvin had recovered from his initial trauma. He was starting to swagger a bit. The little showman recognized the tremendous mileage he could get out of this story, especially with females.

"I got bit by a rat," he announced to the nurse at the doctor's office. She sucked in her breath, looked back and forth between the little boy with shining blue eyes in the button-down Oxford shirt and me, dressed for church. Calvin zeroed in for the kill.

"Yeah, and he wouldn't let go," he said matter-of-factly. "He just hung on. I had to shake him off like this." He waved his little arm back and forth.

The nurse's eyes widened as if she saw a rat still attached there. "Oh, my goodness," she stuttered. "Where did this happen?"

So Calvin told the story again. He got similar results the next day from his first grade teacher, who gasped and fluttered her hands. He repeated the story with great relish to the principal, Mrs. Potter. For weeks, women at church sidled up to him, having heard the story but unable to stop themselves. "Calvin, is it true? I heard you got bitten by a rat."

Rats in the alley are part of the urban landscape, but I drew the line at rats in the house. One night, we heard loud, large-rodent-gnawing noises coming from Craig's home office. This tiny room, formerly part of the wraparound porch, was crammed with books, papers, old magazines, and a massive, 1940s-era wooden filing cabinet and desk. Emptying the floor to ceiling bookshelves to locate a mouse—or in a worst-case scenario, a rat—would take all night. I brought Craig to investigate.

"Maybe they're underneath the porch," he suggested. "I should go check for holes." He trudged down to the basement and scrounged around for old boards.

For Craig, maintaining our house was a Sisyphean pursuit, a home improvement purgatory. As soon as he fixed a broken door or replaced the wooden porch or patched a hole in the roof, another task demanded his attention. Some repairs lingered undone for months, awaiting Craig's day off; others, like broken toilets or rat gateways, received immediate attention whether his sermon was ready or not. Craig found a hole and plugged it. We hoped that was the end of it.

But one morning a few weeks later, as I shuffled down the stairs for a cup of tea, I nearly stepped on a dead rat. In the past, Prince had killed mice and rats outside and presented them to me, depositing them on the porch, waltzing in the front door, or mouthing his prize as he leaped through a broken window screen. This rat looked half his size.

I could hardly bear to form the thought: Rat. Inside. House. I flirted with denial, grasped at straws. "Could he have killed that outside and brought it in?" It was too cold for open windows, but I checked anyway. All shut. I envisioned beady-eyed, long-tailed rats squirming under the porch floor, slinking into the basement, creeping up the stairs to our living room and kitchen, skulking up the carpeted stairs to the second floor, sniffing around the bedrooms for stray Cheetos and Oreos, skittering around my sleeping children.

I called Craig at church. "I just found a dead rat on the kitchen stairs. Prince must have found a rat in the house."

"A rat? Are you sure?" Craig said in disbelief. "Are you sure it isn't a big mouse?"

"Craig! I've lived in this city long enough to know the difference! It's a rat! The question is, how did it get in the house and..." I paused ominously "are there any more?"

He was silent a moment. "I've got a meeting this morning, but then I'll be home."

I picked up the rat in a blue plastic bag and threw it in the trash can.

The children showed great interest in Prince's prey and were impressed with his prowess. Small knots of neighborhood children paraded over to the garbage can, exclaimed over the carcass, and poked it with a stick.

That this hunting triumph had occurred within the confines of our house didn't bother the children as much as it bothered me. My mind replayed a distant childhood memory: the trauma-inducing slide show of inner city toddlers covered with rat bites, part of the Catholic school's attempt to encourage vocations among the poor. I envisioned Juliana sleeping in my bed in perpetuity to protect her from a similar fate. The older kids, I decided grimly, would have to fend for themselves.

I stated the obvious to Craig. "If one got in, more can come in." I half-hoped he would inform me of some unknown one-rat-per-home rule.

"I know," he sighed. "I just can't figure out how it got in." He trudged down to the basement again to inspect for possible points of entry.

A few nights later, I heard loud gnawing and scratching behind the washer and dryer. I pulled Craig from his home office. He tiptoed over to investigate, and stood quietly, almost reverently, before the washer. Soon the gnawing resumed, but with an added reward. A large rat squeezed out from under the dryer and waddled toward the dining room. Craig jumped back. The rat looked him in the eye and scurried back under the dryer.

Craig ran upstairs and grabbed Santiago DeAngulo, the son of our Colombian friends Stella and Miguel. Santi lived with us during his freshman year at a nearby college.

"We need to barricade the whole first floor," Craig instructed. I felt like I'd stumbled into the White House Situation Room. "Then I'll move the dryer and try to kill it. If it escapes, it won't have anywhere to go."

They hauled old boards from the basement, and arranged furniture and sofa cushions to barricade any possible exit.

"Tuck your pants legs into your socks," he ordered Santi. "That way they can't run up your legs." He had learned this tip from a young man, raised in rural Maryland, who helped empty out a rat-infested abandoned van behind our Greenmount Avenue house. I wore a skirt and sat on the dining room table, but wondered if perhaps thigh-high waders would be wiser.

While Santi held an upraised shovel of death, Craig slowly started to remove the clutter around the dryer. Silence. The rats knew we were coming.

Craig grabbed the dryer and yanked it forward. He peered behind it, and amid the dust bunnies and lost socks, saw that a family of rats had built a nest there.

"Will you look at that," he said grimly. "They climbed up the dryer vent and chewed a hole in the tubing."

"You can fix that, right?" I asked. Just checking.

"I'll have to put some kind of grate over the vent," he mused. He knelt down and put his eye to the vent. Just a few inches away, a beady-eyed rat glared back, ready to re-enter. Craig jumped back with a yell. He ran down the basement steps and emerged with a pair of wire snips and a square of wire grating, which he fastened over the dryer vent hole outside. That's the last we saw of rats in the house.

Some women want their men to demonstrate their love with roses or jewelry. I don't need all that. Just give me a man with a hammer, a pair of wire snips, and his pants tucked into his socks.

CHAPTER 30

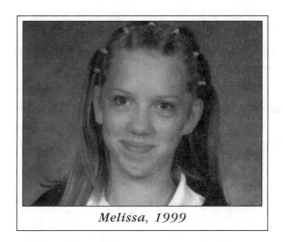

Melissa, 1999

RINGED WITH LOVE

AS Melissa prepared to enter high school, we wondered where to send her. Although she had always been able to make friends easily, middle school had been a difficult transition. In elementary school, she had no difficulty being one of only two white children in the class. But as she moved to a larger, suburban middle school, she found herself pulled between self-segregating racial groups. In the cafeteria, she dreaded having to choose between her elementary school friends (all black) or create new (white) friends with whom she didn't think she had anything in common. She sat with her black friends, but hated the cattiness and labeling from some in both groups. After a tearful seventh grade year, I taught her eighth grade at home. She enjoyed this, and volunteered at BCS under Miss Evie, the kindergarten teacher, but wanted to attend high school.

Becky's high school was not the right fit for Melissa, and neither was the city's magnet high school. We settled on The Catholic High School of Baltimore, an all-girl enclave with a diverse student body drawn from all over the city. While she faced some of the typical opposition—white girls thought she was "acting" black, and some of her black, suburban friends didn't understand her either—Melissa threw herself into activities. She played basketball, field hockey, lacrosse, and ran cross country. Craig cheered her on at nearly

187

every game or meet. She formed friendships with girls from different ethnicities, religions, and backgrounds.

In the fall of her junior year, Melissa announced that her friends were ordering class rings. "How much do they cost?" Craig and I asked.

"About two hundred and fifty dollars. But I'm not getting one. I'm saving for a car."

"We'll buy you a ring when you graduate from college," we assured her. We assumed that a more noteworthy milestone might have more emotional significance. We were wrong. Her father and I, graduates of public high schools, were completely ignorant of the fact that buying a class ring was the highlight of the junior year at schools like Melissa's.

Melissa knew our finances were stretched to afford her tuition. We were also funding Becky's first year in college, Caroline and Calvin's private school tuitions, and Juliana's day care. She didn't ask us to buy her a ring.

A few weeks later, Melissa mentioned class rings again at dinner. "Liz and I and are collecting money to buy a ring for Maggie. She doesn't know about it, but all her friends are chipping in. Her mom can't afford to get her a ring."

"That's so thoughtful," I told her. "I'm proud of you. You girls are really putting the school motto into practice. What is it? About letting your light shine?"

"Yeah, 'Let your light shine.' Maggie is going to be really surprised."

"Are you sure you don't want to buy a ring?" I asked. "Maybe we could go in half with you."

"No, I'm tired of riding those buses. I'm saving my money for a car."

Melissa's school was several miles southeast of us. Caroline's was two miles northwest, and Calvin's ten miles northeast. We couldn't have picked more far-flung schools if we had tried. Melissa had gamely been riding two buses to school. In the winter, Craig drove her to school or walked her to the bus stop and waited with her in the dark. Then he drove Caroline to school. I picked her up as part of my daily, hour-and-a-half before-and-after-work carpool runs. She brought home animated tales of her bus adventures: the drooling sleeper, the off-key singer, the headphone-wearing teens, the mentally ill woman who carried on long conversations with herself. But she told other, more ominous stories as well: a fistfight between two boys, the bus stop shooting, and how other riders had helped her evade the unwanted attention of an aggressive young man. The sooner she could get a car, the better.

Melissa's junior year whirled by, a jumble of classes, sports, and other activities. In early spring, with money squirreled away from summer jobs and babysitting, Melissa and Craig selected her first car, a twelve-year-old maroon

Toyota. She no longer had to take two buses, or rely on her parents for transportation. She had taken another leap towards independence.

At a spring back-to-school night, after discussing Melissa's progress with her teachers, I brought up a question that had been surfacing like an air bubble, a nagging feeling that I had badly misjudged something. I buttonholed Mr. Owens, a tall, African American who taught history and had coached Melissa through several basketball seasons.

"I've been wondering about the Ring Liturgy next week," I began. "Do most of the girls get rings?"

"Oh, *all* of the girls get rings."

I was crestfallen. It was too late for me to fix this.

"I had no idea it was such a big deal here," I stammered. "Our salaries are modest, and with an older sister in college, and tuition or daycare for five kids, money is tight." I squirmed. "If I had known she was the only one not buying one, we would have found the money somewhere."

"I understand," Mr. Owens nodded. "But Melissa's getting a ring. Her friends went around collecting for it. I put in some money, too."

I was deeply humbled. He was a teacher, not a business tycoon. "Please, you must let me reimburse you," I said, reaching for my purse.

"No," he shook his head. "You must accept the gift in the spirit in which it is given. Melissa is a great kid. I'm happy to do it." He reminded me that the ring was to be kept secret from Melissa.

At the Ring Liturgy, Melissa sat with her class. The girls listened for their names, walked across the stage, received a rose from the class advisor and a handshake from the principal, and took their coveted class rings. She clapped and cheered as each girl, including her friend Maggie, received a ring.

When her name was called, Melissa bounded onto the stage, accepted her rose, and breezed by the advisor, who held a small box in her outstretched hand. Thinking the teacher had made a mistake, Melissa waved it away. I could see her mouthing the words, "I didn't get a ring."

But as Melissa walked off the stage, her class erupted. The ceremony screeched to a halt, and the principal, befuddled, pivoted to see what was happening. A sea of girls called out to Melissa. "It's your ring! Go back! We got you a ring!"

Melissa stopped, stunned, tears springing to her eyes. She walked back across the stage and took the ring to the applause and cheering of her friends. "It was overwhelming," she said later. "I finally felt accepted."

The girls had "Let Their Light Shine" in a way that Melissa and her family never forgot. Mark Twain understood that sharing our joys doubles them. "Grief can take care of itself," he wrote, "but to get the full value of a joy you must have somebody to divide it with."

Melissa could have put off saving for a car to buy a class ring. Craig and I could have tightened our belts a little more, and funded it. But how much more beauty and value her silver ring bears because of the sacrifice and love of her peers.

CHAPTER 31

An eviction on Greenmount Ave.

EVICTING EVITA

TO finance the children's education, we depended on the rental income from our Greenmount Avenue house. Craig continued to do all the skilled repairs, and the girls, Calvin, and I cleaned and painted between tenants. Sometimes my screening of potential tenants was motivated more by mercy than good judgment and I had to evict a tenant.

We evicted Evita Jones. She had not paid rent for several months, and we knew she was selling drugs and sex out of the apartment. Cars drove up, honked, and she ran outside for a moment. Callers knocked at her door at all hours. Occasionally, referrals knocked at the wrong door and disturbed the other tenants. What is more, every time I knocked at her door she was either naked or nearly so, and some man or other was just leaving.

Other tenants complained of her activities. When I confronted her about her chronically late rent and asked if she had a drug problem, she shook her head as if I were an over-imaginative child whose fantasies should not be indulged.

"I don't use drugs," she said with a soft chuckle.

"Then how do you explain the steady stream of callers, some of whom don't know your name, or which apartment you live in?" I probed.

She shrugged. "I just have a lot of friends."

We promised to work with her if she would get into a treatment program, but she repeatedly denied any problem.

I had unwittingly rented to drug-abusing tenants before, and watched their lives flame and collapse like spent rockets: a medical school student, a laborer, even a pharmacist left a trail of unpaid bills, trashed apartments, and telltale empty vials and needles.

Baltimore—also known as Charm City—has over 60,000 addicts. It has the highest heroin rate ever found among arrestees in any U.S. city. It also faces one of the nation's most severe crack problems as well. Drug and alcohol abuse are linked to three quarters of the city's crimes, and only Washington, D.C., has a higher murder rate. The city has one of the highest per capita syphilis rates in the world, fallout from addiction-driven prostitution. Soon these figures would have another face for me.

Evita burrowed into a corner of my heart, dragging with her seemingly intractable problems. She provided a face to impersonal nouns: justice, prostitution, poverty, personal responsibility, addiction. In my dealings with her, I struggled again and again with one question: How do I show her God's grace in this situation?

Evita had answered my For Rent ad one afternoon, wearing her brown McDonalds uniform, her nametag pinned above her breast.

"I really, really like this apartment," she effused, boring into me with enormous, almond-shaped dark eyes. She said she was in her thirties, but she looked younger. Two dark braids framed her delicate face. She had long legs and a slender, almost boyish figure.

She circled the rooms slowly, telling me where each piece of her furniture would go. She stroked three-year-old Juliana's hair and pulled a Happy Meal toy from her uniform pocket. Juliana let go of my hand to take the toy.

"How long have you been working at McDonalds?" I asked.

"A few months," she said. "But I'm getting a promotion next week to shift manager." She pulled a crumpled pay stub from her purse and handed it to me. I saw from her heartbreakingly low salary that she could—if she was frugal, had no car or dependents, no loser boyfriend drinking away her cash, no secret addiction—afford this modest apartment.

"Have you ever rented an apartment before? Do you have any rental references?" Something about Evita made me want to overlook her lackluster work history.

"No," she said. "I live with my sister. The lease is in her name. And now her boyfriend moved in, and he's dealing drugs, and…" her voice trailed off. "I just have to get out of there."

I nodded.

"I really want a place of my own, just for me. No boyfriends. No kids. I have a son, but he's grown, lives on his own."

Against my better judgment—wisdom hard-earned from over twenty years of urban tenants— I waived my requirement that prospective tenants have at least a one-year stable job history. I also waived my requirement that tenants show a one-year rental history. I wanted to help her. Also, I was exhausted: problems at work, an active preschooler, four teenagers, church activities, and the stress of the neighborhood were taking their toll. I was beginning to unravel, but didn't know it yet. I just wanted to rent the apartment.

Problems arose within a month. She didn't have the full month's rent. She would pay the rest from her next paycheck in two weeks, she said. Other tenants complained. "Your new tenant? Evita? She has a lot of visitors. A whole lot."

"What do you mean?" I asked.

"People knocking on the door all the time. Maybe ten, fifteen times a day. Even in the middle of the night." The police call this "excessive foot traffic" and consider it a sign of drug dealing or prostitution.

One night, the tenants in the adjoining apartment heard a fierce commotion of brawling, furniture breaking, and Evita screaming. "Help! He's trying to kill me!"

Brad Beier, our pastoral intern who had rented the apartment next door, grabbed a hammer and ran into Evita's apartment. His wife Shannon called the police, then prayed.

Brad entered a chaotic scene. Sonny, one of Evita's boyfriends, held her in a headlock while he rummaged through her kitchen drawers for a knife. Evita flailed against him, trying to pummel him with her small fists, but her blows grazed off his massive frame. The apartment was a shambles. The lock on the door had been kicked open, and a wooden chair lay splintered on the floor.

Sonny's muscles bulged from years of manual labor. Brad, a slender, well-built runner in his mid-twenties, raised the hammer. "Let her go," he demanded. "I don't want to have to hurt you." Another tenant, roused by the noise, appeared behind Brad armed with a huge flashlight.

"Let her go," Brad repeated. "The police are on their way." He could hear Evita choking. Sonny eyed the two men for a tense minute. Finally, he pushed Evita to the floor in disgust.

The police arrived and arrested him for aggravated battery. A week later, Shannon told me that he was out on bail. "He's been staying with her for almost a week." She shook her head. "I've worked with abused women before, but I'll never understand it."

Shannon and Brad stopped by Evita's apartment often to visit. One evening, shortly after the attack, Evita pressed a twenty-dollar bill into Brad's hand. "For you," she said. Brad looked at the money, puzzled.

"Take it," she urged. "I think he was really going to kill me."

The police pursued the battery charge and subpoenaed Brad and Evita. She testified against Sonny in court—a fact that, according to Brad, seemed to surprise him. Shortly thereafter, the police showed up at Evita's door and arrested her on drug-related charges. Evita complained that Sonny had fabricated charges against her. This is inner city justice: you bust me, and I'll bust you.

After a brief stay in jail, Evita got out on bail. Brad and Shannon continued to spend time with her, having long discussions about life and faith, praying with and for her. Sometimes, she lingered when she dropped off a rent check, and we sat on my front steps and talked. Over and over, she expressed appreciation for the intervention that saved her life. "Brad and Shannon," Evita sighed. "I've never met anyone like them. I love Brad and Shannon."

At times it seemed like we were breaking through. When the subject came up, she agreed that drugs were a trap. But she still maintained that she didn't use, didn't sell. Evita agreed to come to church, but never answered the door when Shannon knocked on Sunday mornings. And the "excessive foot traffic" continued.

Evita fell farther behind in her rent, and didn't return my phone calls. When I stopped by McDonalds to see her, I learned she had been fired. After losing this last vestige of a normal life—legal, gainful employment—she stopped making any payments. I reluctantly began the tedious process of filing for past-due rent and eventual eviction.

To evict a tenant requires at least three trips downtown to rent court: first to file a failure to pay rent notice; a trip a week later to wait several hours for the judge to hear the case; and a third trip three days later to file a warrant of restitution. Then several days later, the landlord calls the sheriff to schedule an eviction. The sheriff arrives a week later to serve papers and supervise as the landlord carries the tenant's possessions to the street. The whole process takes over a month. I had to take time off from my job for every trip, and fight rush hour traffic. The only available parking was around the corner in Baltimore's seedy red-light district, The Block. The tenant could avoid eviction by coming up with the money at any time—even at the eleventh hour, when the sheriff arrived to oversee the eviction. Only after the fourth filing could the landlord refuse to accept the money and evict a tenant. I repeated this process three times, filing for past due rents in successive months because Evita would eventually pay some of the money.

Because the sheriff's office did not notify tenants of their eviction date, I stopped by the apartment to tell Evita. "Please find someone to help you move out by then," I said. "You can move in with your sister or a friend for a while." She just looked at me, her expression blank.

The morning of the eviction, I woke exhausted from a series of disjointed dreams: I trudged through a hot, steamy swamp. Several men surrounded me, trying to kill me. I had an old shotgun I kept cocking and firing to no avail.

I wanted Evita out. She needed a treatment program, not free housing. I was uncomfortable with my new status as crack house landlady. Shannon's safety concerned me as well. Brad was frequently out at evening meetings, and men sometimes knocked on their door late at night, looking for Evita.

At 8:15, I appeared in rent court. During this lengthy process, another month had passed, and I wanted to file for additional overdue rent in case Evita paid me. I had also called the police to learn what legal options I had to evict a drug-dealing tenant.

"One of my tenants is dealing drugs out of my apartment house on Greenmount Avenue," I began. The policeman snorted. "Greenmount Avenue? Well, they're all— " he opined, but thought better of it. "You can call back later and talk to the narc unit," he said. "If enough complaints are made, we'll investigate."

At 10:30 a.m., Craig and I waited outside the apartment in the stifling ninety-degree heat for the sheriff. We prayed for Evita's spiritual renewal, for her release from drug addition. I could hear the air conditioner humming in her apartment. Across the street, well-dressed men and women, black and white, began to gather in front of a newly renovated house. A banner stretched across the porch, proclaiming the celebration of a new Habitat for Humanity home. I sighed.

The sheriff arrived, a stocky African American wearing a black uniform with important flashes of silver: badges, nametag, cuffs, walkie-talkie.

"Are you...Garrett?" he asked, looking at his papers.

"Yes. Garriott."

He jerked his head toward Evita's door. "This the eviction?"

I nodded. I stood behind him, not wanting to face her, not wanting to be there. He rapped firmly on the door. "Baltimore City Sheriff. Open up."

Evita opened the door in a tiny, spaghetti-strap t-shirt and underwear.

"Evita Jones? Eviction papers." He thrust them toward her, then began filling out a form on his clipboard.

Evita drew back. "Oh, I went to rent court this morning and got an extension," she claimed.

"No," I stepped forward. "I was in rent court this morning and you weren't there."

"Do you have a receipt?" he asked.

She didn't. The sheriff glanced briefly at Evita's skimpy attire but seemed unfazed.

"Get dressed and get your stuff out," he said. He thrust an eviction form at me. "Sign here." I scrawled my signature across the yellow paper.

We followed the sheriff into Evita's living room.

"You'll have to put all this on the street," he said.

"There's some green trash bags under the sink," Evita called from the bedroom. She acted like we were packing for a picnic. I heard her opening and closing drawers. Craig and I slowly began to put CDs, knickknacks, and old magazines into a bag.

"Can we put her things on the porch rather than the street?" I asked the sheriff. I wanted to save Evita's worldly goods from the scavengers who would descend on the pile like feral cats picking through fish bones.

"Only on the street," he replied. "A city truck will come and pick it up later." The city stores evictees' possessions for up to ten days—if the tenant arranges this in advance, and if the city has space in its warehouse. Otherwise, a trash truck devours the whole pile—clothes, furniture, old photo albums, dishes. All gone.

The sheriff turned to leave.

"That's it?" I asked. "You're leaving?" I worried about being left with an unhappy evictee; the potential for violence always lurks just under the surface like a crocodile.

"I have other evictions to process." He read my unease. "You'll be alright. Any trouble, just call the police." I watched his retreating form. Numbly, I continued to fill trash bags.

I turned to Evita. "Don't you have anyone who can pick up your stuff?"

"Maybe. Can you do me a favor? Can I use your cell phone?"

I retrieved it from my car, where I had locked it in the trunk.

"Hey," she spoke quietly into the phone. "It's me. Look, I need you to come pick up my stuff. At the apartment." She paused, then began to argue. "Forget it." She hung up.

"Can I make one more call?" she pleaded. I nodded. The second conversation was similar to the first; come get me, some arguing, but finally she hung up.

"He's coming," she said. I wonder who "he" was. Sonny, perhaps? Or her son?

Evita piled up several bags from the bedroom and asked if we could put them in the back of the house. I agreed. In the kitchen, Craig dumped pots, silverware, and dishes into Hefty bags. He unscrewed the legs of her dining room table, which was too wide to fit through the narrow apartment door.

I carefully wrapped a milk-white pitcher and washbasin in towels and put it in a large trunk. I pointed it out to Evita. "Your pitcher's in here. You don't want to break that. It's very pretty." She glanced at it, then returned to the bedroom. She emerged a moment later.

"I have to go down the street for a minute," Evita said. She offered no explanation.

I was stunned. What could be more important than safeguarding her possessions? Craig and I kept packing, tugging the heavy bags to the curb, watching the pile spread on the street like an ugly stain. Bags flopped over, spilling shirts and blue jeans onto the dirty pavement.

Evita was especially proud of her large china cabinet. She had shown it to me during an earlier visit, flipping its little light on and off to showcase pretty but unmatched dishes. As we hauled furniture to the street, it quickly became apparent that I was not strong enough to help Craig carry this heavy piece down several stairs.

A truck stopped in front of the house, and two men got out to eye the growing pile. I asked if they would help us put a few heavy items on the street and offered a price. They carried Evita's furniture to the street and lingered a moment. I turned back to the house for another load, and when I emerged a minute later, they were gone.

I paused to catch my breath, and looked across Greenmount Avenue. At the Habitat house, a photographer snapped photos and people smiled and hugged and shook hands. This added to our humiliation: here we were, throwing a woman out on the street, while some fine Christians across the street helped someone move into a lovely, renovated home. Several Habitat employees worshipped at Faith. I hoped no one recognized us.

Craig appeared beside me, hauling several bags. "Oh, great," he moaned. "Great timing for the white pastor to be evicting the black tenant." He shook his head. In Baltimore's racially charged, hyper-segregated neighborhoods, it is easy to feel responsible for all the sins of the white race.

"You know we're doing the right thing," I said.

He shrugged.

Evita didn't return that morning, but her nineteen-year-old son and several of his friends appeared. They burst into the apartment, swarming like wasps. Craig was repairing a broken faucet in the bathroom, so her son zeroed in on me. "Where's my muthah's air conditioner and TV?" he demanded loudly. The two men with him crossed their arms on their chests and muttered angrily.

I felt momentarily flustered. "Uh… outside, with Evita's other stuff."

"They not there! What you do with them?"

"I put them outside! Look around the apartment—you can see they're not here. I put them out."

The men stalked into the bedroom, and saw only a few piles of trash in the empty room. I heard them talking under their breath. It dawned on me that the guys in the truck had helped themselves to Evita's choicest possessions when my back was turned.

Evita's son returned to the living room and stood two feet from my face, yelling. "You sold my muthah's TV and air conditioner to them guys in the truck. That's not right! Cain't be selling my muthah's stuff to them guys."

"No, I didn't." I replied evenly. I lapsed into street lingo. "I paid them cash money to help move her stuff!"

Craig sensed this could quickly escalate, and stepped outside to call the police on his cell phone. Evita's son continued to berate me. "Damn! You sold my muthah's TV!"

"I did not. Look, it's not my job to guard your mother's stuff," I said as calmly as I could manage. "I warned her that today was the eviction. Where is she? Why isn't she watching her own stuff?"

He ignored my question. "That don't be right, selling my muthah's stuff like that!" With loud curses, he continued to vent his anger at me. I thought he might hit me. It would be nothing for him to exact a little vengeance, a little blood. Just get it over with, I thought. Finally, I realized my listening was not helping. "You'll have to leave now."

I pivoted and returned to sweeping the floor. He blustered but stormed out of the apartment, his buddies following.

We found some of Evita's crack vials, both full and empty. When we moved her bed, we also found a pornographic magazine, a monstrous butcher knife, and a hammer. What is it like, I wondered, to have sex with strangers for money, and have to keep a knife at the ready? Drugs had not only robbed her of her job and home, but of her personhood. She was just naked flesh, a means to an end. Young black men on foot, middle-aged white men in sedans and minivans, abusive lover-father figures, all had beaten a path to her door. I found it immensely sad.

While Craig changed the locks, I took stock of damages to the apartment: a broken window, cigarette burns in the floor, holes in the walls. Outside, Evita's son and his friends guarded the pile of furniture and trash bags in the blistering heat. Their angry outbursts floated through the open window. They could easily climb through a window and reenter the apartment, I thought. There were four of them, just two of us.

Craig worked efficiently, but it seemed to take an hour. I felt exhausted and faint from the heat, hunger, and thirst. I wished the house had a back driveway so I wouldn't have to drive by those angry men.

After finishing at the apartment, I went to my office a few blocks away. But I was too exhausted to work, so I left an hour later. Another precious vacation day gone, I thought. On my way home, I circled past the apartment and saw Evita and her son loading some of her possessions on the back of a truck.

The next morning, on my way to work, I returned to sweep up the detritus of eviction that cluttered the curb and shamed my property. Scavengers had ripped open every remaining bag and box, spilling clothes, papers, and household goods all over the street. Broken eggs and oil from her fridge had soaked into everything. I fingered the pieces of Evita's milk-white pitcher before throwing them into my trash bags.

Why, I wondered, had she let it get to this point? Why—even in the midst of her brain-addling cocaine addiction—hadn't she arranged for the truck to arrive the day before, and save herself from the shame and her possessions from the scavengers? Did she hope that she would continue to be able to lie and charm her way into my gullible good graces? Or was everything—jobs, possessions, relationships—subservient to this relentless, fiendish thrill and thrall of cocaine?

CHAPTER 32

Jonathan, 2005

BOYS IN THE 'HOOD
AND THE DREAM DEFERRED

MOST of the girls of Pen Lucy endure and prevail; they graduate from high school, get jobs, and slowly scratch their way up the socioeconomic ladder. They go to school at night to earn certificates or even degrees. They pick up second jobs and buy used cars. Often, they raise babies alone or with the help of their families.

But the boys. The boys haunt me.

The boys, even those with strong fathers at home who try to guide and warn them, often fare poorly. Ten years after moving into Pen Lucy, twenty years after moving into the city, my daughters were halfway through college but many of the boys they had played with as children were dead or in jail, AWOL or on probation, shot or drowned or slow and glassy-eyed from smoking weed. They were just getting out of juvenile hall and trying to find a job. They had gold on their teeth and some change in their pockets, but no visible source of income. They had fathered children whom they might or might not see regularly.

They had been children of promise with possibilities for success and achievement. But so many systems had failed them: fathers neglected them;

schools didn't educate them; the church didn't do enough to help them navigate the perilous journey from boyhood to manhood. The culture polluted them with images of rappers and thuggery, fast money and fast women. They endlessly pushed against invisible barriers, fighting uphill in a white world, a stereotyped world where black urban male equals danger and drugs and failure. The late rapper Tupac Shakur, who lived in Baltimore during his teen years, captured this stark reality in his songs and poetry. Some afternoons, Tupac hung out in Faith's basement while his friend cleaned our day care center. He even performed a song at one of our Community Chill outreach events.

Pen Lucy, like many other urban neighborhoods, offers an array of bad choices. Dealing, drinking, and getting high promise instant gratification. Negative role models shout from drug corners, luring lonely, insecure, or unemployed boys with quick cash and brotherhood. The pool of industries ready to absorb able-bodied but undereducated men continues to shrink in cities like Baltimore.

Positive role models exist though, with less Technicolor hue: men who quietly labor day after day at service jobs or trades or in offices; men who love their wives and invest in their children; men who shovel the sidewalks of their elderly neighbors; men who stand up to the drug dealers. Men of quiet faithfulness, like my neighbor, a long-time member of Faith.

No Small Thing

It is no small thing
to decide every morning
to walk past the men on the corner
who call to you,
remembering that their vials can
in an instant, send you where
there is no more pain, or sorrow, or weeping.

It is no small thing
that when your own son was grown
you seated three nephews at your table
hoping they might not follow their parents
into that white-powder whirlwind,
knowing they would chafe at your bridle,
knowing it might already be too late.
It is no small thing
Not to give up.

It is no small thing
to have to hide your wallet in your own home.

It is no small thing
that you welcomed your brother
when other doors were shut
against his disease;
no small thing
to grieve with him over wasted years
to change his sheets
guide his slow shuffle
and finally, pay the mortician.

It is no small thing
to lie down every night
with the same woman
for twenty years.

It is no small thing.

Calling African American young men in the United States an "at risk" population understates the severity of the crisis. They have a shorter life span because of disease and homicide, and are eight times more likely to be victims of violent crime than their white peers. The unemployment rate for African American males is twice as high as that of white males.

African American youths with no prior offenses are six times more likely to be imprisoned than similar white youth, and are incarcerated for longer periods for the same offenses. Nearly one quarter of black men in their twenties are in the U.S. justice system.

Researchers note that African American males experience massive failure and alienation from America's schools. They are more likely to be placed in special education classes, are suspended from school more frequently and for longer periods of time than other ethnic/gender groups, and drop out of high school at significantly higher rates. They face lowered expectations and negative attitudes from educators.

Not surprisingly, research studies have found high levels of untreated depression in urban, high-minority, low-income areas. Living in a world of racial injustice exacts a psychic toll, draining energy and hope. Beating back despair is exhausting. Perhaps Langston Hughes states it best in his poem, "Harlem," which asks if a dream deferred dries up "like a raisin in the sun? Or fester like a sore—and then run?/...Maybe it just sags/like a heavy load./Or does it explode?"

I see this deferred dream exploding in young men around me, men I know by name.

A young man whom we had not seen in several years stopped by to see Melissa. I remembered him as a sweet child stuck with a derogatory nickname, a boy who made cookies in my kitchen. A boy who wanted to play professional basketball, but whose body betrayed him with average height, average skills. I had written a poem about him.

For Willie, With Love

The first time I met Willie
he hit my four-year-old son.
My boy ran into my arms,
blood tracking down his face.
Willie skulked away.

Everyone calls him Pig
but I make my children call him Willie,
trying to wrap some dignity
around his cringing frame.
He speaks softly, not expecting
to be heard. He has already
put boards over his windows,
wise to hurricanes.

He lives with neither parent;
there is a grandmother,
although I have never met her.

Willie often comes to play,
to borrow our battered bikes
or skates or basketball.

My house is Disneyland,
an orgy of toys and children,
and a real king, too.

We made cookies yesterday.
"Let me put the powder in,"
he asked, stirring wildly.
Carefully, he slipped his treasures
into his torn parka.

Willie, hold out your hands;
I will fill them so you have something
before you realize school is futile
and your teachers, like grandma, are tired;
before the mirage of a basketball scholarship
evaporates, leaving sand in your teeth;
before you believe you are only Pig
but crack makes you a god.

Melissa and Willie talked on the front porch and then moved into the kitchen for a soda. He had recently graduated from the Job Corps, a government training program for adolescents who dropped out of high school, have gotten into trouble with the law, or want further vocational training. He admitted he had made some bad choices, but said that was behind him. He hoped to find a job soon.

Willie appeared dazzled by Melissa. The cute, friendly preadolescent had become a stunning young woman, her blonde hair and vibrant blue eyes set off by a v-neck black t-shirt and jeans. She had street smarts but was unhardened, unspoiled.

When Craig came home, he saw a grown man in baggy pants in our kitchen, talking animatedly with his daughter. He pulled me aside. "Who is that?"

"Oh, that's Willie. Remember him?"

"Willie?" He struggled to reconcile the prepubescent twelve-year-old from the past with the eighteen-year-old in the kitchen. "Yes. What does he want?" He sounded uncharacteristically on edge. Perhaps, as a man, he saw something I didn't.

"He's visiting the old neighborhood, I guess. They're just talking."

"Where has he been? What's he up to now?"

"Well," I sighed, "he just got out of the Job Corps and he's looking for a job."

Craig rolled his eyes. This was familiar territory. "Well, I don't want him sitting there all day," he said firmly.

I felt like I was talking to Rip Van Winkle, who had suddenly awakened to the fact that he presides over a house full of beautiful daughters. "Craig, if you didn't want your daughter hanging out with unemployed high school dropouts, we shouldn't have moved here. Don't worry about it. She's not dumb."

Our church youth group was composed primarily of boys from the neighborhood, who struggled to navigate adolescence against the backdrop of failing schools, street violence, and hard-pressed families. These were the boys that my daughters hung out with at youth group, that they developed crushes on, that they tried to fit in with although their skin betrayed them.

Dion was caught fencing CDs stolen from another camper on a multi-church youth trip. This episode brought shame on the heads of our entire city group, but somehow, within a day the blame slid away from Dion and onto the victim and his youth group—kids from a white, suburban church. The white kids, locked into their own peer groups, were uncomfortable with urban kids who had different social codes, different lingo, different life experiences, different music. After the fencing incident, they pulled away completely. The urban kids, faced with white indifference or obliviousness, slapped in the face by white affluence, rejected because of the actions of one member, circled the wagons.

"They look at us funny," Becky complained, "like we're all guilty." This solidified support in our group for Dion, who morphed, somehow, into the victim. The theft and resulting estrangement became a racial incident, not a moral one. One of the volunteer youth leaders, who was angry and wounded over past racial injuries, reinforced damaging stereotypes: white suburbanites are racist.

When pressed, Becky admitted Dion's theft was wrong. But like many teens, she refused to condemn her friends' actions—especially to her parents. It was easier to believe that all white, suburban people are racist.

A year later, Becky asked Dion to take her to her semi-formal high school dance. My mother-alarm sounded: I remembered the fencing incident.

They were not romantically interested in each other, but he agreed to take her. With money earned mowing lawns and cleaning houses in Guilford, Becky bought a dress and shoes. She spent hours chatting with girlfriends about what they would wear, who would go, who would bring whom. But late in the afternoon of the dance, Dion called. "I'll meet you there," he said. "I have to go somewhere with my mom. Just go without me and I'll meet you there."

Dion never showed up. He didn't have the courage to say he wouldn't come. He did not call to apologize. He avoided, denied, deceived.

Becky was hurt, but not intimidated. She refused to write off the relationship. Sunday at church, she backed him into a corner and confronted him. He apologized.

I was less forgiving. I pictured my daughter desperately trying to fit in with her schoolmates, the daughters of lawyers and investment bankers, girls whose daddies bought them new Acuras for their birthdays. I saw Becky alone, waiting, stalling, putting the best face on things, explaining that her date was late, standing solitary and apart in her new dress and pinching Payless high heels while her friends danced with boys from prestigious Gilman School and Boy's Latin.

At some point, Dion made a decision to follow Christ. Off and on, he attended Bible study with Thurman Williams, our youth minister. But there were troubling indications that perhaps his faith commitment was overshadowed by other desires. Two years later, while swimming in a pool in Ocean City, he drowned. We heard he had been drinking. Still, we wondered: Did the six-foot-five inch Dion, a non-swimmer, wander into water over his head? Was he alone? Or did no one with him understand he was in trouble?

So Becky and Melissa attended another funeral. They kept the bulletin in their drawers, a memento of youth beside the movie stubs, prom flyers, the flowery friendship cards girls send each other, and the bulletins from other funerals of other friends.

I remembered Carl, a teenager two doors down from us. Every day, from mid-morning until late at night, he waited on his porch for business. Cars drove up, and fast as soda shook from a can, Carl raced curbside. Sometimes he passed drugs through a hole in the front basement window; more often, he deftly touched hands with a customer, and the exchange was complete. To protect his business—or perhaps mark his territory—he shot out the streetlights on our block and our neighbor's porch light and car windows. We found his BB pellets on our porch steps, and crack vials on the sidewalk.

I greeted Carl nearly every day but confess I didn't say much. I wanted to do more. I made excuses: I am powerless because I am a woman, I'm irrelevant because I'm white, I don't know what to say. He declined invitations to youth group activities. He had played basketball with Becky and Melissa in our back-yard. But once he started dealing, he rarely left his post. The only time he came to play ball, he wore a beeper and left as soon as it went off. Violence hung over his head like an unpaid bill. Rival dealers beat one of his friends, sending him to the hospital. The threat of the police hovered nearby. Finally, the narc unit caught up with him.

My neighbor, who shared a row house wall with Carl and had no desire to live next to an armed drug dealer, told us of Carl's arrest. It was an answer to his prayers, he said. But it was not an answer to my prayers. I had been pray-ing for a spiritual change in Carl. Becky and Melissa, who heard of Carl's arrest but did not tell me, struggled with it, realizing that prison or juvenile hall would only harden him.

"He knew what he was doing," I argued. I laid out a litany of Carl's crimes.

"I know," Becky said sadly. "I just wish he hadn't gotten into that. I wish it was like the old days. When he used to come around and play basketball."

In Carl's defense, I pointed out that the deck was stacked against him: no father at home, his mother drank, he dropped out of school. I reminded Becky that we were here and the church was here to help young men like Carl. Still, she mourned. And I wished I had been bolder, done more than just invite him to church and to play basketball.

Andy was shot at point-blank range. His execution didn't even make it into the *Baltimore Sun*. To many, he was a statistic, one of over three hundred Baltimoreans killed by violence every year, another twenty-something unem-ployed black male with a scrappy rap sheet, a casualty of the profession employing legions from his demographic group. But to us, he was a neighbor. To my daughters, he was a friend. To others he was son, brother, cousin, lover, father.

We heard the shots and paused, looking up from housework and home-work and storybooks. They were loud and close, from a big gun. But we did not investigate, did not even call the police. We heard shots frequently and assumed someone from the next block would call. We would not know until the girls carried home word from the street that we had heard Andy's execution. His murder was never solved.

Andy's home life had disintegrated a few years earlier. His father was long gone, and his single mother began using drugs. Their food and rent money disappeared. Andy began hanging out on the corner with older youths. Perhaps his involvement was minor at first: watching someone's drug stash, making small deliveries. Aunts stepped in and took in his six-year-old sister, but Andy was already his own man, not to be bridled by female relatives. After some trouble, he was sent to stay with a cousin down South. He returned within a year, back to the 'hood and the tribe and the business.

Andy attended our church youth group for a while, but the streets pulled him back. Even after rival dealers beat him badly enough to put him in the hospital, he returned to the business. He fathered a child, a daughter who will never remember him, who will face forms requesting her father's name all her life, but will have to leave these blank or write "deceased."

Craig and I visited the storefront funeral home in east Baltimore to see Andy laid out in a new denim jacket. We arrived just before closing time, and the two women overseeing the place reluctantly let us in, eying the white interlopers coldly. We prayed by the coffin for a few minutes, and when we left, they locked the door behind us, turned off the lights, and exited. My heart clutched to think of Andy's body lying there, alone and cold and empty.

That night, I fingered a photograph of ten-year-old Andy taken the summer we moved in. I saw a handsome boy in a button-down shirt holding a small garden snake up to the camera, his face intent, intelligent, and sober. While many children mimicked rap stars in front of a camera, he did not mug; he only displayed his treasure, like a future biologist.

Andy's death imprinted a fatalism in his friends, who had already buried other members of the tribe. They wore t-shirts emblazoned with R.I.P. and his name, or a long, black-and-red beaded necklace as a gang insignia of sorts. They became walking memorials, embracing his death even as it contributed to their own.

I saw deadness in their eyes, watched them slam doors of opportunity shut, watched them decide that rising above the neighborhood was betrayal, an abandonment of all the brothers and homies, both fallen and living. Even my own children, more resourced and more resilient, bore a scar. They had hunted snakes and made backyard forts with Andy before the barriers became too high to cross. Becky, Melissa, and Craig attended the funeral in a neighborhood church packed with wailing mourners. They carried home the bulletin, a lovingly crafted final tribute to a short life.

Jonathan and Jay were sons of an activist father and a devout mother. When the boys were young, the parents separated. In early adolescence, they moved in with their father for the male guidance needed in the final lap of the parenting marathon. Jonathan, a slender high schooler with large, thoughtful eyes, appeared on our doorstep after a record two-foot snowfall, swathed in a heavy jacket and hat. "My dad is trying to get residents to come help shovel the street so people can get their cars out," he announced.

As we shouldered shovels and joined them, a friendship began. Jonathan and Jay were hard workers, respectful, and polite. They got involved in our youth group and began attending church. For the next four or five years, Jonathan spent countless hours at our house and at our dinner table. The urban community is rich with kinship unrelated by blood; he became godbrother to Becky and Melissa, godson to me. With some people, I could never forget that I was white. But with Jonathan, we could cross the barrier of race and background.

Jonathan's father, Bill, organized boycotts and marches and wrote a newsletter decrying racism and urging the black community to band together. He attended City Council meetings and demanded the police department publicly burn confiscated drugs, which he feared were cycled back into the community by crooked cops. He tried to interest his sons in his political causes, but they moved into their own orbits.

Through his extensive contacts, Bill found after school jobs for his sons. Both boys graduated from high school, a notable achievement in a city where more than half who enter ninth grade fail to earn a diploma. To pay for his graduation expenses, Jonathan borrowed three hundred dollars from Craig. Although Craig helped him budget a payment schedule allowing several months to repay the loan, Jonathan paid back every penny within weeks. On graduation day, Jonathan knocked on our door in his cap and gown, beaming, holding his diploma. I snapped photos.

The path after graduation was rockier. One afternoon, as we sat in our backyard, I reopened a conversation we had had before, tried to draw him out, hear his plans.

"There's no way I have the money for college. And my grades aren't good enough for scholarships," he lamented. The big adventure—college, dorm life, classes devoted to developing your gifts—was unfolding without him.

"But you can still go to college," I urged him. "You can go to the community college part time, pursue your dream of becoming a graphic artist."

Jonathan just shrugged.

"You're very talented. You should do something with that gift." I tried to connect him with a graphic artist acquaintance, but he didn't follow through. He wasn't ready, and I couldn't force him.

"My dad wants us to join the military, but I don't really want to."

"But that could work for you," I said. "You can get training and money for college." While Bill was not enamored of the armed services, he believed they offered the best hope for his sons' advancement. He took them to a recruiter. Jay's high test scores merited special attention, but he failed his drug test. He never got around to retaking it. Jonathan joined the Navy and spent weeks in basic training.

When he returned home on his first furlough several months later, all traces of the boy had disappeared. Taller and broader, his once-slender frame now bulged with hard-won muscles. He wore his dress uniform to church on Sunday, impressing the women no end. He brought over a video of his graduation ceremony from the Great Lakes Training Academy, and we watched it together.

He shipped out on a tour of duty to the Middle East on the U.S.S. Enterprise, and sent postcards from exotic locales. He came home to visit, bringing two fellow sailors, one African American, one Caucasian. He bought a car. We were immensely proud.

But back in Baltimore, his brother was falling apart. Deeply wounded by Andy's death, Jay became more entrenched in the drug world, and all Bill's threats and entreaties failed to move him. He got high in the alley beside our house and in our back yard when he thought we weren't home. We talked to him, but he pulled farther and farther away. He told Melissa that his dead-end job was good enough because it didn't interfere with getting high. Minor scrapes with the police escalated, and he was arrested several times: minor drug offenses, violation of probation, assaulting an officer.

Bill expressed his frustration to Jay and to us. His voice edged higher and louder, shrill and tense. He was stuck in every parent's nightmare, watching his son hurtle into an abyss of drugs and violence and prison, unable to stop him.

On board ship, Jonathan had his own troubles. He fought with other men and was demoted. He lost faith in the military and in America as a land of opportunity. He told me that I didn't understand, that there were racist conspiracies at the highest levels. Finally, disgusted with Navy life, he went AWOL. Bill, Craig, and I urged him to return to base, take the punishment meted out, and finish the terms of his enlistment. Craig offered to drive him back to Norfolk. But he refused and received a dishonorable discharge.

Back with his brother and his other friends, he pulled away from my daughters. Becky and Melissa felt he shunned them. Craig tried to meet with him, take him out for breakfast or coffee, but Jonathan looked past him, said he "couldn't right now. Thanks, anyway. I'll let you know."

Jonathan had the energy to pull himself up, but he couldn't sustain it. He couldn't bear to have his tribe pull away from him. The 'hood beat him back down with taunts of "Why you tryin' to be somebody?" The 'hood pulled him back into its bosom of disillusion and anger and despair. Sociologists call this the crab-in-the-bucket syndrome: if one crab climbs out of the bucket, the others will pull him back down. His hope extinguished, Jonathan came to believe in vast conspiracies designed to keep the black man down. I was hard pressed to argue with him when so much evidence seemed to pile up.

With his brother in prison, Jonathan moved to St. Louis, his mother's home. We heard he had a job. We heard he lost it. We heard he was dealing. We heard he was in prison. We wrote him, and his long and articulate letters were filled with angry rhetoric against racism, the Man, the System. We wished he were reading Martin Luther King rather than early Malcolm X.

For many young men, the tribe is all. More important than the family, which is often shattered. More important than education, often an underfunded, chaotic environment that squelches any natural desire to learn. More important than the church, which often fails to reach them. More important than sex, which is readily available with multiple partners, so what's the value? More important than the outside world, which is perceived as marked by racist conspiracies. More important than their futures, which seem assured: death or prison.

Sometimes, when I awake, their young faces loom before me, the men we have known and in whose lives we once were entwined. I fear that we have failed to make a difference, that the church had failed to reach them. We once were their pastor and pastor's wife, their friend, neighbor, surrogate godmother, but now we are nothing. I fear we are only white.

Many months later, we received a letter from Jonathan with a dramatically different tone. He had enrolled in a challenging, long-term therapeutic program that included job assignments and classes on social skills, criminal thinking, and empathy. "I have learned and continue to learn much," he wrote. "The program is helping me become more focused and organized, so I truly believe that this whole experience is divine." The program required him to write an autobiography centered on events that contributed to his incarceration. He wrote one hundred and thirty pages. "I consider it to be my greatest accomplishment yet in life!" He had taken on several leadership roles was elected to the Inmate Council. He thanked us profusely for our prayers and love. "You've always been here for me...I am really really sorry for all that I put you guys through when I said what I said and did what I did... I hate that I had allowed myself to become so blinded by frustration and anger. For a moment I had become what I hated most. A HATER! Again, please forgive me." He plans to attend college to study photographic journalism after his release. I wrote him back, and told him he always has a place at our table.

We saw God change the lives of other men, too. Tim was raised by an overworked single mother with an abusive boyfriend, and began coming to church and children's activities as a boy. He often stopped by with his little brothers on his way home from school. With winsome smiles, they would ask for a pickle from the gallon jar I bought at the warehouse supermarket. He graduated from high school, and now holds a steady job.

Casey graduated from high school and landed a white-collar job in a church elder's business. He joined a black church, so we gradually lost touch with him. But he kept the faith, married, and began to raise his own family.

Robert attended our youth group in high school. Craig often hired him to help paint and do repairs, and then drove him across town to the apartment he shared with his mother. Robert graduated from high school, is a devoted father to his young son, and works as a police detective.

Dwayne began attending our church sports leagues in his teens. After his mother died, he moved in with his grandfather. Dwayne returned home from school one afternoon to find his grandfather dead of a heart attack on the kitchen floor. Kevin and Anissa Good took him in until his half-brother, an established professional in another city, adopted him. Dwayne thrived in his new environment.

And I think of Carneal, who describes himself as a "hopeless, homeless drunk and cocaine addict for twenty-three years." Until, like Lazarus, Jesus called him from the tomb.

CHAPTER 33

Carneal Means

CARNEAL'S MERCY SCAR

ONE Saturday afternoon, Carneal Means stepped out of his Pen Lucy apartment to buy a lottery ticket at the corner store, and heard music coming from Mullins Park. Carneal, a recovering alcoholic and crack cocaine addict, generally steered clear of the trash-strewn park where dealers hawked their wares. But the music drew him in.

"What's this?" he thought. "Some kind of a party? Where are the dealers?" Instead of the usual knots of men loitering, he saw tables piled with watermelon slices, neighbors eating hot dogs, and a gospel choir performing on a platform. Men and women manned a row of Weber grills, flipping hamburgers. Children lined up in little cliques to get their faces painted with stars, teddy bears, and rainbows. "Who are all these white people?" he thought. He looked again. "And black people...and Asians? I'm going to check this out."

He liked the racial mix. Not since his days in the military had he seen African Americans, whites, and Asians working together. As he stood on the sidewalk, a woman approached him and struck up a conversation. Christine Harter wore a Summer Youth Ministries t-shirt and baggy shorts, and her straight brown hair poked out from under a baseball cap. She didn't look like a *summa cum laude* Vanderbilt grad, a Johns Hopkins-educated physician who ran a clinic for low-income residents of East Baltimore. He found Christine easy to talk to. A few moments later, Craig strolled up and introduced himself.

"He didn't look like a pastor to me," Carneal later said. "I was used to pastors being stern-looking and authoritative. He wasn't preaching at me, just talking about God."

Carneal had been thinking a lot about God recently. Two years before, when he had gone to Baltimore's rundown Westport housing projects to buy crack, a dealer had drawn a sawed-off shotgun from his coat and aimed it at him. When Carneal turned to run, the dealer pulled the trigger. Sprawled on the sidewalk in the frigid February night, his left arm pinned unnaturally under his back, Carneal felt his life oozing out of the massive wound in his back. An intense, numbing pain sizzled through his torso.

In the first of several divine coincidences, officers in a nearby patrol car heard the shots. As the police stood over him, Carneal begged them to end his life. "Just do it," he cried out. "Finish me off! Get it over with!"

The police refused. As he slipped into unconsciousness, Carneal turned to God. "I knew I was dying, and there was no coming back. I cried out to God to forgive me, not to let it end like this. I didn't bargain with Him—it was just an honest cry. I had never done that before."

He thought of his sister, who had been talking to him about Jesus, telling him that God would help him kick his eight-year crack addiction. He grieved that his death would bring his family unrelenting pain. "They would know that I died a low-life addict in a dope hole. Even in death I would be a burden— they would have to spend their money burying me, knowing I was a crack head." He asked God to comfort them.

Doctors at the University of Maryland Hospital's Shock Trauma Center didn't expect him to last the week, and told his parents to make funeral arrangements. Carneal slipped into a coma. But thirty days later, he regained consciousness.

His prognosis remained guarded. Miraculously, the bullet had not severed his spinal cord. But it had ricocheted through his torso, damaging vital organs. Doctors performed multiple surgeries.

"It seemed like every day something would fail or become infected. The doctors got tired of opening me up and closing me," Carneal recalled. "So they just decided to leave my wound open. They had my organs in a bag laying on the bed next to me, and plastic covering the opening on my chest and abdomen."

Doctors told him he would never walk unassisted again, but Carneal refused to accept this. He kept trying to stand up without buckling, to walk the few steps to the bathroom before crumpling in a heap. The nurses called him "hardheaded." After months of excruciating physical therapy, he learned to walk a few steps with a walker. Then he graduated to a cane. Three months after the shooting, he walked out of the hospital.

But old habits quickly surfaced. "All I wanted was a cold beer. I hated doing drugs. But I loved my beer. I wanted to relax with a cold beer after a day at work, like a normal person." Carneal hobbled to a bar, drank half a can of Colt 45, and was blindsided by an overwhelming compulsion to get high on crack. "It hit me like a ton of bricks." He went looking for crack. He found it.

The next morning, Carneal realized he needed help. He called around to find a drug treatment program. In a short-term program, he faced not only his crack addiction but his alcoholism. He had begun drinking in high school, and alcohol had ruined his military career. "I was a hopeless, homeless drunk and cocaine addict for twenty-three years. When you went downtown and saw people sleeping outside, that was me."

Terrified of using again, Carneal entered a long-term rehab program, but the recidivism rate of many of his fellow addicts struck fear into his heart. "Every time I turned around, one of the guys—even the counselors—was going back on drugs. I kept asking, 'What's going to keep me from using again?'"

His counselor had offered no easy answers, saying only, "that's between you and God." His sister continued to pray for him and visit him, telling him that Jesus would help him stay off drugs. He began to consider embracing this Christ who had transformed his sister. Miraculously, at some point in his recovery, God took away Carneal's compulsion to get high.

"People are always asking me what I did to get clean. I can't answer that—I did nothing," Carneal admitted "This is a God thing. It's not up to me. I know that God has taken away the compulsion for alcohol and drugs."

Carneal thought he should take his sister's advice and find a spiritual home. He visited several neighborhood churches, but felt uncomfortable in each. But then, he stumbled into Faith's Community Chill event.

Carneal listened to Thurman Williams preach about knowing Jesus and following Him. He wanted to hear more. In his heart, faith stirred; he wanted what his sister had. He wanted what these people had. He wanted to know Jesus. He hung around the park and helped clean up. The next morning, he attended services at Faith. He found the sense of Christian community irresistible. "Like a family," he said. "This was a for-real house of God."

That afternoon, Carneal returned to church for a four-hour seminar. He joined one of Faith's small home Bible studies, and met with Tom, an Asian college student, every week to pray and study the Bible. As he grew spiritually, he began to serve in the church, eventually becoming head usher and co-leader of a home Bible study. He volunteered in the church's tutoring and sports programs.

Carneal is quick to assist those struggling with drugs or alcohol. When I told him the brother of my daughter's friend was addicted, he met with this stranger, and then spent an afternoon driving him to a treatment program fifty miles away. He helps lead the church's efforts to open a faith-based drug treatment center—an overwhelming need in Baltimore. Recognizing his gifts and his spiritual maturity as an overcomer, the church elected him as a deacon.

Carneal believes that God spared his life. The only residual effect from his near-execution—a long scar, stretching from below his collarbone to below his waist—reminds him of God's mercy. "Every time I remove my shirt it's a daily reminder," he says. "I'm not supposed to be here." His life shouts out the words of Jesus: "Then you will know the truth, and the truth will set you free."

CHAPTER 34

Ananda Kumar and Djik Maouyo

THE ENDS OF THE EARTH

A S Mary Pipher writes in *The Middle of Everywhere*, "America keeps taking people in. We're becoming a richer curry of peoples. Before 1990 most of our refugees settled in six big states: California, Texas, New York, Florida, New Jersey, and Illinois, but now an increasingly multicultural society is a reality across the United States."

We saw this reality fleshed out in the arrival of shops such as Shyam Foods (Indian), Tienda Rosita (Hispanic), and Waverly's Thai-Philippine Market. *Se Habla Español* signs sprang up in established businesses. Signs in Korean—with or without English translation—appeared over more and more storefronts.

Jesus told his followers to go make disciples in Jerusalem, Judea, Samaria and to the ends of the earth. In 1980, we didn't foresee that the ends of the earth would come to us. Because of its commitment to racial reconciliation, Faith became a magnet for believers and seekers from Sri Lanka, Uganda, Egypt, India, Colombia, Korea, and other distant corners of the world.

With the proximity of The Johns Hopkins University and Medical Institutions, Morgan State University, and other schools, Faith became a second family for students from all over the world. They fell in love with each other, and Craig performed an array of multicultural weddings: Korean-Indian, English-Japanese, Korean-Chinese, African American-Philippine. Many of these young people were missions-minded, and took the Gospel back to their homelands, or to other nations: to Turkey, Japan, China, Thailand, Togo, and Uganda.

Two of Faith's elders are foreign-born: Ananda Kumar, from Sri Lanka, and Djik Maouyo, from Chad. Ananda became a Christian in Sri Lanka, an overwhelmingly Buddhist nation, at an evangelistic meeting when he was eighteen. After earning a master's degree in engineering in Ohio, he came to Johns Hopkins to do doctoral research. He drove into Baltimore on a Saturday night, parked his U-Haul outside his apartment, and came to Faith on Sunday morning. He met Sandy Clark and others, who helped unload his truck after the service.

Because of his spiritual leadership, the congregation elected Ananda an elder four years later. When he returned to Sri Lanka to marry, several members flew over to celebrate the wedding. He returned with his bride, Sahayini, and church members organized a reception for the couple.

Being an elder is "More than I had anticipated," Ananda says. "You see the difficulties of a church. It's like working in the engine room of a cruise ship. There is a lot of work going on" that others don't see. He believes churches should create an environment in which internationals feel welcome. "We are spending money on world missions, but at the same time there are so many internationals sitting in the neighborhood we could reach." Americans must take the initiative to develop relationships. "Even going to young adult meetings can be culturally difficult for a young person just coming to this country," he says.

Faith's other international elder, Djik Maouyo, was born to Christian parents in Chad, a French-speaking nation in central Africa. Because he desperately wanted an education, Djik left his village at age seven to live with relatives. In middle school, he began to consider Christianity even though believers faced severe persecution.

"The president of Chad wanted to force a cultural revolution, going back to traditional rituals and pagan religions," Djik recalls. "The churches were closed and some pastors were buried alive. Some of my classmates were killed." Nevertheless, Djik made a commitment. "I decided whether I die or not... I just wanted to follow Jesus Christ." When the president was killed in the country's ongoing civil war, the churches reopened.

To attend high school, Djik moved to another village and rented a room with no electricity or cooking facilities. For his only meal of the day, he appeared on the doorstep of various church elders' houses at dinnertime. In true Chadian fashion, the hosts would always feed the poor student. "But I didn't want to hit the same house too often," he laughs.

When Djik graduated from high school, he won a scholarship to study in Togo, and soon became a student leader at the university's Christian ministry. While working to develop Bible study groups throughout Togo and Chad, he met frequently with Ann, a young American who developed Bible study curriculum and trained student leaders. Djik and Ann spent a lot of time together preparing meetings, camps, and seminars. He was normally very cautious about relationships with single women. But he thought there was no danger of romantic entanglement with Ann; in his experience, missionaries returned to their home countries to find spouses. "We were going to collaborate and have fun serving the Lord but nothing else," Djik recalls. "I was naïve!"

It gradually dawned on Djik that if he ever did marry, he would want a wife like Ann. He argued with himself. "Why do I have to wait for a photocopy of Ann while she is still available?" He decided to ask her to marry him, even though his job as a student worker necessitated a life of poverty. "She knows I am poor, and don't have a country," he thought. Ann said yes.

Because of Chad's civil war, they went to French-speaking Quebec, where Djik eventually earned a doctorate in biology. They worked in Canada for several years, but when Djik was laid off, they had to leave. The Lord shut all doors except one: the United States.

In 1996, Djik got a job as a researcher at the Johns Hopkins University School of Medicine. They visited several churches, but the biblical teaching, vision, and diversity at Faith resonated with them. "We have many international friends, and this is a place where we can bring them." They could also invite their neighbors. "Since we live in a somewhat disadvantaged neighborhood, and our kids attend a Title I school that is 95 percent black, I didn't want to go to a suburban church where the lifestyle would be so foreign to what they were experiencing in school," Ann adds.

In his role as elder, Djik brings a broad perspective to racial issues. "There is always this kind of polarization of black versus white in the United States. In other countries it is more complicated. The problem is not just a question of black and white. It is the question of sin. Where is your heart? I think the Christian faith … helps us see individuals as people God loves and whom we are called to love," not on the basis of race.

Sometimes, God sends people to Faith for only a short season. Katarína, a twenty-one year old Slovakian college student, was working for the summer in Rehoboth Beach, Delaware, when a hit-and-run accident left her in critical condition. A Medivac helicopter flew her to the University of Maryland Shock

Trauma center in Baltimore, where doctors pieced together her shattered pelvis. A sister church in Rehoboth Beach learned of her plight and called Faith's office to ask if someone could visit her. Unfortunately, the phone message languished under a pile of papers.

A week or two later, the Rehoboth church called back to check on Katarína. Carneal Means happened to be passing through the church office and overheard the call. Carneal—who knows the loneliness of long hospital stays—was irate to learn that no one had visited her.

"The girl didn't speak English, had no friends, didn't know nobody," he says. He called Julie Morris, another member of Faith, and they began to work the phones. "We called every hospital in Baltimore trying to find her because she'd been moved to a specialty hospital." Finally, they called Shock Trauma back. "We demanded to know where the girl was. If they released her, we knew she wouldn't have any place to go."

When Carneal and Julie visited Katarína in the hospital, they saw a frail, broken, young woman lying flat on her back. She had had no one to translate for her, no one to visit her. She feared she might never walk again.

No one had brushed Katarína's long, blonde hair in three weeks, and she had matted tangles the size of softballs. Julie tried to get a comb from the nurses' station, but without success. She asked Katarína how they could pray for her.

Katarína lamented the loss of her $8 per hour lifeguard job, which was seven times her mother's salary in Slovakia. She couldn't afford a plane ticket home, let alone an exorbitant hospital bill. She didn't know if, or when, she would be able to resume her studies. She had no telephone, and no access to her friends in Rehoboth. "I want to speak to someone in my own language," she said.

After the visit, Julie called fellow member Yvonne Harris to ask for prayer. Yvonne exclaimed, "My coworker is Slovakian!" The next day, the coworker visited her. A member of the Rehoboth church sent her the Gospel of John in Slovakian, and another gave her a cell phone so she could talk to her Slovakian friends in Rehoboth.

Other Faith members visited Katarína, including Mike Chen, a medical student. Mike let her check her email on his notebook computer, sang and played worship songs on his guitar, and shared how God had shown his love and grace to him.

"She noted that there was something different about how I worshipped, as opposed to the very formal way of worship in the Slovakian Catholic church,"

Mike later wrote on his blog. "She shared that she really wanted to get back to a right relationship with God." Mike prayed with her, and as he prepared to leave, she insisted that a nurse take a photo of them with the disposable camera other new friends had given her.

God continued to show his tender love and provision. The first five weeks of Katarína's hospitalization cost $700,000. Miraculously, insurance covered the bill. When her insurance coverage ended three weeks before her discharge, the hospital agreed to waive its fees. She left owing nothing.

Because Katarína couldn't afford a ticket home, God made other plans. A Slovakian woman who lives in Baltimore arranged for her to fly home with the president of Slovakia. She flew with Katarína to Boston, where they met the presidential entourage. Wearing a red University of Maryland t-shirt and hobbling on crutches, Katarína boarded the Slovakian equivalent of Air Force One. The press picked up her story and carried it all over her country.

"I have not forgotten about you. Say hello to Julie," she wrote Carneal recently. "I want also to be so strong person like you are." She writes that she is sorry she has not found a church like Faith in Slovakia. But who knows? Perhaps God will use the seeds sown in Katarína to start one. I think of the Lord's words to the prophet Jeremiah. "I am the Lord, the God of all mankind. Is anything too hard for me?"

God has brought the world to our backyards; today, thirty-five million American residents are foreign-born. Ananda, Djik, Katarína, and others show we don't have to travel far to reach the ends of the earth.

CHAPTER 35

Melissa, Jonathan, and Becky, 1998

CROSSING BACK AND FORTH, OVER AND OVER

IN adolescence, Becky crashed.

Maybe it was more like a ten-year plunge down a mountain: long periods of freefall punctuated by bruising collisions. Like watching the cord of her life unravel. As our oldest, she bore the full weight of race in a way our other children did not. She grew up in a hyper-racialized environment where she often felt condemned for being white. At a critical time in her development, when trying to form her identity, she found nowhere to belong.

We did not fully comprehend the depth of her pain. She hid it from us until ominous signs we couldn't fully interpret appeared like cracks in a dike. She had always been strong-willed, but she turned that will against herself, and lashed out with self-destructive behaviors. Some events were too painful to share even with intimate friends. I wanted to rip my heart out of my chest. Even in times of relative peace, my internal background Musak was warning bells, sirens, flashing lights. The depth of our parental pain seemed bottomless. Our lows were previously unimaginable. Fresh wounds left me curled in a fetal position on the bathroom floor, weeping for my child.

For Becky, race was always "in her face." Growing up in hypersegregated Baltimore, she felt she was always to blame, always guilty, could never erase the stain of four hundred years of white-on-black injustice. The childhood biographies I read to her about Martin Luther King or Harriet Tubman or Sojourner Truth, and the school and summer camp field trip to the Great Blacks in Wax museum had burned one message into her brain: white people are bad.

In fifth grade, she was the only white child in her class. When she transferred to a private middle/high school, she looked like most of the kids—but only on the outside. They were upper-class, and whether white or African American, lived in a different world. As what writer Richard Rodriguez calls a "scholarship child," she couldn't fit in with either group. The white kids made fun of her for "acting black." The black kids did, too. "Oh, you're black with too much bleach." A reverse Oreo.

Becky listened to black music, spoke Ebonics, dressed like black urban kids, joined the Black Student Union. She absorbed the pain of African American oppression yet was denied its solidarity. How could it be otherwise? As she and Melissa walked to church, police stopped them for "walking while white." They asked, "Where are you girls going? Where do you live? Are you lost?"

At school, a much older boy sneered sexually suggestive remarks, and used a nickname (an assault weapon) that burned into her. "Hey, Glock-Glock, when are you going to go out with me?" Later, we learned that another classmate had also harassed her. One day he pushed his face close to hers, taunted her. After years of enduring it, she reacted, and slapped him in front of his friends. He stopped, but the damage had been done. Just seeing him sickened her. She told us this long after the fact.

"I should tell the school about that boy," I fumed. "They wouldn't want that kind of behavior."

"If you tell anyone at school," she warned me, "I'll never tell you anything else."

I believed her. I didn't call the school.

We struggled to understand her shifting identities: dutiful daughter, fashion diva, baggy-pants-boy-in-the-hood, tough broad, AfroSheen-wearing white girl, artiste, civil rights advocate, counterculture Christian. And underneath, an anger and depression she couldn't verbalize.

Becky was the only white kid in the church youth group, and for a time, the only female and the only child with two parents at home. When neighborhood kids made prejudiced remarks about white people, some leaders let it pass.

Becky was the only white kid in the church youth group, and for a time, the only female and the only child with two parents at home. When neighborhood kids made prejudiced remarks about white people, they weren't always corrected. Simmering race and class tension and the disparagement of white people was like ingesting a toxin, bit by bit, day after day. Our church was cutting its teeth on how to do youth ministry in a diverse context. But Becky, as an overwhelmed minority, was getting cut.

When our youth attended regional events with suburban kids, clashes invariably arose. During one weekend trip, her group responded to racial insensitivity by boycotting the 50s sock hop because "blacks wouldn't have been allowed" to dance with whites in the 50s. The focus of the weekend became racial protest rather than spiritual development.

At another youth retreat, a volunteer leader bought a bottle of wine and took Becky to the darkened hotel restaurant after hours. They drank it, and Becky returned to her room falling-down drunk. She was sixteen.

Until her early twenties, my daughter couldn't talk about this pain of race and class and identity. When it floated to her consciousness, she pushed it back. "Just buck up," she told herself. "What are you complaining about? Just look around. Everyone else has it worse than you." And they did. Some of her neighbors were being evicted or arrested or dropping out of school or attending dangerous, failing public schools. Or they didn't know their fathers. Or their mothers were using drugs.

She was a third-culture kid, at home in neither culture, needing to find a third way. Like the children of missionaries, she crossed back and forth between two worlds, felt connected and disconnected to each.

I consulted my friend Jennifer Myhre, a medical missionary whose four children saw their village become a refugee camp hosting tens of thousands in war-torn Uganda. "Isn't it hard for your children to be surrounded by such extreme poverty, and then to come home to their grandparents' on furlough? To go from rebel incursions and AIDS to videos and malls and McDonalds?"

"Yes," she said carefully, "but I think it's harder for your kids. Mine understand that they live in two distinct worlds: America and Bundibugyo. But yours have to keep crossing back and forth, over and over, every day."

Although Becky's struggle absorbed much of our parental energy, we had concerns about Caroline as well. By fifth grade, the few other white students had left Caroline's class. She was both academically gifted and acutely sensitive. When other children mocked her as "teacher's pet," she wanted to disappear. So she stopped eating. A school social worker and the teacher addressed class tensions, and diffused the situation. And we made plans for Caroline to attend a more challenging, diverse middle school.

We feared Becky had seen too much, absorbed too many blows. Though our family was safe and stable, outside this cocoon the world was perilous. In middle school, we bought her a new bike so she could ride to school with two male friends, encouraging the independence she craved. We selected a relatively safe route: two blocks through the neighborhood, then cross over to Guilford for the rest of the trip. Two weeks into the school year, a gang of boys assaulted them a block away from our home and stole her friend's bike. There was no more talk of riding to school.

In high school, boys she had played with as children pulled away, began hanging out on corners, and were casualties of the omnipresent drug-related violence. She attended their funerals and flailed at the injustice of it all.

She resisted our attempts to plug her into suburban youth groups where she could be exposed to Christian kids from middle class backgrounds and develop relationships with people who looked like her. White suburbanites were taboo, all racist and insensitive, she maintained. Her few excursions into white, middle-class territory tended to reinforce this prejudice. Once, I persuaded her to visit an informational meeting for a parachurch ministry active in her school. Another parent, who wore a tastefully tailored suit and significant gold jewelry, asked where we lived.

"In the city."

"We do, too," she replied. "In Guilford. What neighborhood do you live in?"

"We live in Govans," I said evasively, citing the larger, slightly mixed region of which Pen Lucy is a part.

"Oh, I know Govans," she replied. "Where in Govans?"

"Pen Lucy."

She gasped. "Pen Lucy? My *maid* lives in Pen Lucy!"

Becky refused to return.

Becky was a talented artist, and her work was to be displayed in a high school art show. I suggested her grandparents go see it. But her art was filled with anger, pain, and darkness, jagged lines and angry words scrawled across writhing images. I found her pieces so upsetting that I called Cleo and Pete back, made excuses, told them not to come. I could not bear to break their hearts, to endure their anguished questions.

When I probed, asked if she was angry or depressed, she dismissed my concerns or lashed out. Conversation was like defusing a bomb. She refused to see a counselor and resented our attempts at intervention. She didn't want to change schools. She knew she was receiving a superior education. "No one's going to take this away from me," she said.

Again and again, behind closed doors, Craig and I agonized: Should we move? Would it help if we left the neighborhood? Should Craig resign? But we were never sure if relocation would help. We had friends in middle-class communities whose teenagers were similarly troubled.

Becky experienced a breakthrough her junior year. She decided she wanted to be a Christian, officially joined the church, petitioned to start a prayer club at her school. The student senate turned down her request: Isn't a Christian prayer club *exclusive*? I mean, won't you *only* be praying to Jesus? The school had other clubs—a Jewish club, a Black Student Union, a gay and lesbian advocacy club—and her sense of injustice flared. She appealed the decision. Two teachers spoke in favor of starting the club, and she won her case.

But a few months later, it all fell apart. She informed us she was no longer a Christian. She took up smoking over our protests. Her senior year was a disaster, a slow torture. She was visibly depressed. She put her head down on her desk during class, struggled academically, gave up and failed to turn in papers. A favorite teacher called: "Please, try to get her to turn her paper in. Something. Anything."

She wore one outfit nearly nonstop—men's scoop-necked t-shirts and baggy jeans. The school sent home interim reports, like mortar shells lobbed through the U.S. mail, exploding in my hand. I had nightmares: a fax machine in my bedroom spit out endless interims, red F's staining each one.

In another dream, a storm raged outside my house, and a tree crashed through Becky's bedroom.

Nothing worked. In private, Craig and I argued, accused. You are too soft on her; you are too hard. You are overwrought. You are too laid back. Craig reasoned patiently, and I flailed at his equanimity. We wrote in our journals. I argued with God in long, fast, walks or runs. Craig woke up in the middle of the night, and trudged through the dark streets to the sanctuary to pray out loud. We tried more restrictions, more freedom. Craig wrote her love letters and took her out for coffee. We sent her to a counselor but she wasn't ready to talk.

She managed to apply to two Christian colleges, neither of which she particularly wanted to attend. You don't have to go, we told her. But she was desperate to be somewhere else. And we were desperate for God's healing in her life.

"Maybe," Craig and I told each other, "in college she will find the strong Christian peer group she never had in high school. Maybe once she's out of the neighborhood, she'll be free of the burden of constantly battling race and class. Maybe she'll grow in her faith. Maybe she'll find healing."

But we were wrong.

CHAPTER 36

Thurman and Evie Williams

LEAP OF FAITH

IN September, 1999, Thurman came to Craig with heart-stopping news. A sister church in West Baltimore, New Song Community Church, had asked him to become their pastor. "I haven't made up my mind, yet, but I'm seriously considering it," he said. "I just wanted to give you a heads-up."

After Thurman left, Craig put his head down on his desk. He had waited so many years for a full-time, African American pastor to share the load at Faith. Thurman had finally finished seminary, and would now be available full time. Craig and the elders were moving toward hiring him as co-pastor. He was needed at Faith—yet Craig could see how much of an asset he and Evie would be at New Song, too. His wordless groanings ended in a final plea: "Lord, what are we supposed to do now?"

Within an hour, the phone rang. It was Stan Long, whose friendship dated back to the earliest days of Faith. Stan had led the InterVarsity Summer Urban Project in 1981, gone to seminary, and now pastored Forest Park Presbyterian Church, which at that time was the only African American church in our presbytery. Craig and Stan had worked together in presbytery to encourage multiethnic church planting and the development of African American leadership.

"Craig, I've decided to turn in my resignation at Forest Park. I feel like I've done all that God wants me to do here, and that it's time to move on."

Craig was surprised. "What are you going to do?"

"I don't know. Hey, maybe Thurman would like to come to Forest Park. He's preached here a few times, and the people were very responsive. Then I'll come to Faith and be your associate." He had several old friends who attended Faith, and he and Terri had visited from time to time during his vacations.

That night, Craig shared Thurman's conversation and Stan's phone call with me.

"Stan Long? Stan might come to Faith?" I exclaimed. It felt like winning the lottery. "God is so amazing. He knew Thurman's leaving would devastate you and didn't let you suffer long. He had Stan call the same day and express an interest in coming to Faith!"

"Well, it's not for certain. The congregation would have to call him."

"Oh!" I exclaimed. "That would take about one minute for anyone who knows him!"

The congregation was saddened when Thurman announced his resignation. He was a gifted preacher and had nurtured a good rapport with the community. Our disappointment was tempered by the realization that he and Evie were uniquely gifted to serve at New Song at this stage of its development.

When Craig announced a few weeks later that Stan Long was considering coming to Faith, those who knew him erupted in applause. At last, Craig had the equally experienced African American partner—what the Bible calls a "yokefellow"—that he had sought for nearly twenty years. Stan and Craig split the preaching schedule, which allowed each man more time to catch his breath, give more of himself to his family, and focus on other aspects of ministry. Stan's gift for steady shepherding complemented Craig's more visionary, outreach focus. Both men, having served as solo pastors for many years, found that emotionally charged conflicts were more easily processed with another brother alongside. Thurman had taken a leap of faith, following God's lead to New Song. The congregation had trusted God and sent him off with their blessing. And once again, in a most unexpected way, God had raised up leaders for Faith.

By 2000, Baltimore Christian School was operating at capacity with waiting lists, enrolling ninety children from kindergarten to fifth grade in classes of fewer than twenty. Nearly every child read at or above grade level. When students fell behind, they received extra help. But parents faced a dilemma when their children graduated: where to send them for middle school. Parents wanted to see BCS expand through eighth grade.

"Can't you put desks in the hall?" one desperate parent asked.

The school's leaders had also harbored a dream to add a preschool to better prepare children for the academic and social challenges of kindergarten. But we had no room.

Starting an academically challenging, Christ-centered school based on faith, not tuition, had been a leap of faith. God had blessed our faltering steps of obedience. To add sixth through eighth grades and a preschool, Faith would need to build a larger facility. Was God calling us to make this leap of faith?

Our Pen Lucy Youth Partnership sports leagues were also bursting at the seams. Because we lacked a gymnasium, Kevin Good relied on partnerships with other neighborhood recreation centers. He scrambled to find open court time, paid fees to use gyms at public schools, and hauled vans full of players and equipment back and forth. Without a central location, juggling schedules became immensely complicated. Sometimes PLYP's equipment was stolen or broken. Several times, one hundred eager children, scores of volunteer coaches, and several paid referees arrived to find that city employees had failed to open up the recreation center.

Kevin wanted to provide additional programs. But we lacked the space. So Craig, Kevin and others began to pray that God would enable us to expand.

Attendance at our worship services had risen steadily. To handle the overflow, we hooked up a camera and large-screen television screen in the church parlor to create an "East Sanctuary." When this room became too crowded, we moved it to the basement. But the worship experience just wasn't the same. We had resisted adding a second service because of the strain it would place on our musicians, nursery workers, and children's church workers. God continued to bring new people to Faith who appreciated the church's vision for reconciliation, justice, and outreach. Our ranks were swelling with young families, students from Johns Hopkins and other universities, community residents, and men and women from the greater Baltimore area. What was God calling us to do? After months of prayer and planning, Faith added a second service. We also began praying about building a larger worship facility.

The idea of building an addition for the school, space for after school tutoring, and a gymnasium/multipurpose facility that would serve our sports leagues and worshipping community was so daunting that the leaders prayed about it for six months. They asked Joe Brandli, a deacon and architect, to draw up a possible building plan. Joe met with the BCS board to determine their needs, and six months later, unveiled his draft at a congregational meeting. Members were asked to fill out a survey to provide additional input. A month later, another congregational meeting was held to review survey responses and answer questions. The congregation voted overwhelmingly to move forward with this vision.

The elders established a building committee, which included a community resident, to move the project forward. The committee invited neighbors in the immediate area to view the building proposal and offer suggestions and concerns. Five months later, Craig and Stan Long hand delivered invitations to nearby residents to provide another opportunity to discuss the building proposal. They submitted the proposal to the Pen Lucy Community Association for several months of review. The elders also established a new community advisory committee, which included a resident, to again survey neighbors and provide an open forum for ideas, concerns, and suggestions about the project. While some of the suggestions—such as traffic flow and parking concerns—were incorporated into the plan, others—such as moving the proposed building outside of the neighborhood—were not.

Most community development projects face some opposition, and we were not immune. Residents may feel threatened by change, or resent that decision-making power rests in someone else. They may suffer from a case of NIMBY (not in my backyard). They may think it's a bad fit for their area. Opposition may even come from those who have been most served by the ministry or nonprofit organization.

One resident circulated a petition accusing Craig and the elders of racism and colonialism. "This is not the 1700's and you are not the then missionaries coming to civilize the natives...You can't think that you can come into someone's home and just tell them what their problems are, what you see as the solution and impose this blessed, unsolicited bounty on them." Night after night, Craig slipped out of bed to pace the floors and pray about the building program. The elders and the congregation agreed to move forward only with strong support from the community. This would be determined through consensus from the community association, parents of children in Baltimore Christian School, and those served by PLYP's sports leagues and Learning Center.

Parents of children enrolled in PLYP and Baltimore Christian School eager-ly embraced the plan. Within several weeks, we had gathered 200 signatures. While we felt that most residents of the community would support the plan, we wondered how many would attend the Pen Lucy Association meeting and vote. The day before the meeting, a former member confronted Craig. Even though his son attended the school, Henry had nurtured a deep personal ani-mosity against Craig for a decade.

"Why are you trying to build this? Don't you know the community doesn't want this? We like things just the way they are." Henry motioned with his arm. "We have our poor housing here, we have some better housing over there, and people can get drugs there. We like things just they way they are. We don't want this."

"Do you think I should just leave?" Craig asked him.

"Yeah, I think that would be best."

At a heated community meeting, a few residents voiced their opposition. Others expressed appreciation for the school, the Learning Center tutoring, and the sports programs. Finally, the association president called for a vote. The expansion was approved 32-8.

CHAPTER 37

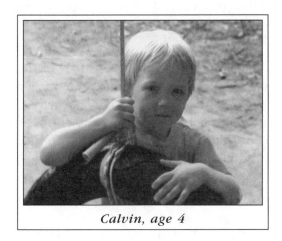

Calvin, age 4

ARE YOU WATCHING MY BOY?

WHEN Calvin was six, Craig had taken him to Memorial Stadium to see a football game one Sunday afternoon. Because we lived less than a mile away, I dropped them off, and they planned to walk home.

The shortest route home took them up Old York Road, through the commercial strip where a drive-by shooting had recently occurred. On a busy Saturday night, several men had jumped out of a van and opened fire with automatic weapons, gunning down eight people. In our family room a block away, we had heard so many explosions that it never occurred to us that it was gunfire. We thought it was fireworks at the stadium. Then we heard sirens, more sirens, and the thump-thump of police helicopters overhead.

Although Calvin had slept through all of this, he had heard the neighborhood boys talking about the shooting. After the ball game, as Craig began to walk up the strip, Calvin pulled away. "No! No! I'm not going up that way!"

"But it's shorter. It's daytime. It will be O.K."

"No!" Calvin was adamant. Tears formed in his eyes. "We need to go the other way! Up Greenmount Avenue."

Craig had relented, and they walked the long way home. Later, he told me about Calvin's terror. My son, I had mourned, my son, his poor little fluttering heart. What are we doing? God, I had asked, "Are You watching my boy?"

At nine, Calvin was afraid to walk the block to his friend's house for morning carpool. He wanted me to accompany him or to watch from the porch. So I stood on the steps, seeing the little blond head, the navy blue pants, the button-down shirt retreating from my view, my grasp, the backpack bouncing as he scurried around the block.

The only times he did not ask were on days the public school was closed. On those days, there were no clusters of middle-school boys clad in draggy jeans and FUBU sweatshirts jostling each other, moving in the opposite direction.

This lodged in my heart. I continued to ask, "God, are You watching my boy?"

At twelve, our son needed outlets, outside opportunities. He didn't want to attend our church youth group. He refused to join Boy Scouts because none of his friends in the neighborhood went. He didn't want to play another season of baseball or any other sport.

For years, he had played with two boys in the neighborhood, Kenny and Shooter. Both slept at our house, ate frequently at our table, and joined us on family outings. But as they entered their teen years, the gulf between them widened. Almost overnight, Calvin pulled away from Shooter. Turned him down when he came to the door. His world became even smaller.

For his birthday, all he wanted was the latest baseball cap worn by the older guys in the neighborhood. Reluctantly, Craig took him to one of the small, trendy shops on Greenmount Avenue, and Calvin eagerly selected his cap. We hated the thought that his life was telescoping down to this, a baseball cap.

God, I asked: "Are You watching my boy?"

We saw—especially in hindsight—the strain that living in Pen Lucy had placed on our daughters, how hard it was for them to fit in, to form healthy identities as nearly the only white children in the neighborhood. We had consoled ourselves that they had each other, a buffer against the outside world. But Calvin had no brother.

Like penniless kids with faces pressed against store windows, we saw the advantages his cousins had—good schools, strong youth groups, safe neighborhoods. We tried to reconstruct all this on our modest salaries: private schools, music lessons, sports teams. We wanted a context that developed character and a passion for following God. We sensed they needed a strong peer group of other kids who were similarly challenged to follow Christ.

Calvin visited his cousin Peter in Oklahoma and took stock: good school, safe, middle-class neighborhood, a vibrant youth group. "It seems so perfect," he said.

Behind closed doors, in endless discussions and in our journals, Craig and I agonized. The church was expanding, with more stable families and a growing youth group—but this had happened too late for our daughters, and even for our son, who complained that he didn't connect with the handful of kids his age at church. His best friends were a group of boys in the suburbs. They attended a Lutheran middle school together, ate at each other's houses, made skateboarding videos, and were generally inseparable. His tribe. They were good kids, the kind of friends parents want for their children. They lived within a few blocks of each other—all except for Calvin. He grew increasingly frustrated.

At various times of the day, he would ask, "Mom! Can you take me to Zach's house? Everybody's there."

"Calvin," I protested, "I can't just drop everything at a moment's notice. It's five o'clock. I have to cook dinner." I had just returned from my daily hour-and-a-half afternoon carpool, retrieving two-year-old Juliana from Vernell's, driving out into the suburbs to pick Calvin up from his school, then doubling back to pick up Caroline after lacrosse practice. "Why didn't you plan this at school? I could have just dropped you off there."

But thirteen-year-old boys don't plan ahead. His social life emerged like a glob of wet clay thrown on a potter's wheel, shaped by five pairs of adolescent hands. His dissatisfaction grew. Even when his friends came over, there was no place in the neighborhood they wanted to go. "I hate living here," he told us. "I can't go anywhere. You have to drive me everywhere."

"In another two years, you'll get your license. We'll lend you the car sometimes," we tried to persuade. But this was like seventy years to him, an eternity, and we knew it.

After middle school, Calvin and most of his tribe planned to attend a larger, Catholic boys' school. It's an old, prestigious school, rich with resources and opportunities. Calvin grinned over his acceptance letter and called his buddies. But somehow, his excitement evaporated on the first day of orientation. I picked him up, eager to hear how my son, my handsome son, was faring now that he was one of the boys in the blazers.

"I hate this school," he announced.

I was aghast. "But Calvin, it hasn't even really started yet. Give it a chance."

"None of my friends are in my classes." He spat it out like a death sentence. He told me other things he didn't like, rituals and rules he pronounced stupid. And no girls.

Craig and I strategized and decided to give him some time. "Maybe after he gets on one of the sports teams..." Craig said. We pushed Calvin to try out. Many of his fellow students had attended lacrosse and basketball camps since they were out of diapers, and although he was a natural athlete, we had not been able to provide the background he needed to compete at this level. He didn't make the final cut.

"Maybe he'll find his niche in the jazz band," we told each other hopefully. "He's so talented." But he didn't. The band had several pianists, and he only performed a song or two in each concert. The rest of the time, he idled on a chair, waiting.

There was nothing to do in the neighborhood, and he felt unsafe venturing beyond our block. His world was shrinking just at the moment he needed it to expand. He needed his horizons to widen, to gain confidence and control.

But he hated school. He hated our neighborhood. He hated feeling like a captive in his own home. He was frustrated, angry, and unhappy. And all our strategies were failing. We began to consider a more drastic solution.

God, I asked, "Are You watching my boy?"

CHAPTER 38

2002

A SNAPPING SOUND

MORE than once, I thought back to my old friend Catherine Watson's pithy comments as she had watched me scurry around tidying the house, teaching the children, and doing ministry tasks.

"Marie, you cain't do it all," she often scolded in that North Carolina drawl. "You got to do some and leave some. Take a break."

"I know you're right," I would say airily. "I will, just as soon as I finish this last thing."

She would eye me skeptically and shake her head. Once or twice, she added a more ominous postscript. "Sometimes, folks that do too much just snap. Just snap! I know you don't want to see that."

I knew Catherine was right. I was overworking myself, and anxiously pondered her remarks. Just what *exactly* did it mean to "snap"? Would I snap? And if I did, would I ever recover?

Becky—now preferring to be called Rebecca—had not found in college the healing we had desperately prayed for. We saw anger eating her soul like a parasite. Each time she returned home for a visit, we girded ourselves for a new identity. She hated her long blonde hair, dyed it red and black, chopped it off. She came home dressed in bizarre biker attire or Goth black. She brought home a boyfriend with a 1.7 GPA. She donned a lip ring, pierced her ears again and again, stretched the holes so that I feared she would look like someone out of *National Geographic*. We expressed both our love for her and our disapproval of the "body art." She didn't care.

"What do you think of tattoos?" she asked us. We told her that we were opposed and if she wanted one, to wait until she was twenty-one and financially independent. But she had a massive tattoo of an angel permanently etched onto her back. I learned of it when a friend, tipped off by her own son, asked what I thought of Becky's tattoo.

"Why do you do this?" I asked her, more in perplexity than anger. "Is it that you don't care what we say? Are you trying to hurt us? Or is it that you know we will love you unconditionally no matter what you do?"

"I know you'll still love me," she shrugged with a sly smile.

At work I felt under attack. My job had been a refuge of sorts, with interesting tasks, an encouraging boss, a mentoring supervisor, supportive colleagues, and manageable deadlines. But that had fallen apart. A project with tight deadlines stressed my supervisor. A new employee whose cubicle abutted mine was overtly hostile, and I found her presence increasingly threatening. I never knew how combative she would be on any given day. My office had felt like the only place in my life that wasn't taken over by my children, the church, or neighborhood crises. My fight-or-flight reflexes stayed on high alert for months.

I needed someone objective and began to take weekly lunch hour walks with my friend Kim, a wise counselor. One afternoon, as we paced the same Hopkins campus quadrangle over and over, I asked her for advice about my stressful life.

"I think you and Craig have no sense of what normal looks like," she said slowly. "You're always on call, and pastors don't have the boundaries or protections that counselors or other professionals have." We continued to pace the brick walkways. "And you—" she laughed, "you mess up all the demographic charts! You're in nearly *all* the life stages at once! Wife, working woman, mother of a small child, mother of teenagers, a kid in college, midlife stresses."

"Everything but the empty-nest stage," I added. "And we'll go from there directly to the old folks home."

We were silent a minute. "I don't see any way out," I told her. "I can't quit my job, we can't afford to sell Greenmount Avenue, and I can't control my kids' hearts or other people's behavior. I feel so stressed my brain cells are burning out like overused light bulbs. Or like mosquitoes lured into a Bug Zapper." I made a buzzing noise. "That's all you'll hear! Just that mechanical frying sound, then the loud quiet."

But my joking couldn't diffuse the stresses that continued to build. At home, consumed by three-year-old Juliana and four teenagers, I ignored my need for rest and renewal. I hated being separated from Juliana, so I overcompensated and gave her everything I had left, then put her into bed before quick quick doing the laundry or cleaning the kitchen or helping with homework. Or if we had a home Bible study that night, I ended up watching four or five little kids of varying ages, trying to keep them happy so that their single moms could get a little peace. Then I fell into bed, and the next morning I got up, started my carpool at 7:30, dropped off Juliana at 8:30, and faced it all again.

The list of repairs needed to maintain our hundred-year-old houses on Springfield and Greenmount avenues was endless. We lacked time and energy for them, or the money to hire the work out. We had owned the Greenmount house for fifteen years, and I longed to sell it and eliminate the strain of managing tenants, but we couldn't afford to.

Craig could see I was falling apart and recognized his own need for boundaries and rest. He was gasping for breath, depleted, desperately needing a sabbatical to recharge his soul after more than twenty years of ministry. "I need a break," he kept saying ominously. "I need a break."

We knew that the building program had unleashed an intense level of spiritual warfare. We had been functioning at an unhealthy level of stress for far too long. At what point, we asked, does living in Pen Lucy become so stressful that it saps our energy for ministry? Craig's thoughts increasingly turned to two questions: Should we move out of Pen Lucy? And if so, should I resign from Faith?

Craig had been assisting a church member and Pen Lucy resident with a personal problem. He called Leon, who was usually a calm, thoughtful man.

Inexplicably, Leon lashed out at him. "You and most of the other families at church have made money their god. These wives should not be working outside the home. Your wife is working. You have—what, three cars?" he asked.

"Uh, actually," Craig admitted, "We have four. Becky and Melissa bought themselves used cars to get back and forth to work and school."

"See?" he exploded. "You're wealthy. You've given yourself to a lifestyle of wealth." He went straight for the jugular. "You're not making any difference in the community. What families and children have really been affected and helped by your presence? Men in the church don't have the guts and boldness to stand up to their wives and take charge! Nobody has the guts! It is clear to me what the scriptures teach. You know but you won't do it."

When people are under enough pressure, they tell you what they *really* think. Sometimes it isn't true. But often there is a grain of truth in what they say. Leon was not in the mood for a discussion about the relativity of wealth, the unreliability of public transportation, or the high mileage on our cars. Perhaps he had no way of knowing how deeply he had cut Craig with his words. But I knew. Craig already staggered under the weight of concern for his wounded children, his fracturing wife, and divisiveness over the church's building program.

One night, picking up supplies in Home Depot, Craig began to question his calling. "What have I been doing for the last twenty years? Is this really what I want to do the rest of my life?" He greeted the store manager, whom he now knew by name. "I could do that," he thought. "I know the building trades. I could make more money managing a Home Depot. Or I could build houses." He reflected on the pleasure of seeing tangible results from construction work. "You build it, and there it is. You work hard on something, and then you can see it." A sermon, on the other hand, might take twenty or thirty hours to prepare, and thirty minutes to deliver. "And then what? It's gone," he shrugged. But the deeper question was not "What is easier?" but "What is God calling me to do?"

Although Faith focused its community development and outreach efforts on the neighborhood, most of our church members lived outside the community, within a few miles. Faith had become a regional church with a community development focus. As Craig considered moving out of the neighborhood, inner voices tortured him. What about our commitment to be incarnational, to live in the community? Were we deserting the neighborhood? Only giving lip service to the Gospel? Would we be capitulating to comfort? Selling out? Craig hated the image of a pastor commuting to an urban church while living in the suburbs.

We agonized over how the MacIvers and Clarks, key church leaders who had relocated into Pen Lucy with their families, would respond. Though their children were still in early elementary school, Pen Lucy had already presented many challenges. They had yet to ride the rapids of the teen years. Would they feel we were deserting them?

American consumer culture moves toward ease and comfort and security, away from stress, danger, and need. We tend to medicate rather than meditate. But Jesus says to follow him, to die to self. Jesus promised we would have tribulation in this world. But what about our children? Were we sacrificing them on the altar of ministry? What was God calling us to do? At various times, during our two decades in ministry, I had been ready to move because of concern for my children. But I had made a deal with God long ago. "If You want us to move," I had told Him, "You tell Craig. Not me. I am not going to drag my husband out of the neighborhood. He's the head of our family, so You tell him."

But now, Craig was listening, probing, taking tentative steps to seek God's will for the next stage of our lives. Should we move out, even if only for a year or two? He asked his father for advice. He asked our treasured old friend Steve Estes, who lives several hours away but appeared unexpectedly on our doorstep one evening as we wrestled with this question. He asked the elders of the church. All were unanimous: You should move.

As great as our love is for Faith and Pen Lucy, we had a higher responsibility: our son. "It's the right thing to do," Craig said. "Calvin has less than four years left in his adolescence. He needs a context of grace. He needs to know that I'll be faithful to him, even if it means changing where we live."

CHAPTER 39

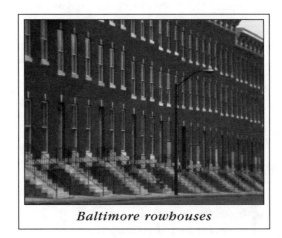

Baltimore rowhouses

NOT WAVING, BUT DROWNING

WHILE the nation reeled from the September 11 attacks, I wondered if I would collapse like an airless accordion. In addition to stresses of family, work, church, and neighborhood, I was embroiled in separate, ongoing conflicts with two women. Such clashes are rare for me, and the fact that I faced two at once was extraordinary. One of the women I had considered a close friend. Psalm 55 seemed most appropriate.

> *If an enemy were insulting me, I could endure it...*
> *But it is you, a man like myself, my companion, my close friend,*
> *With whom I once enjoyed sweet fellowship...*

As my relationship with her fell apart, I realized too late that I had been too trusting. "What is this? I asked Craig through tears. I felt like an emotional hemophiliac, bleeding internally. "Is this the Year of Betrayal? The Expendable Friend? Who's next?"

I wanted to honor Christ and act with integrity—so I constantly evaluated events and agonized over how to respond to them. What does faithfulness look like in this situation? Jesus tells us to love our enemies, to pray for those who persecute us. I begged him to help me do this, because I was not there yet.

Like an autistic child locked into a repetitive private world, I was emotionally stuck, going over the same ground again and again. I could see others rationalizing, self-justifying. Surely I, too, had blind spots. Was I self-deceived in some massive way?

Every time I would begin to make progress toward reconciliation or forgiveness, some new eruption reopened the wound. I took refuge in the Psalms and prophets. A passage from Zephaniah reminded me of God's mercy and restoration.

Night Grace

My anger awakens me.

The slap of betrayal sears.
I replay the words of my enemy,
compose the thousand retorts I will not air
pray for a spirit of forgiveness I cannot summon alone.
I rehearse words of life
but even the Psalms feel impotent.

Unbidden, words memorized long ago
push to the surface:
He will rejoice over you with singing;
He will quiet you with His love.

I began to have serious memory lapses and difficulty concentrating. After more than twenty-five years of accident-free driving, I had two fender-benders in two months, one of which resulted in a lawsuit. My stomach was a constant knot, and my neck and shoulders were tight. I had trouble sleeping and felt overwhelmingly fatigued. When I got my driver's license renewed, my photo showed a tense grimace.

I kept stumbling through my roles at home, at church, at work, then falling into bed. When I awoke, a headache lurked like a malevolent cat, increasing throughout the day. I felt diffused, as if my emotions had been shattered. Rather than gravity holding matter together and pulling it toward the center, I suffered from a perverse antigravity. My mind was flying apart. I inhabited an exploding universe and had to scoop it all back together just to get out of bed.

I read the Bible, prayed, and talked to Craig and a few trusted friends. I saw a counselor. I exercised daily, walking in the neighborhood or shuffling back and forth on the NordicTrack, dragging my angst to Jesus. Some days, fearing deeper despair, I exercised twice, hoping to boost depleted serotonin levels. I felt like I had post-traumatic stress disorder. Like a little rat, I ran on an anxiety treadmill and couldn't get off. Outside forces kept spinning the wheel.

I meditated on the Psalms daily, trying to suck in strength from their promises.

"But the eyes of the Lord are on those who fear him,
on those whose hope is in his unfailing love,
to deliver them from death and keep them alive in famine.
We wait in hope for the Lord; he is our help and our shield."
Psalm 33

I felt emotionally flat, but intellectually I held onto faith. I leaned on Craig's faith and on my friends' faith. I leaned on what I knew to be true about Jesus. That He loves me. That He is both good and sovereign. That suffering has a purpose. I did not understand His actions, but I trusted His character.

Nearly every night, when the house was dark and quiet, Juliana awakened and tiptoed to my room in her little footie pajamas, slipping into bed beside me. I took comfort from her presence: her vibrancy, her softness, her later-in-life appearance an unexpected gift. It was a primal comfort during a cold winter: my husband on one side, my child on the other. Some days, it was the only thing I felt that was not pain.

A darker depression descended, a complete loss of interest in activities that once brought pleasure. I had no energy, no enthusiasm; everything was duty. I leafed through *Women's Day* but lacked the energy to attend to the words. I was reduced to looking at the pictures. Anything more exhausted me and wasn't worth the effort. I thought of the final lines of a poem by Stevie Smith. "I was much too far out all my life/ and not waving but drowning."

My counselor was alarmed. "I think you're depressed," she declared one winter day, and not for the first time. I had denied this, but finally I no longer argued. There was a firmness to her voice, an underlying urgency.

"I want you to call this man." She handed me a slip of paper. "He's very good and will only prescribe medication if he thinks you need it." I nodded dumbly. She continued. "Then I want you to call or e-mail me to let me know you've made the appointment."

At the psychiatrist's office, my narrative of recent events disturbed him. At one point, he dropped his pen and looked me in the eyes. "This is ridiculous," he said gravely. "You must get away from these people." He recommended a leave of absence for six weeks and prescribed an antidepressant. I took it for six months.

While I understood that chronic stress or a genetic predisposition might have brought on depression, the buck-up, suck-it-up side of me was mortified. But taking an antidepressant did not alter my personality, as I had feared. Combined with other disciplines of Bible study, prayer, journaling, exercise, and lifestyle changes, however, it gave me a fighting chance. I waited for God to resurrect me.

> *I waited patiently for the Lord;*
> *he turned to me and heard my cry.*
> *He lifted me out of the slimy pit,*
> *out of the mud and mire;*
> *he set my feet on a rock*
> *and gave me a firm place to stand.*
> *He put a new song in my mouth,*
> *a hymn of praise to our God.*
> *Psalm 40*

C.S. Lewis writes that "God speaks to us in our joys but trumpets in our grief." God had my attention, though I was so accustomed to rush and activity and busyness that He had to nearly slap me silly. My soul felt like it had road rash from being dragged behind the speeding pickup truck of my frenetic life. God was telling me to listen to Him, to obey the speed limit.

Slowly, spiritual truths I had held intellectually soaked into my soul. This God-ordained time clarified my vision and purged me. I had poured myself out for my family and others but failed to set healthy boundaries. I had been too much an activist, too little a contemplative. I had allowed no time to recharge, rest, or write. My inner child had been a worker bee, a machine. I had not rested in God's grace. I had not trusted God, but had taken responsibility for work that was His. I had wanted to save the world, but had lost my joy. What did it *really* mean that "the joy of the Lord is your strength"?

Over time, joy returned, a deeper, sweeter dependence on God, a sober awareness of my limitations, an excitement and assurance of God's calling and direction for the next stage of life. Like a child who has seared her hand on a hot stove, I can remember the singe and the burn. I'll be more careful.

Several months later, I found the missing piece that explained why depression hit so hard. At forty-three, I was in a hormonal free fall. Next to my midlife pregnancy, the "change of life" was the biggest shock of my life.

"I can't do anything on a normal timetable," I complained to Craig. "Isn't this five or ten years early?" I had barely finished reading about toilet training and now I researched night sweats and hormone replacement therapy.

In time, I came to see depression as a loving act, one I would never seek out, but could learn from. "Endure hardship as discipline," the book of Hebrews urges believers, because God disciplines, or shapes, those whom He loves. Unless a grain of wheat dies, Jesus says, it cannot bring forth fruit; only after a period of self-denying, dirt-embracing dormancy and dependence on God can it produce a bountiful crop.

David and other writers cry out to God in the Psalms. God accepts and even welcomes their raw and scraping pain poured out, erupting like a burst sewer line. But within nearly every lament, after a litany of woes, complaints of abandonment, unjust suffering, and the prosperity of the wicked, the psalmist reaches a critical juncture. He understands his suffering only when he enters the presence of God. Psalm 73 pivots in mid-poem:

> *When I tried to understand all this,*
> *it was oppressive to me*
> *till I entered the sanctuary of God*

The psalmist—Asaph, leader of one of David's Levitical choirs—then affirms the presence and sufficiency of God.

> *Yet I am always with you;*
> *you hold me by my right hand.*
> *You guide me with your counsel,*
> *and afterward you will take me into glory.*
> *Whom have I in heaven but you?*
> *And earth has nothing I desire besides you.*
> *My flesh and my heart may fail,*
> *but God is the strength of my heart*
> *and my portion forever.*

At our church, when Bill Bolling leads worship, he often calls out a challenge to the congregation, an exchange passed down from long tradition in the black church.

"God is good," he reminds us.

"All the time," the congregation responds.

"All the time," Bill echoes back.

The people say, in unison, "God is good."

CHAPTER 40

Rebecca, 2005

CROSSING OVER

WE put the Greenmount Avenue house on the market, and Craig looked for a house in the neighborhood where Calvin's friends lived, a few miles away. As we drove down streets lined with single-family homes and row houses, For Sale signs were as scarce as palm trees. And how could we ever afford a house large enough for five children? But a few days later, Craig called me at work with surprising news. "I've found a house in our price range. It's a two-bedroom Cape Cod."

"Two bedrooms?" I tried to figure out how to downsize from a six-bedroom house to a tiny cottage.

"With Dad's help, we could add on to the house at cost. I've called Dad, and made an appointment for the three of us to see it tomorrow."

The next day, I drove to a small, immaculate brick house on a busy street a block away from Calvin's best friends' houses. Pete and Craig had already paced out the size of the lot adjacent to the house.

Life is so odd. As we stood outside sizing up the property, who appeared but Leon. He was scoping out a nearby apartment for a relative.

"What are you doing?" His eyes took in the three of us, and the realtor who had arrived. "Are you looking at a house?" he quizzed.

I winced. No one in the church—except the elders—knew we were considering a move.

"Yes," Craig said. "We're thinking about moving out so that Calvin can attend high school here."

Leon didn't seem surprised at this news. I fluctuated between thinking forgiving thoughts and honestly telling Leon how angry I had been at his personal attack on Craig a few weeks before. Perhaps, like Hamlet's Ophelia, he had been "separated from his own good judgment." "Temporary insanity," I decided. I excused myself and joined Pete, who still scrutinized the property.

"An addition the size you need isn't going to work," Pete announced. "It would overwhelm the house architecturally. But that lot….now that's a double lot. You could build on that. Throw a modular house on there."

After walking through the house, we stood on the front steps. Pete and Craig scribbled figures on a piece of paper. Directly in front of me, two boys rolled by on skateboards: Calvin's best friends. I nudged Craig in amazement.

"Is that a sign?"

Craig and Pete checked the building codes and realized we could build a modular home on the lot. This nearly miraculous ability to afford a house in the exact location we needed was the divine confirmation we so desperately sought.

Convinced that this move was due to God's leading, I adjusted quickly. Craig, however, struggled intensely. Transitioning from being the pastor in the 'hood to the pastor commuting to the 'hood ripped at his soul. After signing papers to buy the house, he came home, threw himself on the bed in exhaustion, and wept.

"I don't want to be on the sidelines," he agonized. "I want to fight on the front lines." He feared the move marked him as getting soft, selling out. Craig recognized that he had created an idol, basing his identity on being the pastor in the 'hood, not just as a child of God.

"Whose plan is this anyway?" I reminded him. "Isn't this God's plan? Hasn't God clearly spoken through the elders, your parents, the church, and circumstances? Or are you arguing with God?"

"I know. I know," he said.

During the few weeks we considered moving, I could not discuss it with even my closest friends. But I did tell my sister in Florida. After Craig and I found the house, I left a cryptic message on Pam's answering machine, fearing that my parents, frequent guests in her home, might overhear. I didn't want to get their hopes up until I knew for certain. They had been remarkably supportive and restrained over the years, but I knew they worried about us.

"Pam, it's me. I just wanted to let you know that things are progressing," I said into her machine. "I'll call back later. Love you."

Sure enough, my parents overheard Pam listening to her messages.

"What's that about?" our father queried. "That's awfully cryptic."

"Dad, I can't tell you," she said in her matter-of-fact way. "But I will say that when you *do* hear, you'll get down on your knees and thank God."

My father's eyes lit up. "She's moving!" he gasped, delight spreading across his seventy-six year-old face.

My parents had longed for this for twenty years. I was grateful that God let them live long enough to see it.

When Craig managed to weave the announcement of our move into his sermon a few weeks later, the church was unanimously supportive. Our friend Vernell, who had taken care of Juliana in her home day care for several years, hugged him after church and spoke through tears.

"I've been praying for this day for years. The thought of Juliana growing up here just weighed on my heart so much..." She could not finish speaking.

After twenty-two years of ministry, the church granted Craig a six-month sabbatical. If pastors in general are on call twenty-four/seven, then community development pastors in particular stand at attention nonstop, ready to answer the next crisis, meet with the next wounded soul, and already behind in preparing the Sunday sermon. Only as he pulled away did he recognize how easily the ministry can become an idol. Only as he pulled away did he recognize the unhealthy patterns established early in our marriage and ministry: the constant overextension, and the lack of boundaries between work and home, a crisis mentality. Only as he pulled away did he realize that he had embraced a wrong paradigm for marriage. Marriage was not just a gift to strengthen a couple so they could do more as a team than as individuals. The whole truth is that marriage is a gift in itself to be appreciated and valued without demanding production. He began to recognize and turn from his drivenness. He began to embrace grace more deeply.

We savored the quiet of our new house, trying to make up for years of too much noise, too much static, too much shaking of our souls. The silt finally settled, the water grew clear.

After twenty-two years in Waverly and Pen Lucy, we moved to an area sociologists call an edge city. Our house fronts a busy street in a diverse middle-class neighborhood a block from a historically African American enclave. Behind us, row houses shelter black and white families, college students, the elderly, single white women, and middle-aged couples. In the apartment complex across the street, middle-Eastern women in long dresses stand at sinks, and women in saris glide out of compact cars. Students trek back and forth to a nearby university. Hispanic grandparents play on the lawn with small children and Asians stoop to gather ginkgo fruit in the fall.

Race and class are not overwhelming issues here. I am not viewed with suspicion as the representative of the oppressor race. I am ignored, passed over, invisible—and I love it. I stand or fall on my own actions, not the accumulated sins of my race.

Suburban plentitude saddens me. It is not fair that my son now receives a better, free public education because of where he lives. It is not fair that in my old neighborhood and others like it, children are hit by stray bullets. It is not fair that residents who can't afford cars have to take cabs or buses miles away because major supermarket chains have abandoned many city neighborhoods. It is not fair that to buy a piece of lumber or a hammer, residents of Pen Lucy have to drive out into the suburbs because all the hardware stores have closed down. It is not fair that at the city's elite private schools, letters to parents are printed on high-grade paper while public school teachers sometimes lack any copy paper at all.

Calvin enrolled in a public high school a block from our home. He picked up the guitar, and quickly became proficient. Our friend Gary Herwig hired him at his kitchen remodeling business after school. He excelled, learning carpentry and computer architectural design. He saved his money, and at sixteen, bought his dream car: an eleven-year-old, five-speed Acura Legend, the fanciest car in the family. His friends still migrated *en masse* from house to house, and several began to attend Faith. He joined a Christian group at his school, and began attending Bible studies and youth meetings several nights a week. He rose at 5:30 every Friday to meet in a small discipleship group. He crossed over from childhood to an adult faith. He found his place.

"God," I pray, "thank you for watching my boy."

Six months after moving, Craig and I took Caroline on an overnight college visit several hours away. Driving home, he was reflective.

"How is it for you, returning home?" he asked

"Great," I replied. "This is the first time I don't have to suck in my breath, steel myself. There's no reentry shock." Often, in addition to facing the culture shock of the neighborhood, to unpacking and gearing up for the hectic pace of our lives, some crisis would surface: a break-in discovered, a hurting child on the doorstep, a shooting, a crisis in a church family. "How is reentry for you?"

"This is the first time," he admitted, "that I've returned not just to a ministry, but a home."

It was a profound shift. Only relocation and a six-month sabbatical enabled him to get enough distance, to change established patterns of a crisis-management lifestyle, to open up more space for a life.

Melissa and Caroline were shaped by the city, but not broken. Melissa is able to relate to people of every hue and background—black and white, rich and poor. Some of her coworkers at a downtown restaurant couldn't understand this. "They can't figure me out. I'm down with the manager, I'm down with the other waitresses, and I'm down with the line cooks. They ask, 'Where are you *from*?'" Her vocation—to teach at-risk children in the city—was first formed when she volunteered at our annual summer camp at age thirteen. She reflected on her upbringing in a college paper.

> *As I grew older, I began to see the oppression faced by friends and their struggling families. I watched my ten-year-old friend taken down and handcuffed, the continuous drug busts next door,*

gang rival fights, and the death of teen friends. My family raised
their five children with a firm faith in the Lord, and that no mat-
ter how difficult the situation may be, the Lord will lift you up and
comfort you. Growing up in Pen Lucy allowed me to find a positive
outlook in any situation...I have witnessed the miracles that take
place daily in my father's church and in my immediate family.

Caroline's cross-cultural background led her in a different direction. While
still in high school, she became fluent in Spanish and developed friendships
with students who had lived abroad. As a student at Johns Hopkins University,
her closest friendships continued to be with other third-culture kids or international students. She majored in Latin American Studies, Spanish, and Art
History. She also picked up French. She spent a summer helping our friends
Stella and Miguel with their ministry in Bolivia, and helped lead a college trip
to Peru and Bolivia. Calvin can't figure out how he got a "Latin American" sister. "You're adopted," he teases her. "We found you wrapped in tortillas, lying
on the doorstep."

Rebecca struggled through three years of college, then decided she didn't
want to return for her senior year. She wasn't sure what she wanted to do with
her life, and how an art degree fit in with her plans. She wanted to be independent, self-supporting. She is a hard worker, and several previous employers
would be eager to hire her full time. "Fine," we said. "We love you."

With this decision, a huge burden lifted from her shoulders. School had
been a place of un-belonging, of emotional pain. She moved in with friends,
delighted in having her own little apartment in Philly, and wanted us to visit.
She became the working poor, like one of Barbara Ehrenreich's subjects in
Nickel and Dimed. She worked full-time and took on several side jobs just to
keep her ailing, donated car on the road. She found a network of friends, built
a life, and got by. But deep inside, old pains still pricked. A year later, she
moved back home to sort it all out. She began to emerge from the suffocating
darkness.

As an adult, she was great company: thoughtful, helpful, and intelligent,
with a sly sense of humor. Though some parents grouse about boomerang kids,
ours became a companion and friend. As Craig and I watched her transformation, we felt as if our prayers, which had been piling up behind a dam, had
finally broken through. Her artwork became lighter, more hope-filled. Her
laugh returned, an unaffected musical sound we had not heard in years. She

began attending church again and asked an older woman to disciple her. The girl who had once viewed God as "someone who kicks you when you're down" now wept in frustration because she wanted to know His will for her life. And she recognized that race was still an open wound in her heart.

"I need to talk to someone about this racial stuff," she said one night.

"Is there anyone in church you can talk to?" Craig asked.

She thought a minute, then shook her head. "I've been away...there's no one there who really knows me, or that I connect with about this."

"I know who you could talk to," Craig said. "Carl Ellis. He teaches seminars about racial dynamics. He's known you since you were a baby. He'll meet with you."

"Yeah, I could talk to Carl," Rebecca said. "So what am I going to do, drive to Chattanooga?"

"I'll go with you," I offered. "We can drive to Chattanooga for a few days."

"He flies all over the country," Craig said. "Let me call him and see when he's next coming to Baltimore." Craig called Carl, and learned he would be in Baltimore the next week.

"This is amazing," Rebecca marveled. "The one person I can talk to about race lives hundreds of miles away, but will be in town next week. You guys are always saying that God goes ahead of me. He sure did."

A few days later, Rebecca and Carl met over crab cakes from his favorite Baltimore restaurant. Carl provided an additional piece of the puzzle. "I can tell you're going to need some healing," he said. "You don't have to figure it all out. You have nothing to prove, nothing to be ashamed of."

She felt affirmed. "I'm not crazy," she thought. Carl explained how the dynamics of dominant and subdominant cultural relations play out in different settings, with especially tense results in America's inner cities, where race and class can form an explosive combination. Suddenly, it all made sense. She had been caught in the crossfire of America's racial war.

Rebecca believes that her cross-cultural upbringing gave her a perspective that would have eluded her in other settings. While her spiritual journey has not been easy, at Faith she has seen Christians who serve quietly for the love of Jesus. She is building on a deeper, truer foundation of grace and hope.

During her sophomore year in college, Rebecca showed us her sketch of an angel, which was later tattooed on her back. The creature knelt, massive wings unfolded above, arms raised in prayer. A broken chain lay under her feet. Two banners flanked her: "Grace" and "Hope." Artistic expression mirrors the soul, and we rejoiced at this spiritual and emotional breakthrough.

God promises to restore the years the locusts have eaten. He promises that his Word does not return void, that he hears our prayers, that if we ask in his Name we shall receive. He stores up our tears. He says that if we train up a child in the way she should go, that when she is old she will not depart from it. Even so, come, Lord Jesus.

Karl and Debbie Dortzbach, who have been teaching and doing medical missions in Kenya for the last twenty-five years, visited Faith. They were relocating to Baltimore, where Debbie's ministry organization is based. They bought a row house nearby, then returned to Kenya to pack. Their son, who had just completed graduate school in the Midwest, planned to move here and find a job.

"He can't move into an empty house," I told Craig. "Tell Karl their son should stay with us for a few days, at least until he has a phone and bed and kitchen."

When Jesse drove up in his red truck, we saw a slender, handsome artist with intelligent blue eyes. During the week he lived with us and in the months that followed, we saw his character. He insisted on helping us refinish the basement to thank us for our hospitality. He rose early and worked skillfully until dark without complaint. He began teaching art to at-risk children in one of Baltimore's most difficult high schools, and grieved over their lives. He volunteered at church and became a member.

Seeking community, Jesse moved into our old house, where a half dozen other young men from church live. The only available room was Rebecca's old room, so he settled in there. When Rebecca and her roommate Keri needed space to paint and sculpt, we suggested they build studios in the basement at Springfield. Rebecca began framing walls and hanging Sheetrock, and Jesse pitched in. During the summer, we hired him to rip off old cedar shingles and hang siding on our Springfield house. He hired Rebecca to help, and they spent several months on ladders and scaffolding three stories high, hammering and playing jokes on each other and having food fights. He had been considering a tattoo himself, and liked Rebecca's so much that he had one of Michelangelo's crucifixion sketches etched onto his back.

Jesse wanted to meet with us that fall, and over bagels and coffee, asked to court our daughter. They were already giddy with each other. Four months later, he wanted to take us out again. After coffee, he pulled a letter from his pocket and read it to us.

Dear Craig and Maria,

I want to marry Rebecca because she is my best friend... I feel more complete and at peace when I am with Rebecca. I want to marry Rebecca because she knows what it is to struggle, to cry, to be beaten down, to finally give up, and yet to persevere, to rise, to grow and ultimately to trust in God's faithfulness to find purpose and joy in each day...

I want to marry Rebecca because she understands me better than any person ever has, because she always sought to know me deeply. She has been patient, forgiving, accepting, and loving...

I love the expression of her faith, the quiet confidence that she has and the child-like faith of always believing in God's goodness and faithfulness...

I want to marry Rebecca because I want to serve and love her for the rest of my life with my mind, body, heart, and soul and I forever want to be a part of her life with all of its drama, its joys, its sorrows and surprises.

I long to discover what sanctification in marriage means with her and to experience what it means to glorify God in how we love and honor and serve each other as man and wife.

And so, would you, Craig and Maria, adopt me into your family, to be your son by means of marrying your daughter Rebecca, so that I might love and serve her all the days of my life, and that I might be one with her as is honorable to the Lord, and is my heart's greatest desire?

Since their birth, our prayers for our children have included the provision of a spiritually mature spouse. During Becky's broken years, I ached at the weddings of our friends' daughters, wondering if she would find such a man. As a missionary kid, Jesse grew up in a culture where he did not fit in. But like Jacob, he has wrestled with God and prevailed. He is exactly the sort of man we want our daughters to marry. He is the other half of Rebecca's heart.

CHAPTER 41

Carmen and Eli Foster

BUILDING TOGETHER

T HE church sent grant proposals to foundations with an interest in urban education or ministry. For the first time in its history, the Van Lunen foundation responded to a "cold call" from an unknown organization, and pledged a $125,000 matching grant towards Faith's capital campaign. The church had one year to raise the $125,000 within the congregation, which numbered about three hundred souls. If we were successful, the foundation promised to give an additional one million dollars and encourage other foundations to join us as well.

People gave checks large and small. Rolls of small bills that looked like they'd been squirreled away in mattresses appeared in the offering plate. Children held bake sales and donated their allowances. Single mothers gave their raises. But by the end of the year, members of Faith hadn't given $125,000. They had given over $180,000. The Van Lunen Foundation pledged half a million dollars for the building expansion, and half a million dollars as an endowment for BCS.

After some initial research, Craig learned that most extensive fundraising ventures, when led by a pastor alone, are not successful and often irreparably burn out the clergy. Faith hired a consultant to guide us through the capital campaign. To encourage the rest of the congregation, a group of key Faith leaders were asked to consider pledging in advance what they could give over the next three years.

Craig, Bill Bolling, and the consultant addressed groups of leaders at a series of meetings in our living room that fall of 2003. I looked around at these faithful, hard-working believers who had already served in countless ways.

"Would this mean," I wondered, "that Stacy and Edward won't be able to move their family of six out of their little duplex into a larger home? Does this mean that Bryan and Cheryl and their five children will somehow have to make their van gasp along for three more years? That whatever tiny financial cushion Helen, a single mom, has will be given to Faith?" Part of me wanted to stop, to shield these dear souls from further sacrifice. I had to remind myself that God was leading, and able to provide for them.

All pledges were held in strict confidence, with only Sandy Clark, our long-time deacon and treasurer, knowing individual pledges. Twenty-five households responded. Nearly all were young families or singles. Most were middle-class, but some had an unemployed member. These twenty-five households pledged to give $430,000 over the next three years—an average of $17,000 each, over and above their regular giving. Some gave their raises; some dipped into retirement accounts; some, like believers in the book of Acts, "sold houses and lands." Sandy said that while opening the pledge envelopes, he had to stop and pray several times. It was too overwhelming. Too humbling. Too big a leap of faith.

The rest of the congregation responded with equal measures of faith and generosity. The pledges continued to come in for several more weeks. At our Advent service, we celebrated God's faithfulness: the saints at Faith—less than one hundred households—had pledged to give a total of $790,000 over the next three years. Combined with the previous $180,000, Faith's members had committed nearly a million dollars towards the building expansion. It was a leap of faith—and more. But God wasn't through with us yet.

The following year, a group of men and women approached Craig about starting a multiethnic church in the neighborhood near our house. Starting a daughter church was not in our plans, but we prayed and waited and studied. Jesus told his followers to go make disciples in Jerusalem, Judea, Samaria, and to the ends of the earth. We had focused on a little section of our Jerusalem; was God broadening our vision to embrace more than one community? Over the next year, we became convinced that God was leading us to hold services at a second location. The multi-site model is a newer, more successful model of starting churches, with one administrative structure and several worship sites. Faith was becoming not only a sending church but a reproducing church.

We began to see significant revitalization in Pen Lucy. Habitat for Humanity, assisted by several members of Faith, rehabilitated twenty homes. After years of effort, the community association's plan to redevelop the blighted Strip gained momentum. PLYP began a G.E.D. program to extend educational opportunities to adults as well as children. For the first time in many years, Pen Lucy experienced no murders in 2005.

Under the leadership of Eli Foster and his wife Carmen, Faith's youth group reached and enfolded young people from both the church and the community. Eli grew up in a white suburb of Chattanooga, Tennessee, and met Carmen while volunteering at a black Baptist church. After earning a Master's of divinity in urban ministry, he came to Faith in 2003. On a weekly basis, his ministry touches eighty kids through Sunday School, Bible studies, and other activities. This group includes African American, white, Asian, and Latin American youth.

"Our youth ministry is a very hard place to be a youth, but also a very rewarding place," Eli says. "Youth are living out the core belief that the gospel not only brings us together across race and other lines but it gives us life in the midst of circumstances that are incredibly difficult...We have youth being raised by their grandmother because the mother is dead or on crack, in the same room with kids whose parents are doctors and are being homeschooled. What we have in common is who Jesus is and what he's done for us." he says.

Eli and Carmen recently led the students on a thirty-hour famine to raise money for World Vision. Forty-five middle and high school students fasted for people they'd never met in the developing world. Eli divided the group into heterogeneous groups—community boys with church girls, community girls with church boys—to learn about issues of power and justice. They played competitive games where some teams were given an advantage over others. "It was fascinating to see them form a sense of identity for their team, and they felt a sense of displacement of justice that was galvanizing. We asked, 'How do we appeal to God when power is abused?'" After work projects, fun times, worship, and Bible studies, the students closed the event with a feast.

True community development is about developing people—changing lives, not just building houses or creating more equitable structures. Community development expands opportunities not only to youth who are isolated but also to those who are considered advantaged. When youth no longer feel the need to self-segregate, and can connect across divides not just in an event but in ongoing relationships, they experience a depth and richness lacking in purely homogenous settings. It is difficult and demanding, but ultimately redemptive.

CHAPTER 42

MY BRAIDED HEART

GOD uses his church in spite of our pettiness and immaturity. In one of the most faith-filled transactions in the cosmos, God designates his followers as the hands and feet of Jesus. At Faith, I see these hands and feet at work.

I see Kim, whose son broke her heart afresh every day in an endless free fall into pot and other vices his parents warned him against. Kim and her husband served and hoped even when God seemed silent to their anguished pleas. They prayed and fasted when he was kicked out of high school, when they sent him to treatment programs, when he quit trying in community college. And then one night he had a conversion experience to rival Paul's on the road to Damascus. Within a month, his mind was clear, his spirit strong and tender toward God. Now he reaches out to younger adolescents.

I think of Joyce, who wakes up every morning to take care of her five children, including the youngest, who has Down's syndrome, even though a tumor lies malevolently inside her pituitary gland, neither growing nor shrinking, but perhaps... waiting.

I see Jocelyn, a veteran of numerous operations, cancer survivor, mother of a child with Asperger's syndrome. With every step, her knee bones grind against each other without benefit of cartilage. Yet she soldiers on, gracious and cheerful, taking joy in the incremental but significant victories of her son.

I see Addie, born in Korea, and her husband David, a convert from Judaism, who moved into the city with their four young children to be part of God's work here and to invest in the lives of urban children. They put down roots here even though Addie daily battles three life-threatening illnesses that decimate her liver, immune system, and heart.

And I think of Linette, who overcame drug addiction and reaches out to others. She tries to get Gina to leave the drugs alone, to stay away from the men who offer that free first hit that utterly enslaves so that you don't care whether or not your son has breakfast or lunch or a winter coat for school. Linette stands at the edge of the broken ice of Gina's life, extending a hand to the skater who one moment ago was exhilarated by speed and the chill of the air but who now has slipped through a jagged, shattered hole into frigid waters and is sucking ice into her lungs.

I think of Karim, who came from an Islamic nation to study engineering and met Jesus. He grieves for his countrymen, who do not have the hope of forgiveness of Christ. What will happen when he returns to this closed nation, where he could be beaten or beheaded for owning a Bible? Will his family disown him for embracing Christ?

I might tell about Irene, who sings with us on the music team. Irene adopted a seven-year-old daughter twenty years ago, a beautiful, shy, sweet girl who will always need support because of emotional and mental limitations. And her daughter has her own mind, as daughters do, but Irene never lets go. Irene also takes care of her ailing aunt. Yet she still serves, and sings, and shares her heart with younger women who seek her advice, even when she probably wants to take to her bed. She has enough faith not only for herself but to stir up those around her. Her life demonstrates an enduring obedience.

I think of Howard, who leads our Gospel choir, taking a motley assemblage of blacks and whites and teaching them to *shout*! unto God. Howard and his predecessor J.T., graduates of Johns Hopkins, raised in the black church, took a chance on us. They agreed to shape a dozen singers, then two dozen, into a sound good enough to pierce us, to rip our sorrows out and cleanse them, to give voice to our joy. They write arrangements and teach each part, reaching down for the bass line and singing falsetto for the sopranos. Both emanate an unfettered joy and openness that I can only dream about. When Howard directs, his back arches and dances under his suit jacket with grace and looseness, as though every muscle has been summoned to participate. These men are not performing, but somehow relaxing and opening up so that the praise inside can come out. Their love for Jesus is so infectious that even white people from very straight, liturgical, formal backgrounds stand up and clap and sway. When I get to heaven, I want to be in their choir.

Irene, Linette, and the others would not want me to write about them. They would shrink away, say no, I am just doing what God has laid on my heart. Perhaps, like me, they often feel like frauds or failures. We have done so little. We have not done enough.

But perhaps we have awakened every morning, sometimes only in pure gut obedience, and risen to do the next thing next, to take up whatever God has put in our hands to do, without thinking it would matter much to anyone but Him, trusting that His pleasure was enough. But somehow, God has designed a blueprint, a plan we didn't see and never expected. We are each hammering away in our own little corners with bent nails and balky hammers and sore fingers but then suddenly, we look up and realize that we have been building a cathedral.

These people share their faults, their griefs, their joys, giving me their most valuable offerings, their hearts. *Pray for me*, they say. *I scream at my kids. I lost my job. I want a husband so badly. My son is in jail. I've been praying for a wife. My daughter is addicted. I am infertile. The cancer is back. My daughter was raped. My father just left my mother. The doctors don't know what's wrong with my daughter. My mother is dying. My friend is dying. I am dying.*

They are recovering from addiction, from childhood sexual abuse, from being ridiculed or excluded for being too light or too dark. They live with chronic pain and unfulfilled dreams, bring each other meals during illnesses, slip each other twenties when times are hard. And they all love Jesus.

In his poem, "Mending Wall," Robert Frost writes that good fences make good neighbors. For twenty years, I had trouble figuring out how to build neighborly fences, how to serve while maintaining healthy boundaries. The Apostle Paul writes, "We are not trying to please men, but God." Usually this verse is interpreted to urge believers to resist the pull towards comfort and people-pleasing at the expense of obeying God. But it also means we must choose between the good and the best. We must chase after and obey God's call for our lives. Our goal must be, as the Westminster Shorter Catechism states, "to glorify God and enjoy him forever."

I never thought I was a messiah come to save the city. I wanted to obey the words of the prophet Micah: "And what does the Lord your God require of you? To do justice, to love mercy, and to walk humbly before your God." I wanted to be faithful to the call.

I am thankful for my beloved neighbors in Pen Lucy, who demonstrate generosity of spirit with their welcome, who persevere in the face of unjust systems, who still want to reach out, to redeem young men caught up in a culture of drug dealing and violence, to invest in children who need a drug-free adult to come alongside them. They give unstintingly from their own modest resources, and teach me how to live abundantly with less. They are entwined with me, part of me no matter where I live.

Several months after our move, a medical missionary spoke at Faith. While discussing her work with the Dani tribe in Irian Jaya, Indonesia, Dr. Brenda Sharritt told of her early attempts to communicate there. She began doodling, and her new Dani friends quickly mimicked her drawings.

"I wonder what they'll think of this one," she thought, as she traced two interlocking links, a three-dimensional doodle she had learned as a child. Turned on its side, it looks like two hearts braided together.

"Every time I drew it they would exclaim, 'niniki kiniki kunik.' I learned it was a Dani expression of affection, of connection. It means 'my heart, your heart, knit together.' That's how I feel about the Dani," she explained. "Only God can do that sort of knitting."

That's how I feel about the people at Faith, whether from Pen Lucy or Baltimore or the ends of the earth. They are braided into my heart.

I still believe it is all worth it—the struggle to educate our children, the endless leaching of Craig's time and energy. I still believe that Jesus answers all the questions we ask ourselves, whether we live in Pen Lucy or Guilford or the ends of the earth: Why am I here? Does my life matter? Can anyone really know me and love me unconditionally?

There is always hope. Even in our darkest times, some small sliver of light remains, like a crescent moon or a nightlight burning in a child's dark room. A conversion. An influx of one or two believers eager to serve. And the moments of sublime joy, when I see Jesus through a passage of Scripture or a sermon or song and I am resurrected.

DISCUSSION QUESTIONS
by Ann Maouyo

1. Garriott describes herself and her husband as "woefully unprepared for urban ministry" (page 29). What do you think was most challenging for them to adjust to initially? Ultimately? What valuable (perhaps hidden) resources did do you think they brought with them from their own backgrounds and upbringing?

2. The author admits that she and her husband struggled with finding the balance between ministry demands, family needs, and personal renewal. How did this imbalance affect each of them? What lessons did they learn over time? What principles can you take to heart from their experience?

3. Garriott quotes her husband as saying "It's a whole lot easier to focus on one people group... It's just not in the Bible" (page 38). Do you agree or disagree? Why? How would you qualify or expand on this perspective?

4. Craig Garriott invited his friend Bill Bolling to the young mission church, believing that strong, diverse leadership was crucial to developing an authentically diverse church. Do you agree? Why or why not? What does "diverse" mean in your context? What are some ways that people of different ethnicity, class, or gender can be encouraged and empowered to take a significant role in your fellowship or church?

5. John Perkins' "three R's of Christian community development"—Reconciliation, Relocation, and Redistribution—were key to the developing vision of the young church. Define these principles and give specific examples of ways they were applied in practice. How important do you consider them to be in the ministry of your church or fellowship?

6. Economic hardship and disparity are recurring issues in the book. To what extent do you believe an incarnational lifestyle (identifying with the struggles of the people they were serving) was helpful or even crucial to the young church's urban ministry? Does this

principle carry through in other ministry contexts? How do you think it applies to your own church or fellowship?

7. Garriott says, "Some mornings, as I jogged or walked our streets, crossed into Guilford [a wealthy neighborhood] and then back again, I felt immensely grateful to live on the Pen Lucy side. I knew I was richer for seeing life through the eyes of my neighbors. Pen Lucy was teaching me to be less selfish, and to focus on God's value system... It forced me to depend on God's provision rather than my own competence, to be broken before God, to see with spiritual eyes" (page 126). How do you react to this statement? How do you relate it to Jesus' teaching—for example, the Beatitudes (Matthew 5:1-10)? Also, why is it important not to tear down the rich in order to build up the poor? Are there "poor" rich people?

8. Many members of Faith Christian Fellowship had life experiences that enabled them to identify with the hurting community around them: financial hardship, dysfunctional families, a past history of substance abuse. The apostle Paul wrote that God "comforts us in all our troubles, so that we can comfort those in any trouble with the comfort we ourselves have received from God. For just as the sufferings of Christ flow over into our lives, so also through Christ our comfort overflows" (2 Corinthians 1:4-5). How have you seen this principle worked out in your own life? What present trials are you facing that enable you to respond more compassionately to others?

9. In the Gospel accounts of Jesus' ministry to the oppressed, we see radical, miraculous deliverances. Steve Stahl's spiral into depression and eventual suicide led Craig Garriott to anguish over the validity of his ministry. How should we respond when those to whom we minister experience tragic setbacks or return to bondage of various kinds? Is this necessarily an indictment of our lack of faithfulness? Can you think of biblical figures who faced similar challenges?

10. Particularly in its early years, the fledgling mission church attracted a number of believers struggling with mental illness. How can the church become a safe haven for those marginalized by society? What do you see as the biblical basis for this? What was the cost of being a church where this was a reality?

11. In one instance the author recognizes, "There is an intersection between faith and foolishness, a fine line between trust and presumption. I suspected then, and know now, that I crossed that line. Compassion offers oneself to another; presumption takes unnecessary risks" (page 169). To what degree do you believe risk-taking is an unavoidable part of walking by faith? What are some of the risks of a life of obedience? (Physical? Emotional? Financial?) In the heat of the moment, how does one discern between necessary and unnecessary risks?

12. Many of the Garriotts' friends and family members questioned their decision to raise a family in a blighted urban community. From their children's perspective, what were some of the costs and heartbreaks of growing up white in a struggling, overwhelmingly African-American neighborhood? In what ways do you think this experience may have contributed to giving them a richer heritage or a broader view of the world?

13. Garriott laments the despair of young men in the urban environment, citing economic hardship, fatherless homes, a failed educational system, and the overwhelmingly negative messages of popular culture as almost insurmountable barriers. What is the responsibility of the church—both urban and suburban—in addressing these needs? What resources need to be brought together to bring hope to these young men and develop their God-given potential?

14. How do you view the Garriotts' decision to move out of the community when their son was in high school? (A sell-out? A long-overdue capitulation to good sense? Or another step in a walk of obedience to God's call?) What are the warning signs that a worthy principle is in danger of becoming an idol? Why was this decision such a difficult one, especially for Craig?

15. The author says, "… had I not remained utterly convinced that [Craig] wanted to follow Jesus above all, that he wanted to love me, wanted me to feel loved, and that Jesus could intervene… our marriage would not have survived. Leaving him—breaking my marriage vows, depriving my children of their father, dishonoring the name of Christ—was not an option" (page 105). What factors—commitments, practices, attitudes of mind and heart—kept

the Garriotts' marriage alive? Are there things that in hindsight the author wishes they had done differently?

16. What role did older, experienced believers like Catherine Watson, Pastor Tony Dorsey, Bob and Jean Jenkins, and Bruce and Marlene Gustafsen play in Maria and Craig Garriott's lives amidst the turmoil and stress of ministry? Who plays this role in your life?

17. In relating the young church's search for an adequate facility, Garriott says, "Intellectually I knew that God would provide, and yet I sometimes felt we had slipped his mind altogether" (page 68). Do you sometimes feel this way? How do you keep your grasp on God's faithfulness when your prayers seem to go unanswered?

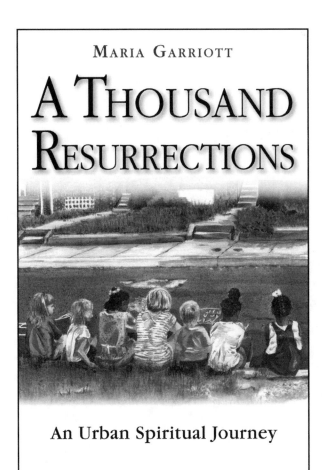

MARIA GARRIOTT

A THOUSAND RESURRECTIONS

An Urban Spiritual Journey

For more information
or additional copies of this book:

Maria Garriott
c/o Faith Christian Fellowship
505 East 42nd Street
Baltimore, MD 21218

www.AThousandResurrections.org